Personal Letters for Business People

Third Edition

Personal Letters
for
Business People

Third Edition

Mary Bosticco

Gower

First published as *Personal Letters for Businessmen* in 1965 by Business Publications Limited.

Second edition 1966

Third edition published 1986 by
Gower Publishing Company Limited,
Gower House,
Croft Road,
Aldershot
Hampshire GU11 3HR,
England

Gower Publishing Company,
Old Post Road,
Brookfield,
Vermont 05036,
U.S.A.

British Library Cataloguing in Publication Data

Bosticco, Mary
  Personal letters for business people. — 3rd ed.
  1. Commercial correspondence
  I. Title
  808'.066651021   HF5721

Library of Congress Cataloging-in-Publication Data

Bosticco, Mary
  Personal letters for business people.
  Rev. ed. of: Personal letters for businessmen. 2nd ed. 1966.
  1. Letter-writing.   2. Commercial correspondence.
  I. Bosticco, Mary. Personal letters for businessmen.   II. Title.
  PE1483.B67   1986   808.6'02465   85-14776

ISBN 0-566-02593-0

Contents

v

Acknowledgments

First of all, I should like to thank Sheila Morris, for without her timely intervention I should never have written this book.

The following companies have very kindly allowed me to use one or more of their letters, for which I am most grateful: Austin Reed Limited, The Direct Mail Group, and Lily-Tulip Cup Corporation.

My sincere thanks also to D. A. Bartlett and Michael Ivens for contributing letters and encouragement, and to Anthony and Robert Morris for practical help.

Finally a very special 'thank you' to Peter Townend, former Editor of *Burke's Peerage, Baronetage and Knightage*, whose helpful and knowledgeable advice on matters concerning proper forms of address was invaluable to me.

Preface

It is a great satisfaction to an author to write a book that proves useful to many people over a long period of time. This has been the case with *Personal Letters for Business People*, which now appears in a third edition.

In 1965, when it was first published, the standard of business letter-writing, at least in Britain, seemed to have been frozen in a mould established in the nineteenth century. Neither were writers in this field giving any worthwhile guidance. While scouring the bookshops to see what competition I had, I actually saw with my own eyes specimen letters recommended as models which began: 'Your esteemed favour of the 11th inst. to hand'! I then knew that not only did I *have* no competition, but that my book was sorely needed. Subsequent sales of the book proved this to be the case.

This book contains over 900 specimen letters for all occasions. They are arranged under main headings according to subject matter: 'Letters of Introduction', 'Letters of Invitation', 'Letters of Welcome' and so on. Each main group is also subdivided, so that if you wish to write a letter introducing a friend, all you need to do is look up 'Letters of Introduction' in the Contents starting on page v. Below this main heading you will see the sub-heading 'Introducing a Friend'. Turning to pages 17–20 you will find eight specimen letters. One of them should, with only a few minor changes, suit the case you have in mind. Otherwise simply use whichever idea appeals to you most and best fits the occasion.

As the title of the book indicates, these are not – with few exceptions – routine business letters, but 'courtesy letters', letters of introduction, congratulations, Christmas greetings, invitations and messages of condolence and sympathy.

Such courtesy letters help the wheels of business turn more smoothly, create goodwill and add an element of friendship to a business relationship. They can mean a great deal to the recipient and take but a few moments to write. But how often do *you* sit down and write such a letter?

Most of us often *intend* writing such notes, but postpone the task, ostensibly because of 'pressure of work', but in reality because we do not know what to say and how to say it. We repeatedly make excuses until it is too late. The opportunity is missed. If only we had an Aladdin's lamp we could rub while reciting: 'Letter of condolence to Bill Brown who has lost his wife!' This book aims to be such an Aladdin's lamp for the busy executive.

About 98 per cent of the specimen letters included I have written myself. A handful of them have been reproduced by kind permission of various companies and individuals, which I have acknowledged separately. In some instances the names of real clubs, societies and publications have been used, while in others the names are fictitious.

In the preface to the first edition of this book, I expressed the hope that it would prove a boon to business people. That hope was fully realized and I can do no better now than to re-echo it.

Bourne End.   Mary Bosticco

1

Getting Off
to a Good Start

The art of letter-writing, much like the art of conversation, is dying. Television no doubt gave the art of conversation its *coup de grâce* and perhaps the furious pace at which we now live is taking its toll of letter-writing.

Unquestionably the number of purely business letters written today is astronomical. The kind of letter-writing that is suffering is the courtesy letter, the goodwill letter – the letter that you do not *have* to write, but is a gracious gesture bringing pleasure or solace to its recipient. This kind of letter-writing is a habit well worth cultivating and if you persevere in the practice you will soon find yourself dashing off friendly notes with no effort at all.

If you want your letters to be fresh, sprightly and readable there is no better way to begin than by a thorough 'housecleaning'. Begin by throwing out all surplus words. Read over every sentence of your letter and ask yourself: 'Is this word really necessary? Will the meaning change if I throw it out?' If your answer is 'No', then ruthlessly remove it. Every word must earn its keep and there is absolutely no place for parasite words in a crisp piece of writing.

Avoid such phrases as *along the lines of* – use LIKE instead. Cut *for the reason that*, substitute SINCE or BECAUSE. Throw out *on the grounds that* – use SINCE or BECAUSE once again, and in place of *with a view to* say, simply, TO.

After a little practice you will be amazed at the number of surplus words you will be able to discard and how often you can make one short word take the place of three, four or even five.

The next housecleaning exercise involves giving up as many worn-out clichés and dreary relics of 'commercial English' as you possibly can. Some of the choicest specimens are the following:

and oblige (as a close)	at the present time
as and from	at this writing
as per	at your earliest convenience
as stated above	attached please find
assuring you of our best attention	avail yourself of this opportunity
at an early date	await the pleasure of a reply
at hand	awaiting the favour of your further esteemed commands

1

beg to acknowledge
beg to advise
beg to announce
beg to remain (before
   complimentary close)

carefully noted
communication (instead of
   letter)
complying with your request
contents duly noted

deem it advisable
desire to state
due to the fact that
duly noted

enclosed herewith
enclosed please find
esteemed favour
even date

far be it from me to . . .
favour (instead of letter)

has come to hand
has gone forward
has greatly helped
have before me
having regard to the fact
herewith enclose
herewith please find
hoping to be favoured

if and when
in answer to same
in connection therewith
in due course
in receipt of
in reply to yours
in reply I wish to state
in response to your favour
in the near future
in the not too distant future
in this connection
instant

kind favour
kindly advise
kindly be advised

kindly inform

meet your approval

note from your letter
note with interest
note with pleasure

of even date
our records show
owing to the fact that

past favours
permit me to state
please advise
please be advised
please do not hesitate
please find enclosed
please note
please rest assured
proximo
pursuant to

recent date
referring to your favour
referring to yours
regarding your communication
regret to advise
regret to state
replying to your favour
replying to yours

said (e.g. said package)
same (used as a pronoun)
submit herewith

take pleasure in advising
take this opportunity
thank you kindly
thank you in advance
the writer
this is to advise you
to hand
trusting this will

ultimo
under separate cover
upon receipt of

valued favour
valued patronage

we are pleased to advise
we note
we take pleasure
well and truly
when and as
wherein we state
wish to acknowledge
wish to advise
wish to state
would advise
would state

would suggest

your esteemed communication
your esteemed favour
your favour to hand
your letter of even date
your valued inquiry
yours just to hand
yours of the fourth
yours to hand

The next thing to avoid using, as often as possible, is the passive voice. Never use it unless you have to. Do not say: 'It was decided by the Board . . .'. 'The Board decided . . .' is far more forceful and shorter to boot.

Now you have removed all surplus words, all worn out clichés, and every passive voice you can do without, you are left with the task of word selection. Which words shall you use by preference? As a rule of thumb you can safely choose the short word in preference to the long one, the simple word in preference to the complex one. Beware of long Latin-derived words. Prefer the short Saxon ones.

'Begin' or 'start' are preferable to 'commence'. 'Urge' is better than 'encourage'. 'Get' is better than 'procure'.

Beware of long words with prefixes or suffixes, such as *pre*, *re*, *de* or *ousness* and *ization*. They can often be replaced by two short words or even one short word of Saxon origin. Many verbs of Latin origin can be replaced by a combination of verb and adverb in tandem which is characteristic of the English language and consequently more forceful. Here are some examples:

Get down instead of *descend*
Go up instead of *ascend*
Get about instead of *circulate*
Carry on instead of *continue*
Carry out instead of *execute*

There are hundreds more, of course, and it will do your English nothing but good if you learn to identify them and give preference to the short, simpler words or pairs of words. But do not be misled into believing that it is easy to write simple, direct English, for no ideal is harder to attain.

Jointly with short words, favour short sentences. The English sentence has been getting shorter and shorter over the past centuries and by adopting the short sentence you will not merely be moving with the times, but, far more important, you will give your English a shot in the arm.

In fact, according to the studies carried out by Rudolph Flesch, short words and short sentences are two of the ingredients which make your English readable. And, unquestionably, in spite of some quite famous modern authors, whose works are almost unintelligible, the purpose of writing, whether it be a simple letter to a friend, or a lengthy tome, is to communicate. There is no merit in obscure, involved prose which only its perpetrator can understand. Neither is the complexity of a subject an adequate excuse for not explaining it clearly.

Using concrete words will help no end in making your meaning clear. Colourful, definite words will also help. Cultivate the habit of looking up the word you want to use in the dictionary. You will be surprised at how often the word you have chosen is not *exactly* what you mean to say.

Finally, and perhaps most important of all, cultivate the 'You' approach. So many letters are peppered with the word 'I' as if the writer had no thought in the world but himself. Yet the recipient is interested not so much in you, as in *himself*. Try, then, talking about *him*, or *her*. Write: 'You will be happy to learn that your order is ready for shipment', instead of 'I am happy to inform you that . . .'

Particularly when writing a personal letter, it is most important to write as you speak, complete with contractions. If you put on a special 'written English' mask, your friends will not recognize you – you will not come across. Your letter will be cold and distant, as if from a stranger.

If you can make time to think before you write, your letter cannot help but benefit, and the time spent in thinking will be saved in a shorter, more concise letter. It is surprising how many executives are like the French philosopher Pascal who wrote long letters because he had no time to write short ones!

If you want to save time you can save it by not worrying unduly about the so-called rules of grammar. So many letters become stilted, cumbersome, and dull because their writer has scrupulously married every infinitive and carefully embodied his every preposition within the sentence.

Capital letters

The modern trend is to cut down on capital letters. Capitalize:

Proper names of persons, countries, towns and cities, counties, rivers, mountains, lakes, seas and oceans.

The names of months and days of the week.

The titles of books, plays, articles, magazines, chapters, speeches, operas, songs, etc. e.g. 'He wrote a book called *The Art of Readable Writing'*. 'She spoke on "How to Improve Your Letter-Writing".'

The names of ships, houses, hotels, restaurants, inns, etc.

A common noun when it is used in conjunction with a proper name, e.g. Westminster Bridge, Lake Constance, Mount Everest. Or when it is used in place of a proper name, e.g. 'The Company (meaning Company "X") was founded in 1917'.

A designation of rank or position when it is used in conjunction with a proper name, e.g. 'The first to arrive was Arthur Smith, Chairman of Stephen Miller and Company'. Or when it refers to a specific person, e.g. 'The Queen visited Canada last week.

Do *not* capitalize:

a common noun when it is used to indicate a general class of person or thing, e.g. 'There are not very many large universities in England'. 'His experience as salesman and marketing executive was invaluable to him when he took charge of the business'.

a designation of rank or position when it is used as a common noun, e.g. 'Most sales managers have spent several years on the road'.

the names of various fields of learning when used in a general sense, e.g. 'His studies had included philosophy, psychology and ancient Greek'.

Punctuation

The trend is to cut down on punctuation as much as possible. The only exception is the full stop, which will occur more frequently if you write short sentences.

As a rule of thumb you might say that if the omission of a comma alters the meaning, then put one in. Otherwise leave it out. Certainly use a comma to separate a list of items, e.g. 'Our third floor boutique has an excellent stock of ladies' suits, dresses, coats, and rainwear'. A comma belongs before the 'and' in the example given, but is omitted when only two items are listed, e.g. 'Bacon and eggs'.

Nowadays many good writers do not enclose parenthetical expressions between commas. If the meaning is easy enough to grasp, by all means leave the commas out, but do one thing or the other, not half and half. So many people use a comma before the beginning of the parenthetical remark, but not after. Write: 'Our Midland representative, Mr Edward Williams, will be calling on you soon'. 'George Fellows, whom you met at the Annual Dinner, will be moving to Scotland early next month'. Clearly, both sentences benefit by the insertion of a comma before and after the parenthetical remark.

You should also use a comma before a direct quotation, e.g. 'He said, "I shall be there at noon".' A comma should also separate the remarks which come between a direct quotation, e.g. 'I shall not be late', he said, 'at least, not *very* late'.

The semicolon is supposed to be used to indicate a pause somewhat longer than that of the comma, but the modern short sentence has all but made it obsolete, particularly as far as the business letter is concerned. If your sentence is so long and complicated that it needs several semicolons to make it clear, better re-write the sentence.

Sometimes, however, you may be listing things which fall naturally into several groups. In such a case clarity will be helped if you separate the groups with semicolons and the items between groups with commas, e.g. 'We have three top executives only: George White, chairman and managing director; Wilfred Warren, secretary, treasurer, and chief accountant; Fred Allen, in charge of sales, advertising, and public relations.

At times the omission of a word calls for a semicolon to bridge the gap. If you say: 'We have ten branches in the United Kingdom, but only two throughout the rest of the world', a comma will do admirably. If you omit the little word 'but' a longer pause will be needed and you consequently need to use a semicolon instead, e.g. 'We have ten branches in the United Kingdom; only two throughout the rest of the world'.

The colon indicates a pause somewhat longer than a semicolon, yet not so long as a full stop. You need not worry too much about it in business letters. You will probably only need to use it before a list of examples or explanations, e.g. 'The qualities we seek in our sales representatives are: enthusiasm, determination, friendliness, energy, and ambition'.

The colon can also be used before a direct quotation, instead of a comma.

The full stop is the longest pause of all and should be used at the end of a sentence, after initials, and most abbreviations. If the abbreviation ends the way the word normally does, then no full stop is necessary; e.g. Sept., Wed., A.D., but B'ham, Xmas (no point). However, in the interests of speed, points after initials or abbreviations are almost always omitted nowadays.

The other punctuation marks are: the interrogation mark, the exclamation, inverted commas, the hyphen, parentheses, and the dash.

The interrogation mark is used only after a direct question, not after an indirect one. It can also be used between parentheses to indicate that a word or statement is in doubt.

The exclamation should be used very sparingly. It denotes that the preceding word or sentence expresses strong emotion.

Inverted commas are used before and after direct speech.

The hyphen is used to unite two separate words into a compound one. In time such compound words become one and the hyphen is dropped.

The dash is often scattered all over the place or used willy-nilly instead of other punctuation marks. It should rightfully only be used to signify a sudden break in the reasoning, the resumption of a scattered subject, or an omission.

'I could tell you more — but I must close now'.
'Sales representatives, clerks, accountants — all were there'.
'Mr — said he was d—d fed up with it'.

As with herbs in cooking, dashes should be used sparingly.

Forms of address

You are now all set to write your letter and in case you still feel that all personal letters must be written by hand you should dispel this thought from your mind. If this were so, very few personal letters indeed would be written nowadays. There simply is not time to sit down, pen in hand, to write a letter and everyone understands this. It would be a pity indeed if you were to refrain from writing a letter which might bring pleasure to its recipient simply because you could not spare the time to write it by hand.

A typewritten personal letter is accepted nowadays in all but the most punctilious circles. Certainly, you will want to write most letters of condolence by hand, as well as short thank-you notes. But all other letters can safely be typewritten.

A rather pleasant compromise is the 'topped and tailed' letter, that is, a typewritten letter with the 'Dear Mr So-and-So' and the complimentary close written in by hand. This is an excellent idea, which gives an added personal touch and injects a note of warmth into letters. Many executives use it even for strictly business letters to people they know well.

Letters beginning 'Dear Mr So-and-So' or 'Dear Ms So-and-So' should end 'Yours sincerely', 'Sincerely yours', or simply 'Sincerely'. The American 'Cordially' is frowned upon in British circles, but just why is not quite clear. In fact once you embark on a letter which begins 'Dear Jim' or 'Dear Jane', there's no reason at all why you should not end it however you like. Most such letters in this book stick to the conventional 'Yours sincerely' and variations, but this does not mean that any other ending should be avoided.

On the contrary, why not try ending a personal letter in a completely personal way for a change? Why be a slave of convention? George Bernard Shaw was an outstanding letter-writer and he very seldom bothered with meaningless 'Yours faithfully's and 'Yours sincerely's.

As for addressing your letter, for men you have the choice of the traditional British Esquire or the American Mr. The latter form seems to be taking hold in business, but it appears that men rather like to be addressed as Esquire, so no doubt this form of address will linger on for some time yet.

Women usually indicate in brackets after their surname whether they wish to be addressed as Miss, Mrs, or Ms. In such cases, you know exactly what to do. If you are not given a guideline, then settle for Ms. This form of address was sanctioned for women Members of Parliament, if they so wish, as far back as 1976 and it is also offered as a choice when applying for a passport.

At times you will need to write to someone with a title of some sort or you will want to know what to do about all those initials some people sport after their names. The Appendix will give you some guidance on such matters. In addition, you might want to have a specialized reference book at your elbow. One such is *Titles and Forms of Address, A Guide to Correct Usage*, published by A & C Black.

2

Letters of Introduction

A letter of introduction is a courtesy extended to a friend, colleague or business associate visiting or moving to another town or city. If there is time, send the letter by post and give a copy to the person introduced. Otherwise give the letter, unsealed, to the person you are introducing, for him or her to hand personally to the addressee on arrival.

In asking a friend or associate to spare time to meet someone he or she does not know, you are, in effect, asking a favour. Your letter should therefore be couched in these terms and it should thank him for any kindness he may wish to extend to the person you are recommending.

In addition the letter should state:

1 The name of the person introduced;
2 The reason for the visit;
3 Any relevant background material, whether of a personal or business nature, according to the kind of introduction involved.

The tone of the letter will depend not only on the degree of friendship between the correspondents, but also on the the purpose of the introduction. If you are introducing a personal friend to another personal friend for purely social reasons, then, obviously, your letter will be quite informal. A purely business introduction, on the other hand, will be formal, though friendly.

A letter introducing a new sales representative is not, strictly speaking, a personal letter at all. Its purpose is quite obviously promotional. It should include a summary of the new employee's background and qualifications and stress his or her eagerness to be of service to the recipient of your letter.

Sometimes you will have occasion to write a letter introducing yourself. Such a letter will usually ask for an appointment or a favour of some sort and should therefore follow the same rules as other letters of introduction.

Introducing a new sales representative

Dear Mr McGuinness,

Within the next few days, Ms June Abel, our new Northern representative, will be calling on you.

You will find Ms Abel a very likeable person, helpful and eager to please. She is well qualified to serve you, having spent the past ten years in the domestic appliance field. In addition, she has just completed our ten-week Sales Training Course, which makes her thoroughly well versed in everything connected with our products.

Ms Abel looks forward to maintaining the very friendly relations between our two organisations and will be only too pleased to do anything she can to co-operate with you. I may add that she has the full support of all of us here at Head Office.

I wish you an excellent summer season.

Yours sincerely,

Dear Mr Newton,

May I introduce James Stannard, our new representative for hospital equipment?

James came to us from Institutional Dishwashers Limited when we took over their line of hospital dishwashers and bedpan rinsers. He is thoroughly familiar with all aspects of operating and servicing these machines, and was, for a while, our sole expert. He has been calling on hospitals for over five years and is therefore well acquainted with their special problems.

Intelligent, enthusiastic, and knowledgeable, James Stannard brings to the job that professionalism and seriousness of purpose which we know you appreciate. He is eager to serve you and we know you will enjoy dealing with him.

Yours sincerely,

Dear Mr Jones,

This is to announce the forthcoming visit of:

Harry Welch

our new representative for your area.

He replaces Tony Everett, who has left us to start his own business.

In selecting a replacement for Tony we were very much aware of the importance of the Midlands area and the need to have a first class man there. Harry Welch is such a man and will, I think, impress you with his extensive knowledge of heavy equipment. Certainly, he is a man of his word, whom you can trust and will surely like.

He will be calling on you soon, both to make your acquaintance and to see what he can do to be of service. I'm sure you will reserve for him the same welcome you always extended to his predecessor.

Thank you for your continued patronage.

Yours sincerely,

Dear Ms Jones,

We are pleased to introduce:

Mr George Rose

our new sales representative, who will be calling to see you shortly.

Mr Rose is no newcomer to the printing industry. He joined us some eight years ago, starting in the composing room. After a short spell in the reading room, he transferred to the production and buying department, where he has been for the past six years.

You will find Mr Rose well equipped to advise you on print problems and he will be pleased to arrange for you to have quotations for all types of book printing. He looks forward to being of service to you.

Yours sincerely,

*This letter had a
photo of the new
sales representative
here.*

Dear Mr Baker,

The smiling face at the head of this letter belongs to Mr Iain Bain, the latest recruit to our team of direct mail consultants.

In his leisure hours Mr Bain puts his weight (16 stone) into hammer throwing – he's a member of the Achilles Club and only just missed representing his country at last year's Olympic Games.

During business hours Mr Bain will be putting all his weight, and his very considerable ability, into promoting better and more successful direct mail advertising.

Greatly to my regret, it is some time since one of our representatives came to see you and Mr Bain will endeavour to make amends by calling on you within the next few days. I hope you'll like him and find him a great help in all matters relating to postal publicity.

Yours sincerely,

Dear Miss Bruce,

In order to give you better service we have decided to split the Midlands territory into two. This means that Mr James Lawrence, who has called on you for so many years, will no longer be doing so. In his stead, you will soon be getting a call from Ms Joyce Williams, who has recently joined the ranks of our sales force.

Ms Williams feels keenly that it will be a difficult task to step into the shoes of so popular and capable a person as Mr Lawrence and is the more determined to help you in every way possible.

You will, I am sure, find Ms Williams a very likeable person, extremely knowledgeable and well-informed. I am confident you will do everything you can to make her as welcome as her predecessor.

Yours sincerely,

Dear Mr Spiller,

In view of the extent to which my business has grown and the additional expansion plans for this year, I am regretfully no longer able to call on all my customers myself, as I have been doing for the past five years.

I have therefore decided to appoint a sales representative to cover Scotland and the North of England, while continuing to take care of the rest of the country myself. I shall certainly miss seeing you, but such is the price of success.

The representative I have appointed is Mr Charles Butterworth, who will be calling on you shortly. He is very capable and will unquestionably be able to help you considerably with your production problems. He looks forward to being of service to you and I'm sure you'll like him.

Yours sincerely,

Dear Mr Sanders,

Ms Mary Whithers, our new office furniture representative, will shortly be calling to introduce herself.

Ms Whithers is extremely well equipped to advise you on any office outfitting problem you may have, from installing a new filing system to refurnishing the chairman's office. You will find she takes a keen interest in your problems and is eager, capable and willing to help.

Should there be anything you would like to take up with Ms Whithers before she calls, why not give her a ring on 01-343-3626? She will be only too pleased to be of assistance.

Yours sincerely,

Introducing a business or professional associate

Dear Mr Watson,

This letter will introduce Mr John Seymour, my friend and colleague, who is doing some research for his forthcoming book on sales management.

Since you are one of the leading British experts on the subject, Mr Seymour is naturally eager to meet you and have a talk with you.

I'd be most grateful for any courtesy you may wish to extend to Mr Seymour, as I am sure he will be.

Yours sincerely,

Dear Mr De Angelis,

I am happy to introduce:

Mr Henry W. Baldwin

one of our authors. (You may have noticed his name on some of our books.)

Mr Baldwin is making a business-cum-pleasure trip to Italy and I should be most grateful if you would do what you can for him on the business half of his trip. He is planning to investigate the Italian labour organizations, or should one say syndicates? Any help you may be able to give him in the way of introductions, and perhaps in interpreting, would be very much appreciated. It will also, we hope, lead to the publication of another book to our mutual benefit.

You'll find Mr Baldwin very likeable and interesting and I'm sure you'll enjoy meeting him. Many thanks for your kindness.

Yours sincerely,

Dear Mr Sullivan,

This is to introduce Signor Carlo Bianchi, our Italian agent, who is over here on a brief visit.

He is most anxious to visit your plant as the first stage in his study of the whole operation, from the raw materials you supply us with to the finished product we supply to him.

I'd therefore be most grateful if you would arrange for him to be shown round and for any courtesy you may be good enough to extend to him. You will find his English quite fluent, if rather picturesque at times, and I'm sure you'll enjoy his visit.

Yours sincerely,

Dear Dick,

The bearer of this letter

Mr Charles F. Baker

has been my right-hand man at the plant here for some seven years.

Unfortunately for me, however, he is now leaving to try his luck in the big city.

Charles Baker is not only a first-class engineer, but has a very special way with him in dealing with the workforce. I can therefore recommend him highly and I would greatly appreciate anything you can do to help him get resettled in London.

Many thanks and I look forward to seeing you at the conference later in the year.

Sincerely,

Dear Colin,

Frank Haynes, my friend and a good client, is making a pleasure trip to Turkey with his wife. He has promised to look you up and I am hoping that he will do so.

Any courtesy that you extend to him will be most appreciated both by me and by him. It will be his first trip to Turkey, so a guide such as you would be invaluable to him. Do introduce him to some good Turkish food and show him some of those features of your city which the average tourist never discovers.

Thanks a lot, Colin, and let me know if ever I can reciprocate with any friend or client of yours.

Sincerely,

Dear Mr Harris,

May I introduce to you Dr Leslie Carson, my fellow teacher and neighbour?

Dr Carson has been elected chairman of the Bourne End Community Association. While discussing the project with him yesterday evening, I happened to mention to him that you had done a good deal of work on a very similar project in Gerrards Cross, whereupon he expressed a desire to meet you. He feels that your valuable experience would be of great help to him – and rightly so, no doubt.

Any courtesy that you may be able to extend to him will be greatly appreciated by us and, indirectly, by the whole community of Bourne End.

Yours sincerely,

Dear Miss O'Brien,

Joseph McGuire, who does a splendid selling job for us in the North, was telling me the other day that he was planning to add some allied lines to enable him to increase his turnover.

I immediately thought of you, since unquestionably your lines 'marry' well with ours. He jumped at the idea and he will be calling on you when he gets back to Yorkshire.

I very much hope the meeting will prove mutually beneficial.

Yours sincerely,

Dear Mr James,

This is to introduce my colleague

Mr Geoffrey Walker

who is visiting Edinburgh with a view to finding premises for our new branch and carrying out other spade-work.

I would greatly appreciate any guidance you can give Mr Walker as to preferred sites, reputable dealers, current rents, and so on. Your many years' residence in the city, coupled with your lengthy experience of doing business there could be of tremendous help to him in carrying out his task.

Many thanks in advance,

Yours sincerely,

Introducing a friend

Dear Otto,

I have taken the liberty of giving your name and address to a friend of mine, Dr Paul Neiman, who will be making a brief visit to the USA at the end of this month.

Paul is an economist and just about your vintage, so I'm sure you'll soon be burning the midnight oil together straightening out the affairs of the world. It will be Paul's first visit to America, so he would obviously appreciate any steering you can give him. Though he is calling it an 'exploratory' trip, not really business, it is certainly not just a pleasure trip.

I'm sure you'll enjoy meeting Paul. Do let me know how you make out. Hope all is well with you and the family.

Sincerely,

Dear Jean,

My good friend John Siddons has suddenly decided to make the Grand Tour, having been left a small legacy. He has never been out of the country before and insists on going it alone – no package tour for him, he says. However he speaks not a word of French, German or Italian and I'd hate to see him stranded.

I am therefore writing to friends in each of the countries he is visiting in an attempt to pave the way for him. Would you be good enough to look him up when he descends on Geneva? He'll be staying at the Baur au Lac from the 12th to the 20th May, inclusive. I have taken the liberty of giving him your name, address and telephone number.

John is a jolly good sort and does not need elaborate entertaining. The excitement of being abroad for the first time will be quite enough to keep him happy. He'll also enjoy your wonderful Swiss cuisine.

Thanks a lot, Jean, and do let me know when I can do the same for any of your visitors to England.

Sincerely,

Dear George,

This is to introduce an old college friend, Jill Hobson, who will be making a short stay in your town.

Jill is researching for her next book on office systems and procedures and when I told her about that splendid system you have in your office, she insisted on my giving her this introduction.

I'm sure you'll be happy to supply her with the information she needs, and I think you'll find her excellent company besides.

Hope business is keeping up at your end. When will it bring you back to London?

Thanks for anything you can do to help Jill with her book.

Sincerely,

Dear Brian,

My friend and business associate, Guido Gironi, is spending six months in England with the double purpose of improving his English and carrying out some research in physics. He is a doctor of physics and, although only 31, a highly respected member of the Montecatini research team.

He is naturally most anxious to visit your plant, whose fame has reached Italy and beyond, and I promised to write to you and announce his visit. He will be in your town next week and will most certainly give you a ring. You will find his English quite adequate and you'll have no difficulty understanding him.

I'm sure you'll be delighted to show Guido around and you'll find his quick sharp brain and Latin animation quite stimulating. Unquestionably you'll learn every bit as much from him as he will from you.

Many thanks. Hope to see you soon.

Yours sincerely,

Dear Joe,

My friend, Alan Jones, will be speaking at the E.D.A. National Sales Conference in Harrogate during the week of April 14. Since both of you are keen chess players, as well as marketing men, I thought you'd enjoy getting together.

He will be staying at the Old Swan Hotel and you might care to get in touch with him. I've also given him your name and phone number.

Sincerely,

Dear Philip,

My friend and neighbour, Stan Huxley, will be attending a conference in Brighton next week and I have taken the liberty of giving him your name and address as I think you two might like to get together. You are both old Etonians, keen golfers, inveterate travellers and above all, outstanding financiers so it was probably on the cards that you should meet sometime.

Stan will be staying at the Metropole as from next Tuesday if you care to make the first move.

Sincerely yours,

Dear Mireille,

Sheila Atkins, a close friend of my daughter's, will be in Paris next week on her first buying trip for Bloomingtons and I have ventured to give her your name and address.

I'd greatly appreciate any help you can give in steering her through the intricacies of the world of fashion. She is terribly excited about the trip, as you can imagine, but she is also rather inexperienced, so I'm sure she'll greatly welcome any help she can get from an 'old hand' – no offence, meant, of course!

Sheila's full of the enthusiasm of youth, and works hard at her job and seems to know her stuff where merchandising is concerned.

Many thanks and all the best to you.

Yours sincerely,

Dear Tom,

I have just learned that my good friend, Michael Torrington, is being transferred to the Western Area and will therefore no longer be calling on me. My loss, it seems, will be your gain, and I have recommended him to make a special point of looking you up.

Michael is an absolute mine of information in the pharmaceutical field. He has been calling on me for almost ten years and during that time we have become firm friends. He will do anything to help you and you have only to ask his advice and guidance on any problem. He is definitely not the type of salesman who is only interested in selling to you.

I'm very sorry that Mike is moving away from London and can only really find comfort in the thought that he will henceforth do for you what he has been doing for me all these years.

Sincerely,

Introducing yourself*

Dear Mr Dean,

I am in the process of doing some research on my next book, which will deal with financial investments. My work will be taking me to Manchester on May 16 and 17 and I am wondering whether you would be good enough to spare me a few minutes of your time on either of these dates.

I would certainly deem it a privilege to make the acquaintance of so outstanding a financier as yourself and hope you will be good enough to see me. Needless to say, I have read all your books on the subject and have been wanting to meet you for some time.

If you would mention the most suitable day and time for my visit I will gladly fit it in with my programme.

I shall look forward to your reply with interest.

Yours sincerely,

---

*The only real difference between the letters that follow and those appearing in Chapter 12 under the heading 'Making requests – for business appointment', is that the recipients of the letters below are not acquainted with their correspondent.

Dear Dr Fletcher,

I shall be attending the International Symposium in London at the end of the month and am most anxious to seize the opportunity to make your acquaintance. As it will be all too easy to miss you in the hustle and bustle of the meeting, I am wondering whether we could make arrangements to meet. I would particularly like to discuss with you some of our work here at the Hospital.

I shall be arriving in London on the 25th and staying with friends until early December – well after the symposium ends. If you will therefore kindly let me know when and where I might call on you I should be most grateful.

I look forward to hearing from you.

Yours sincerely,

Dear Ms Jackson,

As fellow authors in the Progress Publications 'stable' and workers in two such closely-allied fields, I really feel it is time we met.

I shall be in Scotland next Monday for about a week and I'm hoping you will be able to spare me a few moments in your busy day. I shall be visiting our Glasgow plant, so it will be easy enough for me to arrange my schedule to suit you.

Do let me hear from you.

Yours sincerely,

Dear Mr Springer,

I understand that you are planning to increase the number of your dealerships in the United Kingdom and since it happens that I shall be doing some business in Birmingham early next week, I am wondering if I might call on you to discuss whether our two companies could not profitably work together.

Would 3 p.m. on Wednesday, April 21 suit you? I am keeping that time free on my calendar until I hear from you.

Yours sincerely,

3

Letters of Recommendation

Nowadays it is customary to check references by telephone and the all-embracing 'To Whom it May Concern' letter handed to a departing employee is quite literally a dead letter.

Sometimes, however, you will have occasion to extend the courtesy of writing a letter of recommendation on behalf of a business associate, former employee, or friend.

In writing to recommend a former employee, you will need to give specific details, such as dates of employment with you, position occupied, qualifications and pertinent information on character, temperament and any other relevant details you may have observed. If you have any reservations about recommending a former employee, you should not hesitate to mention them, for it would be unfair to your correspondent – and indeed to your former employee – wholeheartedly to recommend a person for a position you knew he or she was unsuitable for.

In recommending a friend or business associate you will dwell more on qualities of character and personal integrity. In other words, you will be a little less specific. However, do not make the mistake of being too vague and indulging in meaningless generalizations. It is always a good point, for instance, to mention the number of years you have known the person concerned.

In any event, the tone of your letter should be warm and enthusiastic. Write as if you mean every word you say – sincerity is recognizable by all. The specimen letters which follow cover all three cases mentioned, i.e. letters recommending a business associate, a former employee, and a friend.

Recommending a business or professional associate

Dear Mr Wynne,

I have just received your letter of October 12 and am very pleased to learn that you are considering Mr Henry Lawrence for a position in your Bank.

It has been my pleasure to know Mr Lawrence for almost ten years, and when he was living in Leicester, until about two years ago, I had business dealings with him almost daily. Without exception I found him to be a person of the utmost integrity, scrupulousness and accuracy. Whenever I left a business matter in his hands I knew it would be dealt with expeditiously and efficiently.

In addition Mr Lawrence is a man of quiet charm and unfailing good humour – all qualities of great importance in dealing with the public.

I have no misgiving whatsoever in thoroughly recommending Mr Lawrence for the position you have in mind. Thank you for writing to me.

Sincerely yours,

Dear Mr. Wirsig,

It is a pleasure to recommend Miss Paula Hartley for the editorial position you mention. I have known her for about eight years, during the first four of which we were colleagues on the editorial staff of C. C. Winston (Publishers) Limited. After that, we each went our separate ways and soon afterwards it was my pleasure to be connected with publishing her first two books.

Miss Hartley is a woman of ideas, with a distinct flair for recognizing a saleable one and the ability to nurse a promising author through the birth pangs of a book. At the same time she has a sound technical knowledge, a well-organized mind, and a taste for hard work.

Unquestionably, if you succeed in persuading her to join your company, you will have acquired a valuable employee.

Yours sincerely,

Dear Dr Winters,

I was very interested to learn that you are contemplating engaging the services of Mr Harry Le House for a term at your Summer School.

I do not hesitate to say at the very outset that if you do so it will rank as one of the most successful ideas you ever had, and I am quite convinced that, given the opportunity, you will want to have Mr Le House back for every term thereafter. For your pupils will be clamouring for him.

Mr Le House has a rare, almost magic, magnetic personality, which attracts and wins people in a most extraordinary way. Many a time have I seen a group of youngsters actually fall out of a dance to run down the road to meet him as he approached.

I know little, if anything, about his subject, of course, but unquestionably, his pupils of all ages and both sexes, listen to him entranced and I cannot see how he can be anything but an asset to your Summer School.

Incidentally, I only knew him for the three months of the California Summer Course we both attended. Later we dined together a couple of times, then he was off to Mexico and I saw him no more. In spite of my brief acquaintance with Mr Le House, I am firmly convinced he would be a great drawing 'attraction' for your School.

Yours sincerely,

Dear Mr Wynn,

I have known John Fennimore for over ten years, in fact ever since he joined the firm of Winslow, Cooper and Winslow. He has handled many of my business matters and we have also been associated in civic affairs. I have always found him to be a man of the highest integrity and a very able solicitor.

His standing in the community is very high indeed and he has put in a good deal of work in the general interest, both with the Chamber of Commerce and the local Community Association.

I thoroughly recommend Mr Fennimore and have never heard anything to his detriment.

Yours sincerely,

Dear Ms Stallard,

Your letter regarding Walter Taylor was on my desk on my return from a business trip to the Continent. I hope the slight delay in replying will not have inconvenienced you or prejudiced Mr Taylor's chances of securing the position with your Company.

I have known Mr Taylor for about six years and have worked with him on several occasions on Rotary and community affairs. I have found him to be an excellent organizer, an enthusiastic leader and tireless worker. If Walter Taylor headed a committee, we always felt that something was sure to be done. Not merely a man of action, but a man that gets things done – that is my assessment of Walter Taylor.

From what you tell me of the position you are considering him for, I would have no hesitation in saying that Walter Taylor is the man for the job.

Yours sincerely,

Dear Mr Knight,

Thank you for your letter of March 15, asking me about Stanley Wright. I have known him for many years, ever since he sold me my first car over 20 years ago. We have both travelled far since those days and we have not been in constant touch throughout these years. Yet I have watched Mr Wright's progress since his early years as a salesman and I know his signal success has been due to hard work, perseverance, a desire to be of help to others and a winning, charming manner.

Mr Wright is a born leader. Unquestionably, he could motivate and inspire your sales force as few other people could. He is quite an expert on salesmanship and frequently speaks informally at the Marketing Association and at sales training centres throughout the country.

In securing Mr Wright's services, your company will unquestionably be acquiring a great asset.

Sincerely yours,

Dear Ms Whitlow,

I am very happy to have the opportunity of giving you my appraisal of Miss Ethel Thornton. I have known her since her childhood, or since <u>our</u> childhood, I should say, for we were neighbours even before we became associated in social work.

Miss Thornton is an utterly selfless person, completely dedicated to service to her fellowmen. Young people are her special interest and for this reason I am convinced she is the ideal candidate for the position you mention. Miss Thornton is a person of the highest moral standards and in every way suited to influence the young.

She is an excellent organizer and an indefatigable worker. Her charming manner and dry sense of humour endear her to all who come in contact with her.

In all, I have no hesitation in recommending Miss Thornton most highly.

Yours sincerely,

Recommending a former employee

Dear Mr Hart,

I am pleased indeed to recommend Miss Renata Vericchio for the position of translator in your Export Department.

During her three years with my company, from January 1978 to February 1981, she demonstrated an excellent grasp of Italian, French, and Spanish, and was soon translating all our rather technical material from and into any of these three languages and English. In addition, we found her to be an excellent shorthand-typist, a fast and cheerful worker, thoroughly well-versed in all export matters. On many occasions she acted as interpreter for us when agents and buyers from abroad visited our works.

She left for personal reasons and we were sorry indeed to lose her.

Yours sincerely,

Dear Ms Payne,

I am very pleased to answer your inquiry as to the qualifications of Ms Sheila Lennox for the position of Word Processing Supervisor.

Ms Lennox was employed by our company as a senior typist from March 1978 to June 1981. We found her a proficient and very fast typist, and a willing and industrious employee. When we introduced Word Processing we realized that she had other assets as well, namely organizing ability and marked qualities of leadership. This led us to put her in charge of the more junior operators in the company. However, ours is rather a small concern with very little further scope for Ms Lennox's abilities. She therefore decided to leave us to pursue her career elsewhere.

I have no hesitation in recommending her for the position you have in mind. I'm quite sure she will be equal to any supervisory challenge put before her.

Yours sincerely,

Dear Mr Goldberg,

I am happy to give you the information you request on the suitability of Ms Margaret Winnet for the position of executive secretary.

Ms Winnet was my secretary from March 1969 to September 1975, when she left for an extended trip to the Continent to improve her language abilities. I can wholeheartedly recommend her not merely as a competent secretary, but as a true executive assistant, able to use her own initiative, judgement and imagination.

Her secretarial skills are excellent and she ran my office efficiently and unobtrusively. Gradually, as she got to know my work, she became invaluable to me in taking care of a hundred and one details I would normally have had to attend to myself. I could confidently leave on quite a long trip in the knowledge that everything would run smoothly in my absence.

I need hardly say that I was sorry to lose her. I'm sure you will soon find her invaluable to you and my loss will indeed be your gain.

Yours sincerely,

Dear Mrs Herriot,

I am happy indeed to recommend Mr George Farley for the position in your accounts department.

Mr Farley was with our company for three years – from February 1975 to March 1978 – and during that time we found no cause to complain of him whatsoever. Punctual, neat and accurate in his work, a stickler for detail, methodical, Mr Farley is indeed the ideal man for a job in accounting.

We certainly would not hesitate to re-engage him and can recommend him to you unreservedly.

Yours sincerely,

Dear Mr Stephens,

I have your letter of April 15, asking for information on Mr Jacques Vittel and am happy to comply with your request.

Mr Vittel was employed as sauce cook at our hotel from November 15, 1978 to January 21, 1980. During that time we found him to be a capable and efficient cook, punctual and reliable and thoroughly well versed in Continental cuisine. He was apt to be a little temperamental at times and occasional flare-ups occurred in the kitchen, involving the usual feuds between head waiter and kitchen staff, but as you well know, a cook without a temperament is just as rare as an artist without one and you have no doubt learned to live with this phenomenon.

I'm sure you will find Mr Vittel well worth having on your kitchen staff, temperament notwithstanding.

Yours sincerely,

Dear Ms Green,

I am pleased to give you the information you request on Ms Sally Howarth.

Ms Howarth was on our sales force for five years, from March 30, 1979 to April 15, 1984. After a slow start, she became one of our best sales representatives and we were sorry indeed to lose her when she decided to move North after her marriage. Ms Howarth is the embodiment of the up-to-date salesperson: enthusiastic about her product, friendly and helpful with her prospects and clients, thoroughly imbued with the spirit of service. There is nothing Ms Howarth will not do to oblige a client and this quality has served her well over the years.

I do not hesitate to say that your sales force will be greatly reinforced by the addition of Ms Howarth's services and I recommend her wholeheartedly.

Sincerely yours,

Dear Mr Given,

In reply to your letter of June 15, I am very happy to recommend Ms Griffiths for the position in your personnel department.

She was employed by our company from April 1, 1978 to May 31, 1984 and we were always extremely satisfied with her services. She has a real gift for personnel work and, although very young, she progressed rapidly with us. She began as secretary to Mrs Young, our Personnel Officer in charge of women staff, and later on, as the company expanded and began to hire more and more women, Ms Griffiths took on some of the interviewing and staff welfare work.

Ms Griffiths is an extremely diligent, conscientious, and enthusiastic worker and we have no hesitation in recommending her for the post you have in mind.

Yours sincerely,

Dear Mrs Jones,

I am happy to answer your questions regarding Mr Frederick Allen.

He was in our employ from February 1, 1979 to May 31, 1980 and was doing extremely well in our tie department. His easy manner, fine speaking voice and innate good taste made him an excellent sales assistant and, in spite of his youth, many of our clients came to rely on his recommendations.

Always punctual, courteous and co-operative, Mr Allen is the type of young man we would have liked to keep with us. Unfortunately, however, like many young people nowadays, he decided to try his luck in the 'Big City' and we had to resign ourselves to losing him.

I can heartily recommend him for the position at your store.

Yours sincerely,

Dear Mr Dean,

I was very interested to learn that you are considering Mr Harry Simpson for a position as driving instructor at your school.

Mr Simpson was my private chauffeur for about two years, from December 1, 1979 to November 30, 1981. I was extremely pleased with him for he is an excellent, smooth driver, kept my two cars in very good condition, was always punctual, respectful, and neatly turned out.

Whether he would make a good driving instructor I cannot tell. Certainly he is an intelligent and ambitious young man and I have no hesitation in recommending him both as a driver and as a person.

Yours sincerely,

Dear Ms Yates,

I am happy to let you have the requested information on
Mr Harry Selwyn.

He was employed in our Export Department for about a
year, from January 6, 1974 to February 28, 1975 and we always
found him a hard-working, reliable, and conscientious young man.
He is well-versed in the preparation of most export documents,
can use his own initiative when necessary and does not mind
occasional long hours caused by last-minute scrambles to meet
shipping deadlines.

He has a fair knowledge of French and German, which are
certainly useful in the export business.

All in all, I feel that he would be a distinct asset to your
export department and am happy to recommend him for the
position.

Yours sincerely,

Recommending a friend

Dear Mr Pritchard,

I am writing to you at the request of Alan Freeman, a
young friend who is anxious to learn the publishing business.

I have known Alan all his life, his parents having moved
next door to me before he was born. He is a very studious and
sincere young man, mature, diligent, and as keen as mustard to get
into publishing. I was telling him about the special trainee scheme
your company has and he gave me no rest until I agreed to write
to you about him.

I am quite convinced that my young friend would make an
excellent publishing trainee and that you would have no cause to
regret taking him on. He took one of his A levels in English and
has shown a marked interest in literature from an early age. He is
extremely intelligent, industrious, and meticulous, all virtues
which I know you appreciate.

Shall I ask him to come in to see you? I'd greatly appreciate your having a chat with him.

Hope business is keeping up well.

Kindest regards.

Yours sincerely,

Dear Miss Wilson,

I am happy to reply to your letter of March 5, requesting information on the character of Mr Geoffrey Parker.

Mr Parker has been a friend and neighbour of mine for some five years, and we have been active together both in church and community affairs. He is a man of the utmost integrity, an able organizer, and tireless worker. His gift for leadership makes him an excellent man to entrust with a task.

I am quite convinced you will find Mr Parker worthy of any trust you may place in him and I have no hesitation in recommending him to you.

Yours sincerely,

Dear Ms Finlay,

It is with great pleasure that I write to recommend Ms Joan Bridie, in reply to your request of February 28.

Ms Bridie is a childhood friend of mine and I have watched her steady progress through school and college, and then on to a career in publishing. All her life Ms Bridie has been a zealous worker, throwing herself into every task she undertakes with zest and enthusiasm.

She is loyal to a fault, scrupulously honest, a stickler for detail, conscientious, and reliable. Indeed, if your company decides to offer her the post, I am convinced it will have secured a most desirable asset.

Yours sincerely,

Dear Mr Vance,

If your company gets Mr Williams on its sales force it will indeed have picked a winner.

I have known Jim Williams for about ten years and I would describe him as having the classical sales personality. An out-and-out extrovert, friendly, cheerful, interested in his fellowmen, he is none the less persistent, determined, ambitious, and methodical.

Moreover, he is a man of absolute reliability, thoroughly honest and trustworthy in every way. I cannot recommend him too highly.

Sincerely yours,

Dear Ms Riley,

I am happy to reply to your letter of March 1, asking me for information about the character of Mr John Wentworth.

He has been a friend and associate of mine for about five years and I can assure you that he is a man of unimpeachable character and extremely high moral standards. He enjoys a high reputation in the whole community, for which he has done a good deal. He has given much time and energy to maintaining and improving business ethics through his work for the Reading Chamber of Commerce and he is also secretary of the local Rotary Club.

An able organizer and tireless worker, he is the right man to entrust with a difficult task. I can heartily recommend him in every respect.

Yours sincerely,

Dear Mr Stewart,

It is a pleasure to reply to your letter requesting information about Mr Charles Fox.

I have known Mr Fox for some seven or eight years, as we are members of the same golf club. He is certainly a most popular man, with a winning personality, always cheerful and eager to give a helping hand wherever it is needed. He is both willing and able to take his share of responsibility and has, in fact, gone far beyond the call of duty to help run the club.

An honest and trustworthy man, he is well liked and respected by all who know him. I have no hesitation in recommending him to you.

Yours sincerely,

Dear Mr Greenely,

I very much welcome this opportunity of recommending Mr Eric Sweeny, for I have appreciated his sterling qualities for many years.

We met in 1963 when I joined the Leicester Rotary Club and our friendship has matured and deepened over the years.

Mr Sweeny is a man of outstanding intellect and drive. He joined his present company as a salesman and within three years was in charge of their whole selling operation. A fanatic for work, he still finds time to devote to community affairs, in which he takes a keen interest.

Mr Sweeny is a man of integrity, forthrightness and determination and I should very much like to see him offered the position you have in mind.

Yours sincerely,

Dear Ms Arnold,

I am taking the liberty of writing to you on behalf of a young friend, Peter Evans, who is most anxious to secure a place in your management trainee programme.

I have known Peter since he first went to grammar school, where, incidentally, he achieved a splendid record. He is a very industrious and conscientious young man and his school record shows evidence of qualities of leadership. I truly believe he is the kind of young man who would benefit from your programme and quickly become an asset to your company.

I can highly recommend Mr Evans and hope you will be kind enough to consider him for inclusion in your programme.

Yours sincerely,

Dear Mr Giles,

Thank you for your letter of July 15, inquiring about the character of Mr Max Young, who has applied for a position as science master at your school.

Mr Young and I were at London University together and have been close friends for three or four years. He is an extremely bright young man, serious beyond his years, with impeccable morals.

He is unquestionably the right kind of person to have young boys in his care, and I am sure he would be an asset to your school.

Yours sincerely,

4

Letters of Invitation

Letters of invitation should be easy enough to write, for they carry no bad news, do not risk hurting or offending, and usually announce a pleasant or even festive event.

They should be cordial and friendly without being too gushing, but as with other letters, the degree of informality used must depend upon the relationship and degree of friendship between the correspondents.

Letters of invitation should never fail to specify the date, the time, and the place of the event in question. In some cases the reason for the event should also be specified. This applies in particular to invitations to customers to attend an opening, or other essentially business occasions.

Invitations to the more formal type of dinner or other evening event should go out three weeks ahead of time, if at all possible. This enables more people to accept the invitation, gives them time to prepare for the event, and precludes the need for them to cancel other engagements when they feel duty-bound to accept – such as in the case of invitations to members of your staff.

Try to add a note of gaiety, warmth and welcome to your invitation letters. Enthusiasm is catching and engenders goodwill.

The specimen letters of invitation which follow include one formal third person invitation, because many people are not quite sure how to word them.

To customers

To open charge account

Dear Mrs Rogers,

That the things you buy from Swallow are of the finest quality and good value for money is something you have known for a long time. Now we are offering you yet another reason to shop at Swallow: the Swallowcard. Buy what you want when you want to at any Swallow store anywhere in the United Kingdom, produce your Swallowcard and have your purchases charged to your account.

Every month you will be sent a statement and you will have a choice either of clearing up the balance right away, without any interest added, or else you can pay as little as £10 a month on the balance outstanding.

Take your choice of three easy ways to pay: (a) by direct debit; (b) by post; or (c) through any bank in the United Kingdom by using the Giro slip at the bottom of your statement.

The enclosed leaflet tells you more about Swallowcard and includes an application form and direct debit mandate, should you select this way of settling.

We look forward to welcoming you as a charge customer.

Yours sincerely,

Dear Mrs Ballantine,

Thank you for your letter of January 6 asking about our Charge Card.

As you will gather from the enclosed leaflet, our Charge Account is especially designed for the convenience of our customers. It offers you not only an easy way to shop, but also an easy way to pay.

Choose your own credit limit and your own rate of repayment. Use your Charge Card in any Super Store. What could be more flexible?

The Super Store Charge Account works like this:

- You agree a credit limit with us. It can be anything from £200 to £1,250 or more.

- When you get your monthly statement, you can settle in full by the due date, earning yourself at least 25 days of interest-free credit a month. If you prefer, you can spread your repayments, paying as little as 5% of the outstanding balance. In this case an interest charge will be added to your account.

Apply for a Super Store Charge Card right away and see how much more convenient and pleasant it makes your shopping expeditions.

Yours sincerely,

Dear Mr Spencer,

This is a cordial invitation to become one of Myers' charge account customers.

As you know, charging your purchases is a very convenient way of shopping. It not only saves time, but offers you the added convenience of having a record of every item bought for budgetary or other purposes.

Normally we ask a customer wishing to open an account to fill in an application form, but for special people like you, we like to make it even easier. All you need do is mention this letter to the assistant next time you come in to make a purchase and she will do the rest.

Your Charge Card will be ready for you on your next visit. Why not try this convenient way of doing your shopping?

Do be assured of our desire to serve you well at all times.

Yours sincerely,

Dear Miss Burnett,

You are missing something,

. . . something that is being recognized every day by more and more of our good customers – it's the convenience of simply saying, 'Charge it'.

You would really enjoy this special service – so many of our customers do – but as yet you haven't let us show you its many advantages. We'd like the opportunity to do this, so we've taken the liberty of opening an account for you, ready to use at any time.

You will find your charge account simplifies shopping amazingly, but there are other advantages too: special fashion previews for Charge Account customers, advance notice of bargains and instant credit of up to £1,000, if you need it.

Just try it and see: next time you are shopping, present the enclosed card and say, 'Charge it, please'.

Yours sincerely,

Dear Mrs Wilkins,

It has been a pleasure to have you as a regular customer for so long and we much appreciate your support.

We have been wondering what we can do to make your shopping expeditions even more enjoyable and it occurs to us that if you were to open a charge account at our store, the result would be quicker, easier, smoother shopping for you.

The way it works is this: first of all you agree with us the spending limit you think you'll need for all your shopping over the months ahead. Then you can spend up to that amount by producing your Charge Card and signing for your purchases.

Every month we send you a statement, itemizing your purchases and the balance outstanding. You then pay a minimum of 5% or £5 (whichever is the greater) against the amount outstanding – or you can pay more, just as you choose.

An application form is enclosed and we look forward to hearing from you soon.

Sincerely yours,

Dear Ms Fillmore,

I was delighted to learn that you visited our fashion floor last week and hope you will return often.

I have just got back from my continental buying trip and the fashions I have selected will be in the store within the next two or three weeks. I know you will like them.

It occurs to me that you might like to avail yourself of our credit facilities to make your shopping even simpler. All you need do is fill in the enclosed card and mail it back to our Credit Department in the enclosed addressed envelope. Next time you come in just call at the Credit Department and your Charge Card will be ready for you.

I hope you decide to avail yourself of this invitation to become one of our many satisfied charge account customers.

Yours sincerely,

Dear Ms Bloch,

Business people like yourself are well aware of the value of time: writing out cheques for small items or waiting around for change are both time-wasters. They can be avoided by opening a charge account with our store. This will enable you not only to pop into any of the Lilley stores and make a purchase without loss of time, but also to charge your purchases at any of the Wilkens' chemist shops and Allegro shoe shops. The Lilleycard is a passkey to them all.

Around the 10th of each month you will get an itemized statement of all your purchases during the previous month. Just one cheque takes care of the lot. How's that for speed and convenience?

Further details about the Lilleycard are given in the enclosed leaflet. An application form is also enclosed.

We hope we shall have the pleasure of welcoming you as a charge customer.

Sincerely yours,

Dear Miss Greenall,

Our charge account customers are like members of a very select club, for we do not welcome anybody on our books. But you have been a loyal customer for a long time and we should like to invite you into the inner circle of account customers.

This method of shopping is a great convenience, as many of our account customers will testify. It means that you can pay for all your month's purchases with a single cheque and need no longer waste time waiting for change or writing out cheques for small amounts.

Why not try this easy, time-saving way of shopping?

Yours sincerely,

Dear Mr Ferris,

It was a pleasure to have you as a member of our Christmas Club and we should now like to invite you to open a charge account with our store.

All you need to do is fill in the enclosed form and return it to us in the business-reply envelope provided. Your account will be opened immediately and will be ready for you the next time you pay us a visit.

You will find this a very simple and easy way to shop.

Sincerely yours,

Dear Miss Freeman,

As the Christmas shopping season approaches we feel you will be visiting our store more often than usual, for it really has an extremely wide selection of gift ideas.

In order to facilitate your shopping we invite you to open a charge account with us. This will mean you can make a purchase at any time, without bothering to carry the cash around with you.

If you just mention this letter to the assistant next time you wish to make a purchase, she will take care of the details and your account will be ready for your use.

We are eager to do all we can to make each of your visits to the store as enjoyable as possible.

Yours sincerely,

To reactivate account

Dear Mrs Green,

You have been missed! It is almost six months since we had the pleasure of serving you and we are wondering why.

Could it be that we have incurred your displeasure in some way? If so, we would deem it a favour if you came into the store and told us about it.

Come upstairs to the Credit Office on the fourth floor and ask for me. If there was anything about your last purchase which made you unhappy, I shall be very pleased to straighten it out to your satisfaction even after such a long time.

We'd like you to know that we value our customers very highly and miss them when they cease to visit us.

May we look forward to seeing you again soon?

Yours sincerely,

Dear Mrs Jones,

You know the saying: new friends are silver old ones are gold. That is just the way we feel about our customers and when one of them stops coming into the store for several months we wonder what has kept her away.

Our new spring collections have just arrived and everything is looking so fresh and inviting that we hate to think of your missing all the excitement.

Do come along, if only to browse among the wonderful Paris and Italian-inspired fresh spring numbers.

Yours sincerely,

Dear Mrs Goldberg,

Several months have passed since you made use of your charge account at Nyman's. We are naturally concerned as we value your custom and have always done our best to serve you well.

Could it be that something happened to upset our good relationship? If so, do please tell us frankly and give us a chance to put things right to your satisfaction.

We look forward to your reply with great interest.

Sincerely yours,

Dear Mr Wilson,

We've missed your business.

In checking over our records we cannot find any charges to your account for the past three months.

Do please let us know if there is any reason why you haven't been buying from us lately. We'd greatly appreciate your using the bottom of this letter and returning it to us in the enclosed reply-paid envelope.

Thank you very much for past business and we look forward to filling your orders again.

Yours sincerely,

( ) I haven't bought because ....
( ) Nothing wrong – I simply haven't needed anything.
( ) Please send me the items listed hereunder:

Dear Mrs Cash,

I thought you'd like to know that our spring collection is now on display at the store – and a mouth-watering one it is! I'm sure you will want to come in and see it, even though you haven't been our way for quite a while.

Perhaps you thought we hadn't missed you, but we certainly have. We value our regular customers too much not to miss them when they stop coming.

Your charge account is still open and we hope you will pay us a visit soon. We shall all be pleased to see you.

Sincerely yours,

Dear Mrs Roscoe,

Our new Christmas stock is all in place and the whole store is simply bursting with exciting new gift ideas. Do come in to see us soon. You will certainly find something for almost everyone on your list.

Your charge account will make your Christmas shopping easier, too.

Please pay us a visit. We look forward to seeing you.

Sincerely,

Dear Miss McCall,

I am writing to tell you how much you have been missed at the store. Several months have passed since you used your Goodall charge account and we are naturally worried.

May we inquire the reason? If you were not entirely satisfied with one of your purchases, do please let us know, as we are most anxious to set things right.

The summer sales will begin on July 15 for two weeks and we would not like you to miss any of the bargains we are planning to offer.

We hope you will come in soon.

Sincerely yours,

Dear Ms Hunter,

We had always regarded you as one of our best and most loyal customers, when suddenly you stopped coming to our store.

You may have moved out of town, but on the other hand you may have been dissatisfied for some reason, either with the service or with the goods supplied.

I would certainly consider it a favour if you would kindly write and tell me what happened, as I am most anxious that it should be put right. If you will enclose your letter in the attached stamped and addressed envelope it will come directly to me. If you prefer to see me, do please come along to the store and ask for me.

I do hope you will give me a chance to put the matter right and look forward to hearing from you.

Yours sincerely,

Dear Mr. Selwyn,

Could it be that you've given up smoking? We really cannot believe it. Was your last box of cigars not up to par? We certainly hesitate to believe that. Have you moved out of town? Surely not! Then do please let us know why we have not had the pleasure of serving you for three whole months?

As you know, we pride ourselves on the excellence of our products and would not knowingly tolerate anything inferior passing across our counters. If for some unaccountable reason you failed to be completely satisfied with your last purchase, I should appreciate it if you would kindly let me know, in confidence, and permit me to put it right.

If nothing is wrong, why not drop in to see us and put our mind at rest? I can assure you that we value our regular patrons very highly.

Very sincerely yours,

To attend special function

Dear Mrs Grayson,

I have good news for you! During the week of March 13 Monsieur Marcel Duchat, the famous Parisian hair stylist, will be in attendance at our Salon de Coiffure on the 4th floor. He will advise you absolutely free of charge on the best hair style for you and give you any advice you may require on hair colouring, permanent waving, hair pieces or, indeed, anything connected with the coiffure.

Monsieur Duchat has brought with him from Paris the very latest and most exciting hair styles and we are happy indeed to be able to offer you this opportunity of meeting him and letting him help you to even greater beauty and allure.

Don't fail to come in on the week of March 13.

Yours sincerely,

Dear Miss Gift,

Won't you please be our guest at the Studio next Monday evening, April 22, at 8 p.m.?

I have a very special event lined up for you: George Irving, the British champion modern sequence dancer, has kindly agreed to come along and give us a talk entitled 'The Professional Touch'. His lecture will be illustrated, of course, or, rather, he will illustrate the points he makes with his partner, Isabelle Weston.

After the talk I am sure we shall be able to persuade George and Isabelle to give us a full demonstration, after which there will be general dancing, as on a normal Monday evening.

I look forward to seeing you at the Studio.

Sincerely yours,

Dear Mrs Gilchrist,

Our spring models are all ready for unveiling – and what a collection they are!

We have arranged a special showing for selected customers on Tuesday, March 5, at 3.30 p.m. in the Oval Room. Tea will be served during the parade and the Room will be closed to everyone without a special invitation.

Do please come along, bringing this letter with you for identification. You will be thrilled with the delightful models our buyer has brought back from Paris and Milan with her.

Yours sincerely,

Dear Mrs Rome,

It is a pleasure to invite you to be our guest next Wednesday, May 13 at 3 p.m. in the Auditorium on the eighth floor of the store. We have a very special treat for you.

Miss Laura Lavelle, chief housecraft adviser of the Simplex Company, is going to demonstrate a series of quickie dishes on her company's new SUPERBA cooker.

Miss Lavelle, as you may know, is noted not only for her skill as a cook, but also for her delightfully dry wit. You may have seen her on television in one of her Thursday evening shows.

We look forward to seeing you and can assure you of a very enjoyable hour.

Yours sincerely,

Dear Miss Freeman,

Won't you please be our guest at a special event for brides-to-be and other young ladies?

Ms Priscilla Hall, noted expert on home furnishings, will be speaking on: 'Furnishing your New Home on a Budget'. The meeting will take place in the fourth floor lounge, adjacent to the furnishing department, on Wednesday, March 17, at 6 p.m.

After her talk Ms Hall will be happy to answer questions or advise on any individual problem.

We are sure you will enjoy the event and look forward to seeing you. Why not bring a friend along?

Yours sincerely,

Dear Mrs Young

We have been in business just one year. It has been a truly successful year thanks to you and to many good customers like you. For this reason we want you all to join in our celebration.

On March 1 it will be Fiesta time at Casa Sevilla and you are cordially invited to attend at any time during the day. There will be stalls run by gay señoritas in Spanish costumes offering the ice-cold Spanish orchata and other delectable refreshments, fortune tellers, gipsy dancers, guitars – everything, in fact, except the Fiesta Brava itself.

We look forward to welcoming you to our Fiesta, which is dedicated to you, señora, our valued patron.

Sincerely,

Dear Mr Greer,

This year's harvests have been excellent and they are expected to produce fine clarets and outstanding burgundies.

Rather than wait for them to mature, we have decided to celebrate now and are happy to invite you to our wine-tasting party on Wednesday, November 2, between 12 noon and 2.30 p.m.

You will be able to taste many of the best wines in our cellars and, in addition, there will be some special bargains to celebrate the occasion.

We look forward to seeing you.

Yours sincerely,

Dear Ms Mason,

Miss Lucette Chandos, the best selling novelist, will be in our book department on Wednesday, March 25, between 1 p.m. and 4 p.m. to autograph copies of her new novel <u>A Candle in the Sun</u>.

We thought you'd like to know this, so that you can make a point of calling in. You'll find Miss Chandos quite unassuming and very easy to talk to.

Yours sincerely,

Formal invitation

To dinner

The formal third person invitation is usually engraved on a card, the guest's name being written in by hand.

Mr and Mrs John Cooper
request the pleasure of
the company of
Mr Frederick Allen
at dinner on
Friday, October 25
at eight o'clock

R.S.V.P.
'The Haven'
Cherry Lane
Chalfont St Peter, Bucks.   Black tie

Informal invitations to business or professional associates

To lunch, dinner or banquet

Dear Mr Springer,

Sir George Holden will be speaking at the next meeting of
the Sixty-Six Club and, as I know how much you would like to
hear him, I am wondering whether you would care to join me
there for lunch. The meeting is on March 13 and we could meet in
the lobby at 12.30. I do hope you can manage it.

Yours sincerely,

Dear Mr Smithers,

If you are free for lunch next Tuesday, September 11, will
you join Mr Griffiths and me at the Publicity Club around noon?
Mr Griffiths will be passing through Nottingham and I think it
would be useful for the three of us to get together.

We shall be in the bar at 12 noon and will keep a lookout
for you. Hope you'll be there.

Yours sincerely,

Dear Rachel,

I am planning to meet several of our authors for lunch at the Duke of Wellington at 12.30 on Thursday, March 23, and am hoping that you will be able to join us.

There is nothing iron-clad on the agenda. I just feel it is good that several of you should get together on occasion, and if between us all we manage to come up with some ideas for new books, so much the better.

Do let me know whether you can make it.

Yours sincerely,

Dear Mr Brown,

The B.I.M.C.A.M.'s annual banquet will be held this year at the Hyde Park Hotel, on Tuesday, March 21, at 8 p.m.

We are very much hoping that you will be able to join us. The guest of honour will be Mr James Kipping, OBE of Cambridge University. Dennis Reynolds will also be there, and is receiving his B.I.M.C.A.M. prize at the dinner.

I look forward to hearing that you will be able to join us.

Yours sincerely,

Dear George,

The subject of Bill's talk at the Marketing Association's dinner next Friday is 'Selling Within the Broader Marketing Concept'. Will you be my guest at dinner so that you can hear him?

We can meet in the bar at 6.30, if that suits you.

Sincerely,

Dear Dr Shelley,

I think it would be an excellent idea if we could get together while you are in town for the symposium and exchange ideas privately. Will you join me for dinner at White's on Monday, the 18th?

We could have a pleasant meal and then retire to a quiet corner of the smoking-room and discuss our respective projects, and, indeed, compare notes on the symposium's progress.

If the idea appeals to you, will you meet me at the club at around 6.30? I'll leave word that I'm expecting you.

I very much look forward to meeting you personally after such a pleasant long-distance association.

Yours sincerely,

Dear Mr Atkins,

I have just heard from my sales manager that you are planning to be in town next week and am wondering whether you would like to join us at our top-management monthly dinner on the 13th?

We'd all very much like to have you with us and I feel that it would be useful for you to join the discussion which takes place afterwards.

We usually meet at the Café Royal at 7.30 p.m., in the Blue Room. May we count on your presence?

Yours sincerely,

Dear Fred,

I was very pleased to get your note announcing your fleeting visit to London next week. I realize you will be very busy, but do hope you can spare the time to lunch with me on one of the days. I could manage Monday, Tuesday or Wednesday of next week, so pick whichever one you like and I'll meet you at Sweeney's at 12.30, if that suits you. Let me know which day it is to be.

I very much look forward to a long chat with you.

Sincerely,

Dear Ms Wilkins,

Your suggestion for a series of articles on homemaking for the career woman sounds very well worth exploring and I'd like to discuss the idea with you in more detail.

Perhaps we could talk more easily away from the interruptions and noise of the office and I wonder whether you would care to join me for lunch at the London Grill next Wednesday, May 12. Would 1 o'clock suit you?

Yours sincerely,

Dear Miss Harrison,

Both our area representatives will be in town next week and I think it would be most useful if the four of us got together. Problems never seem to loom so large once you know personally the people you're dealing with.

Could you join us for lunch on Thursday, May 20? We usually eat at an excellent little restaurant in Soho called L'Escargot, in Frith Street. May we expect you there at 1 o'clock?

Yours sincerely,

Dear Bill,

      I am lunching with Mr Frank Williams, Editorial Director of the Simmonds Group, next Wednesday at the Athenaeum and I am hoping you will be able to join us. Mr Williams is a very interesting person to talk to and, in addition, I feel he is a man you ought to meet.

      Do therefore try and arrange it. I am picking Mr Williams up at his office and we can meet you at the club at 12.30.

                Sincerely,

To attend lecture, talk or other event

Dear Mrs Lloyd,

      September 15 marks the end of Thomas & Watson's first financial year in France. We are planning to celebrate the event with a cocktail party at the Hotel Georges V on Friday next, between 6 and 8 p.m.

      We shall be honoured to have you as our guest, if you can manage it, and shall look forward to seeing you in the Salle Louis XV.

              Yours sincerely,

Dear Mr Lewis,

      I have two tickets for the Cup Final on Saturday and knowing what a football fan you are I am hoping you will be free to accompany me. I could quite easily pick you up at your home just before two o'clock. It should be an exciting game, so I hope you can get away.

              Yours sincerely,

Dear Jeff,

I understand that Dr Carruthers will be speaking on 'The Silicon Office' next Wednesday at 8 at the Town Hall. How about coming along? Perhaps we could meet in the lobby just before 8, if you are free. What do you say?

Sincerely,

Dear Shirley,

I am asking a few of our best customers to join me for a drink at our stand at Olympia immediately after the opening on Monday. I do hope you will be able to join us. Just make for the back of the stand, where I shall be waiting to welcome you.

Sincerely,

Dear Joe,

As soon as I heard that the School of Printing was sponsoring a lecture on 'The Human Side of Printing', I thought of you and hopefully secured two tickets on the off-chance that you'd be free on that particular evening.

The evening in question is Friday week, March 30; the time 8 p.m., and the venue the main hall of St Bride Institute in Fleet Street. Knowing how interested you are in every aspect of printing, I hope you'll be able to come along. Give me a ring and we can probably have a bite and a beer together before we go along to the lecture.

Sincerely,

Dear Mr Ferris,

At long last our brand new plant in Bracknell is finished and ready and we are planning to celebrate the occasion on Monday, May 27 with a buffet luncheon, followed by a conducted tour of the works.

May we count on your attendance? We are very proud both of the new building itself and of the fine, up-to-date equipment in it, and are eager to show you round.

The new plant is located on the Southern Industrial Estate, just off the Bagshot Road. You will see the huge royal blue sign above the building. May we expect you about noon?

Yours sincerely,

Dear Chris,

I thought you might be interested to learn that the National Trust is holding its annual meeting at Conway Hall on November 6 at 6.30 p.m.

I plan to go along myself and, knowing how interested you are in their work, I thought you might like to come along with me. May I pick you up at your office about 6.0 p.m.?

Sincerely,

Dear Fred,

I have been reading in Thamesman that Slough College of Higher Education is offering to tailor courses to the individual needs of small and large companies. The courses they offer include various sectors of marketing, including export.

There is to be a one-day seminar on the subject at the college on May 15 and it occurred to me that you and I might go along and get them to tailor an export course which would suit both our companies and perhaps another small local company or two.

What do you say? I am enclosing my copy of Thamesman with the article in question marked up. Perhaps when you have studied it you would give me a ring and we could arrange to go along, if you are interested.

Sincerely,

Dear Bob,

Fred Gillow will be giving his popular talk 'No close, no sale' at our next Sales Managers' Club meeting at the Café Royal on Wednesday evening.

Will you be my guest at dinner so that you can hear him? We could meet in the Long Bar at 6.30 for a private chat beforehand.

Sincerely,

Dear Mr Fisher,

I wonder if you have heard about Dr Byrd's lecture next Friday at the College of Technology? His subject is to be 'Electric Power in the Atomic Age'.

Both Jack Stowell and myself are going along and we thought you might like to join us. The lecture starts at nine and we'd be happy to call for you at your home at about 8.45.

Hope you can manage it.

Yours sincerely,

To spend night at home or club

Dear Peter,

      I was very pleased to learn that you will be in London in February to attend the national sales conference. It has occurred to me that you might prefer to stay overnight at my home, rather than bed down in a strange hotel.

      Both Cathy and I would be delighted to have you and are hoping you'll say 'yes'. If you're being sensible and coming by train, Cathy says she'll pick you up at the station. What more can you ask?

Sincerely,

Dear Mr Carstairs,

      I understand you'll be in Scarborough for the annual engineering conference and if your plans for the trip have not yet been completed, my wife and I would be delighted to have you as our guest.

      We realize you'll be a very busy man with little time for social activities and we won't stand in your way at all. Our only thought is that hotels will be pretty fully booked at the time and we flatter ourselves you'll be rather more comfortable in our home than at a hotel.

      Do let me know if we may expect you.

Yours sincerely,

Dear Roy,

Having looked forward to seeing you for so long it is very
disappointing indeed that your next trip to town happens to
coincide with my business tour of the Continent. It really is too
bad and I'll be very sorry to miss you.

I do insist, however, that you be my guest during your brief
stay in London and I've already reserved a room for you at White's
in my name.

I hope you have a very successful stay and that your next
trip will not be too far in the future.

Sincerely,

Dear Ms Fox,

My wife and I are hoping that your trip to the West Country
will include a stay in Bath and if so that you will accept our warm
invitation to spend as much time as your plans permit as our
guest in this delightful spot.

The guest room is ready and we very much hope that you
will come.

Yours sincerely,

Dear Ship,

Madge and I and the children are just back from three
wonderful weeks of sunshine and relaxation at our villa on the
Costa del Sol. Since we are lucky enough to own the villa, but not
lucky enough to be able to live there the whole year round, we feel
we would like to share it with as many of our friends as possible.

Bill and Phyllis will be spending a couple of weeks there in
August, but after that the place will be empty and you and Jean
are most welcome to be our guests there for as long as you wish.
There is no resident maid, but perhaps you would not mind taking
care of yourselves.

Do let me know whether you would like to go.

Sincerely,

Dear Dr Girone,

I am very pleased to learn that you have decided at last to come and see our plant for yourself. We shall all do our best to make you welcome here and to dispel the Italian notion that the English are a cold people.

My wife and I are hoping, in fact, that you will accept our cordial invitation to be our guest for the length of your stay in England. My wife is already busy studying an Italian cookery book.

We both very much hope you'll decide to come and look forward to your visit.

Yours sincerely,

Dear Dr Jones,

Thank you for your letter of the 12th accepting our invitation to conduct the two-day management seminar at our Institute.

May I extend to you a cordial invitation to spend the night of the 15th at my home? My wife and I would be delighted to have you and we are sure you would be more comfortable with us than in one of the guest rooms at the Institute.

May we look forward to welcoming you?

Yours sincerely,

Dear Charles,

I very much look forward to your visit next month and would like you to be my guest at the Club for the length of your stay in town. I shall be living there myself that week because the family's away, so we shall be able to have some good old chin-wags in the evenings. Is it on?

Sincerely,

To make speech or give talk

Dear Mr Dickens,

I've heard such glowing reports about your recent Middle Eastern tour that I am hoping you will be good enough to share your experiences with us at our next Rotary meeting, on March 15.

Dinner begins at 7 and we'd very much like you to be our guest and speak to us informally afterwards for about half an hour.

I can assure you of a large and enthusiastic audience and I very much hope you will be able to come. I could pick you up at your office and we could drive to the meeting together.

Yours sincerely,

Dear Mr Falkner,

I am now planning our next sales meeting, to be held in our school room on Thursday, April 21, and I am anxious to secure an expert of your calibre to address us informally.

Could you be persuaded to give us a talk lasting 30 to 45 minutes on a pertinent subject of your choice? I do hope your schedule will allow you to accept, as I know the sales team would benefit greatly from hearing you.

I could arrange your talk either at 11.30, just before we adjourn for lunch, or at 2 p.m. We will in any event count on having you with us for lunch in the executive dining room.

If you find you can manage it, will you kindly let me know what time you prefer and the title of your talk?

I look forward to hearing from you.

Yours sincerely,

Dear Ms Stevens,

I read your report on the psychological aspects of accident prevention with a great deal of interest and feel that all our members would greatly benefit from hearing your story.

I wonder if I could prevail upon you to give us a talk on the subject at our next week's meeting on Wednesday, May 21? Meetings usually begin at 6.30 and continue for a couple of hours. So important do I consider your approach that I would gladly give you as much time for your talk as you require.

As I have to organize the rest of the programme, I would greatly appreciate hearing from you as soon as possible, with an indication of how long your talk will be. I very much hope we shall have the pleasure of having you as our guest speaker.

Yours sincerely,

Dear Dr Crawford,

I have just read that you are shortly to visit the United Kingdom and I hasten to write to you before all the other management schools do so in the hope of inducing you to lecture at our College, if only as a 'one night stand'.

Your schedule, no doubt, will be very crowded, yet I sincerely hope that you will be able to devote one evening to our institution. There will be week-end courses in progress during the whole time of your stay – assuming, that is, that the papers have the dates correctly – and I'd be happy to fit you into any one of them, if you will only agree to come.

The subject of your talk will obviously be the amazing Crawford 'How to' technique, as yet little known in Britain. No doubt your visit here will change this state of affairs quite rapidly. You may have as long as you like for your lecture, but please let me know soon, giving me the date and the time required.

Wishing you a very happy stay in Britain. I look forward to your good news.

Yours sincerely,

Dear Mr Robbins,

I have just put down your latest book, <u>Self-Development for Potential Leaders,</u> and have been most impressed by it. May I offer you my congratulations on a very thorough, thoughtful and practical work?

By sheer coincidence two of our week-end courses for industrial supervisors will be devoted to just that topic – simply substitute the word 'supervisors' for 'leaders' and you have the theme of our meetings.

I should be gratified indeed if you could come along on both week-ends and talk to our delegates for about an hour. The week-ends concerned are April 19/21 and May 12/13. At this stage I could give you a choice of time if you will let me have your reply very shortly.

You can be sure of a good turn-out and an audience most eager to listen and learn – <u>and</u> ask questions! I <u>do</u> hope you will come.

Yours sincerely,

Dear George,

After several years of struggle our fine new Community Centre is being opened at last. It has fallen to me to organize the programme for opening day on March 17 and it seems to me that you, our most distinguished citizen, should be the man to talk to us.

Would you do this for us? We really would be honoured. Fifteen to 20 minutes would be about right. I can arrange for you to speak at 8, if that would suit you.

May I hear from you and please make the answer 'yes'.

Sincerely,

Dear Mr Swanson,

Our next conference, to be held on June 2 at the Esso Cinema, Holbury, Southampton, will be devoted to the business upturn. We are extremely anxious to secure a speaker of your distinction for the occasion and I am writing to ask whether you would consider speaking to our Association for 30 to 45 minutes on that date.

The conference begins at 8 o'clock and I'd be honoured if you'd be my guest at dinner beforehand. It has to be rather a rushed affair under the circumstances, but it would still allow us a little time to talk.

You'll find our audience attentive and enthusiastic and I do hope you will be able to come.

Yours sincerely,

Dear Fred,

It has occurred to me that a report on your recent selling tour of the Near East would be of great interest to our Young Conservatives. Would you be willing to address them at the next meeting? As I believe you are aware, we next meet on June 21 at 8 p.m. at the Club House.

A talk of half an hour or so would be fine, plus 10–15 minutes for questions. I have an idea there will be plenty of these. Please say 'yes' so that I can begin spreading the news among the members.

Sincerely,

To staff

To attend a company social event

Dear Mr. Sweeney,

As you may know, Robert J. Forster is retiring at the end of next month after serving the company loyally for 25 years.

As a send-off I am planning a little dinner for all company employees with ten or more years' service and all company directors. I'm not quite sure which heading you come under but I'd like you to be with us.

The date is March 23, the place the Café Royal, and the time 7.30 in the Napoleon Room.

I look forward to seeing you there to give Bob a right royal farewell.

Yours sincerely,

Dear Ms Fields,

This year the Company plans to hold its Christmas dinner and dance at the Palm Court, Hotel Waldorf, on December 21.

We shall all be meeting there at 7.30 for cocktails, and dinner will be served in an adjoining room at 8 sharp.

You are cordially invited to attend and I hope you will let Joyce Maxwell know right away that you will be with us.

Yours sincerely,

Dear Fred,

I am asking my colleagues on the marketing team to join me for lunch on Thursday to celebrate Joe Crawford's recent promotion. The 'Bunch of Grapes' are reserving their private dining-room for us and we shall be meeting there at 12.30 sharp.

Please join us and help to give Joe the appreciation he deserves.

Sincerely,

Dear Mr Elliott,

As you know our new building on the Cressex Trading Estate is nearing completion. It will be formally opened on October 12 with an Open House for some of our best customers. The following week, on October 19, that is, it will be Open House for the Staff.

We all meet in the lobby at 4 p.m. and then tour the building in small groups, stopping for tea and biscuits en route. Afterwards we all get together again in the canteen for drinks.

I look forward to seeing you there as I want all the staff to share the management's sense of accomplishment and pride in seeing the new building finally complete.

Yours sincerely,

Dear Mr Bannister,

This is the Company's Golden Jubilee. Fifty years ago Oscar Watson, my grandfather, began the business as a small grocer's shop. Little did he then foresee what giant strides the business would make in his lifetime, much less after his death.

We are planning to celebrate the anniversary with a dinner and dance for the whole of the Company personnel. We have reserved the Killarney Room at the Connaught Hotel and I invite you to join us there, in the bar at 6.30 on Friday, November 11. Dinner will be served promptly at 7. Dress will be informal.

I hope you will be able to come. I'm sure we'll have a very pleasant evening.

Yours sincerely,

Dear Mr Boyle,

This is to ask you to be a guest of the Company on January 6, at 7 p.m. for dinner. We have reserved the Oval Room at the Piccadilly Hotel and hope you will be able to join us there.

Important expansion plans will be announced at the dinner and I am especially anxious that our own people should be the first to hear about them.

I look forward to hearing from you.

Yours sincerely,

Dear Mr Soames,

February 22 marks the Chairman's tenth anniversary as head of the firm and we are planning to honour him with a dinner at Rules on that evening.

They are reserving the upstairs dining-room for us at 6.30 p.m., so we can all meet there after the office. Ms Jones is helping us to make the dinner something of a surprise to the Chairman, although the news will probably have to be 'leaked' to him ahead of time, otherwise he might be off on a business trip leaving us to hold the stuffed boar's head, as it were.

So, don't forget – February 22 at 6.30 p.m. at Rules – come as you are!

Yours sincerely,

Dear Miss Riley,

This year again I am happy to ask you – together with all the other members of the staff – to join me for an afternoon at my country home, 'The Oasis', on Saturday, June 10, at 3 p.m.

My wife will have a 'spread' waiting for us and then you will all be free to wander round the grounds, have a game of croquet or tennis or even take a swim in the river.

My wife and I look forward to welcoming you once again to our home and I, for one, feel convinced that the weather will co-operate again this year as it did last.

Yours sincerely,

Dear Mr Bruce,

Well, you all picked straws and the river trip won, so here's your invitation to join me and the rest of the staff on the M.V. 'Victoria' for a cruise up-stream to Windsor.

Please be at the landing stage at Kingston at 2.30 sharp on Saturday, June 21, ready to sail at 2.45. Bring your sunglasses, your camera and your guitar, if you have one, and let's make it the very best staff outing yet!

Yours sincerely,

5

Acceptance Letters

Letters accepting an invitation to a banquet, to lunch or dinner at someone's home, or to any other event requiring prior preparation, should be sent within two days of receiving the invitation.

While conveying pleasure at being invited and anticipation of the event, their degree of formality or informality should take their cue from the invitation itself. Obviously a chatty note inviting you to lunch at a friend's club will be answered in an equally informal way, while a more formal invitation to the Company's annual banquet will require a more formal reply.

It is a good plan to reiterate the time, place and date of the meeting just to make sure there will be no misunderstanding, and if some of these details have been left to you, then do not forget to specify them in your reply.

The specimen acceptance letters which follow include two examples of formal third person acceptances, since many people are a little unsure of themselves when faced with the task of replying to a formal invitation.

Accepting someone's resignation from his or her job or from a board, committee, club or association is, of course, an entirely different situation. Unless you are glad to get rid of them, the formula calls for your expressing regret at losing their services, saying a few kind words about the qualities they brought to the office concerned and conveying your good wishes for their future.

Formal acceptances

Of invitation to dinner

Mr Frederick Allan
has much pleasure in accepting the kind invitation of
Mr and Mrs John Cooper
to dinner
on Friday, October 25 at eight o'clock

70

Mr and Mrs French
accept with great pleasure the kind invitation of
Mr and Mrs Gordon Walker
to dinner
on November 29 at eight o'clock

Informal acceptances

Of invitation to banquet, lecture or other event

Dear Mr Greenley,

I am delighted to accept your kind invitation to the
B.I.M.C.A.M.'s annual banquet at the Hyde Park Hotel on March 21.

I shall be there at 8 as you suggest and look forward to a
very interesting evening.

Thank you very much for thinking of me.

Yours sincerely,

Dear Fred,

I very much appreciate the invitation to attend your
Company's annual banquet on March 15 and am happy to accept.

I shall be in the Palm Court at about 7 and greatly look
forward to the event.

Sincerely,

Dear Mr Keenan,

How good of you to remember my literary leanings and how
right you are; I'd be happy to hear Sir Allen Wickers speak and
gladly accept your invitation for March 13.

I shall be in the lobby punctually at 12.30 and look forward
most keenly to the occasion. Thank you again.

Yours sincerely,

Dear Chris,

Yes, I <u>would</u> like to hear Bill's talk before the Marketing Association and I gladly accept your kind invitation to be your guest at dinner on March 13.

As you suggest, I'll meet you in the bar at 6.30. I'm most eager to have a chat with you before the evening's events begin. Thank you for asking me.

Sincerely,

Of lunch or dinner invitation

Dear Mr Stanley,

Many thanks for your letter of March 4.

I'd be happy to have lunch with you during my brief visit to town next week. Both the day and the hour suit me admirably and I will be in the foyer of the Piccadilly Hotel at 12.30 as you suggest.

I look forward to seeing you.

Sincerely yours,

Dear Peter,

How kind of you and Muriel to ask me to dinner during my visit to Harrogate next month. Quite apart from the pleasure of spending the evening with you, a home-cooked meal begins to take on the aspects of manna from Heaven after a few days of 'conference' food.

Thank you both and I'll be there at sevenish, as suggested.

Best wishes to both of you.

Sincerely,

Dear Mr Stevens,

I'd be delighted to have lunch with you and Mr Graham on April 12.

It is kind of you to suggest calling for me at my hotel and if this really does not inconvenience you too much, I will wait in the foyer for you at about one o'clock.

Many thanks for asking me.

Yours sincerely,

Dear John,

I was glad to get your letter asking me to have lunch at your home when I arrive in Oxford on May 11.

I accept with pleasure and greatly look forward to seeing you and Madge again.

My train gets in at 12.15 so, unless something unforeseen happens, I should arrive at 'The Coppice' by 12.45 at the latest.

See you then.

Sincerely,

Dear Dr Fraser,

I was very pleased to receive your letter asking me to have dinner with you and your husband when I visit Washington next month.

I'd be delighted to come, of course, and any of the evenings you mention would suit me. I leave the choice to you and I will keep all three evenings open until I hear from you further.

I'm very much looking forward to my trip to the States and seeing you again and meeting your husband.

Yours sincerely,

Dear Mr Whiting,

It was good of you to suggest lunch at your club during my fleeting visit to London. I accept with pleasure and Wednesday, the 22nd, at 12.30 suits me perfectly.

I shall await you in the lounge and look forward to a long chat. It is so long since we last met that we have a lot to catch up on. See you next week.

Yours sincerely,

Of invitation to spend night at home or club

Dear Herr Schneider,

Many thanks for your letter of May 21.

It is most thoughtful of you to ask me to spend the week-end at your home during my brief stay in Hamburg and I accept with great pleasure.

However, I do beg of you not to put yourself out to meet my plane. I have been to your city many times before and I shall have no difficulty in making my way to the hotel unaided.

I very much look forward to seeing you and to meeting your wife on the week-end of June 20–21.

Yours sincerely,

Dear Signor Pacelli,

Your charming letter has just reached me and I'm delighted to accept your kind invitation to spend a night at your villa during my business trip to Italy next month.

I shall be in Milan from May 12 to May 18, so Saturday, May 15, would be ideal for me.

It is most generous of you to offer me the hospitality of your home and I greatly look forward to the visit and to meeting your wife.

Sincerely yours,

Dear Mark,

Thank you for your note. What a thoughtful suggestion that I make my headquarters at your club during my overnight stay in London. I gratefully accept and very much look forward to seeing you again.

Sincerely,

Dear Henry,

I cannot tell you how happy and relieved I was to get your letter. Quite frankly I dread these conference trips more and more each time but your kind invitation now makes the prospect infinitely more attractive.

I gladly and gratefully accept. You cannot imagine how much I'd rather spend my nights at your home than in this or that hotel bed.

Thanks, Henry, you're a real pal. Tell Jean I'll be as good as gold and will put her out as little as possible! I very much look forward to seeing you both.

Sincerely,

Dear Mrs Miles,

Thank you for your letter of March 16.

It was most thoughtful of you and your husband to invite me to spend the night of the lecture at your home. It would indeed have been a little late to return to town afterwards, as you say.

I gratefully accept your generous hospitality and look forward to seeing you and your husband again.

Yours sincerely,

Of invitation to make speech or give talk

Dear Mr Reynolds,

I feel honoured by your invitation to speak at the Marketing Society's meeting on March 13, and gladly accept.

I recently gave a talk called 'The Advent of the Hypermarket', which went down rather well and since the subject is a timely one, I would like to use it at your meeting, if this is agreeable to you. The half-hour allotted to me should be ample and I will do my best to give your members an interesting talk.

I shall be there at 7.30 as you suggest.

Yours sincerely,

Dear Fred,

Thank you for your letter of February 13.

I'd be very pleased to talk at the Rotary luncheon about my recent selling trip to the Middle East. I realize I must keep strictly to half an hour so that everyone can get back to his office; I will therefore limit the illustrations to just one large map, so that the audience can follow my trip, and one or two photographs, which I can pass round.

I'll be there at 12.30 on March 22 with bag and baggage and will do my best to give a good talk.

Sincerely,

Dear Mr Squires,

It was good of you to ask me to take part in your annual Sales Conference at Scarborough next month and I'll be happy to do so.

You suggest I tackle something connected with the spirit of service and I shall accordingly use my well-worn, but none the less effective, talk entitled 'Serving, not Selling'. Half an hour, plus 15 minutes for questions suits me fine.

I greatly look forward to the occasion, as your Sales Conferences are always so dynamic and brimming with enthusiasm.

Yours sincerely,

Dear Mrs Guinness,

Thank you for asking me to speak at the February meeting of the Librophile Club. I am quite flattered by your invitation.

I shall call my talk 'Are books doomed?' In case you are worried, I hasten to add that the gist of my argument will be that in spite of heavy competition from visual and aural communications, books are definitely here to stay.

As you kindly suggest picking me up at my office about noon, I will wait for you here.

Yours sincerely,

Dear Ms Chambers,

I should be delighted to talk to the Young Liberals on April 21. I am keenly interested in the Liberal movement and only too happy to make whatever contribution I can.

As you suggest, I will tackle the subject 'Why not a Coalition Government?' and will endeavour to squeeze all I have to say into the 45 minutes allotted to me, plus 10–15 minutes for questions.

I very much look forward to the occasion and hope you have a good attendance. I shall be there by 7.30, so we can go over the arrangements beforehand, as you suggest.

Yours sincerely,

Of invitation to attend meeting or conference

Dear Mr Charles,

Thank you for inviting me to attend your workshop meeting on Wednesday, May 22. The technique you are planning to use sounds most interesting and it will be an experience for me to attend. I am, of course, also gratified that you should think my contribution valuable and I will do my best to give the meeting all I've got.

Yours sincerely,

Dear Mr Cousins,

I shall be happy to attend the Birmingham Chamber of Commerce meeting on Friday week at 2.30 p.m.

Your export project is a very useful and timely one and I am only too anxious to give it all my support.

Yours sincerely,

Dear Ms White,

I shall be very glad to attend the opening day session of your annual Sales Conference on January 9.

There is always much to learn from an aggressive, far-sighted organization such as yours and I consider it a privilege to be asked to attend.

I look forward to seeing you and my other Clary friends at Scarborough.

Yours sincerely,

Dear Margaret,

Thank you for your letter of March 16. Your scheme sounds very interesting indeed and I'll be glad to attend the meeting you have scheduled at your office for Wednesday, March 28, at 5.30 p.m.

Let me know if there is anything I can do before this date to help things along.

Sincerely,

Dear Miss Griffiths,

I was very interested to learn about your plans for enlarging the magazine in the New Year and shall be delighted to attend the planning meeting next Wednesday at 10.30 a.m.

As you know, I am keen to participate in PM&M and would be only too pleased to contribute to its continued success in any way I can.

Yours sincerely,

Of invitation to join professional or civic bodies

Dear Mr Skinner,

It was very kind of you and your Committee to ask me to stay on as an Honorary Member of the Birmingham Chamber of Commerce.

Although I am semi-retired, I cannot help still being keenly interested not only in our own business, but in business in general.

I am therefore very happy to accept your kind invitation and look forward to attending a great many more meetings in the year that lies ahead.

Yours sincerely,

Dear Mr Carver,

I greatly appreciate your cordial invitation to become a member of P.E.N. and gladly accept.

Realizing how many writers of distinction from every corner of the earth are P.E.N. members, I am aware of the honour extended to me and am eager to be a part of the association.

I will certainly attend one of the lectures or discussions soon and will otherwise participate as often as business activities permit.

Yours sincerely,

Dear Ms Taylor,

Many thanks for your letter of March 21, inviting me to become a member of the Marketing Association.

I must admit that I have long toyed with the idea of joining, as there is no doubt that your Association has a great deal to offer members.

I therefore gladly accede to your suggestion and my membership form is returned herewith, duly filled in.

Yours sincerely,

Of invitation to serve on committee or board

Dear Ms Harwood,

Many thanks for your letter of March 15 informing me that my name as been put forward for the Club's membership committee.

I am glad to accept nomination and if elected will do all I can to serve the Club well.

Yours sincerely,

Dear George,

I cannot tell you how delighted I was to receive your letter inviting me to join your editorial board. You wonder whether I have the time? Don't worry for I shall certainly <u>find</u> time for such an exciting project.

I note that you meet quite informally about once a month and look forward to being informed of the date and time of the next meeting.

Thank you for your confidence in me. I really am honoured and will do my best to make a useful contribution to your team.

Sincerely,

Dear Mr Shinwell,

I have your letter of January 25 asking me to serve on the Park Estate Residents' Association Executive Committee.

This is to confirm that I shall be very happy to serve a term on the Committee, since I am quite anxious to further the aims of our Association.

Yours sincerely,

Dear Mrs Clifton,

Thank you for your letter of December 2. I greatly appreciate your suggestion that I should agree to be nominated to serve on the Club's Executive Committee. I gladly accept your invitation.

Although I cannot hope to be a regularly playing member of the Club much longer, I shall always take a keen and active interest in its welfare.

Yours sincerely,

Dear Mr Weeks,

International Organization for Standardization
Space Heating Appliances

Many thanks for your letter of January 12 about the setting up of a U.K. Steering Committee in connection with the IOS Technical Committee, to study the above subject.

I shall be pleased to serve on this committee and look forward to receiving further details in due course.

Yours sincerely,

Of resignation from job, board or committee

Dear Ms Giles,

I am very sorry to learn from your letter of March 15 that you wish to resign your position as Assistant Sales Manager.

All of us here at Grenfell House will miss you, for you have put a good deal of enthusiasm, hard work, and skill into your job since you joined us five years ago.

I do like to see young people move ahead, however, and I cannot help but agree with you that the opportunity offered to you is too good to miss.

I therefore wish you the very best in your new post, and congratulate W. H. Wood on their acquisition.

Yours sincerely,

Dear John,

I have just received your letter of yesterday and very much regret to learn of your decision to leave Hartman's.

Your qualities of leadership, enthusiasm and sheer dedication have been an inspiration to your department and I know the Company will be diminished by your departure.

I would not wish to stand in your way, however, and the position you have been offered sounds a wonderful opportunity for you. I know you will make a success of it and you certainly take with you my best personal good wishes.

Sincerely,

Dear Rex,

It is with sincere regret that I accept your resignation from my Editorial Board.

Over the years you have contributed some most valuable ideas, offered constructive suggestions and wise counsel to our group and we shall miss you sorely at future meetings.

I do realize, however, that pressure of work no longer allows you the time for this pleasant avocation and I can but say 'thank you' for your valuable contribution to our deliberations and wish you the very best for the future.

Sincerely,

Dear Liz,

I have your letter of December 2, telling me that you wish to resign from the Club's Entertainment Committee at the end of the year.

You have done splendid work for the Club during your tenure of office and we hate to see you relinquish it. On the other hand, the work involved in running the Club should be shared equally between members and, as you have devoted a good deal of your spare time to the Club during the past year, we cannot complain if you now feel the need to hand over to someone else.

May I take this opportunity of thanking you on behalf of all our members for the splendid work you have done for us during the past year?

Yours sincerely,

Dear Mr Gross,

The Board of Directors has reluctantly accepted your resignation as Research Director, as from August 1 next.

Every one of us sincerely regrets your departure, for you have led the Company to the very top place in the industry through your remarkable talent, insight, and tenacity. You will be hard indeed to replace, for individuals like you are not born every day.

None the less, our first concern must be for your health and our heartfelt wish is that, once you have laid down the burden of work, you will soon find yourself on the road to recovery. All the members of the Board join me in extending this wish to you, as well as in thanking you for your tireless devotion over the past years.

Yours sincerely,

Of resignation from club or association

Dear Mr Powell,

     We very much regret to learn that mounting pressure of business makes it difficult for you to attend meetings and that you have therefore decided to resign from the Heat and Power Club.

     We certainly have missed you over the past several months and, while you will no longer be a member, we would like to make it clear that, if ever you <u>do</u> get time to attend a meeting, you will be most welcome as a guest.

              Yours sincerely,

Dear Barry,

     Your letter of resignation from the Reading Chamber of Commerce was read at this afternoon's meeting.

     We shall all miss you greatly, for you have contributed a great deal to the organization since you joined some five years ago.

     At the same time we are happy to learn of the splendid opportunity which has made you decide to move to London. The good wishes of all of us go with you.

              Sincerely,

Dear Stan,

     We were all sorry to learn of your resignation from the Rotary Club.

     Your high spirits and good humour will be very much missed at future luncheons and now that you are leaving we realize more than ever how fortunate we were to count you as a member.

     As you take the road to the milder climate of the South, all our thoughts and best wishes go with you.

              Sincerely,

Dear Mr Hynes,

We were sorry to receive your letter of resignation from the Marketing Association and accept it with reluctance.

The Association owes a great deal to your loyal support over the past 15 years and your active interest will be sorely missed.

Our good wishes go with you and may your overseas post give you a great deal of satisfaction.

Yours sincerely,

Dear Mr Soames,

We regretfully accept your resignation from the Institute of Directors, the more so since the reason for your retirement is ill health.

You have given generously of your time and talent to the Institute, both in and out of office, during the past 10 years and we feel very sad indeed to see you go.

All our members join me in wishing you a speedy recovery and once you are feeling your old self again, we hope you will wish to attend some of our meetings as our guest. You will be more than welcome.

Yours sincerely,

6

---

*Refusal Letters**

If they are not to offend, letters of refusal must be both tactful and friendly. They should leave the recipient with the impression that the invitation was not only welcome, but flattering and that it is turned down with genuine regret.

One way of achieving this effect in the case of invitations to lunch, dinner or some sort of function or entertainment, is to indicate your availability on another occasion. In other cases, it helps if you give a valid reason for turning down the invitation. But, above all, let 'the kind word turn away wrath', or rather, let it cement good relations even while saying 'no'.

Once again, the formal third person reply has been included to dispel all doubt on how this kind of situation should be handled.

Formal refusals

Of invitation to dinner

> Mr Frederick Allen
> thanks
> Mr and Mrs John Cooper
> for their kind invitation to dinner,
> but very much regrets that he is unable to accept
> as he will be abroad on that date.

---

* The letters in this chapter are all concerned with turning down invitations. Letters refusing requests will be found in Chapter 12, under the sub-heading 'Refusing Requests'.

Mr and Mrs George White
greatly regret that a previous engagement
prevents them from accepting the kind invitation to dinner of
Mr and Mrs Henry Fletcher.

Informal refusals

Of invitation to banquet, club or other event

Dear Ms Forsythe,

I very much regret that I shall be unable to attend the banquet honouring Mr Cameron.

Our annual Sales Conference at Scarborough is taking place this year from January 6 to 9 inclusive, which means that I shall unfortunately be far away on the evening of the banquet.

I cannot tell you how sorry I am, for nothing would have given me more pleasure than to be with you. Do please excuse me and accept my best wishes for a very enjoyable occasion. I cannot think of anyone who more richly deserves the tribute being paid to him on January 8.

Yours sincerely,

Dear Mr Greenwood,

Many thanks for your kind invitation to be your guest at the Chamber of Commerce luncheon next Friday.

Unfortunately I leave for a brief business trip to the Continent on Wednesday and will not be back until the following Monday. I am therefore unable to accept your welcome invitation, much as I would have liked to do so. I hope another opportunity will present itself in the near future.

Yours sincerely,

Dear John,

I very much appreciate your invitation to be your guest at the Sixty Six for lunch and informal talk. I had been hoping for an opportunity to go one day, but now that you have asked me, however, the date unfortunately coincides with that of our Board meeting and I dare not leave the office at all on that day.

I'm terribly sorry and do hope you will ask me again some other time. Don't forget to let me know the gist of Victor's talk.

Sincerely,

Dear Miss Holmes,

Thank you for your kind invitation to attend the showing of your latest sales training film. Unfortunately, however, I shall be out of town all day on March 25, visiting our 'outposts' in Devon and Cornwall.

I'm very sorry about this, as I would have been extremely interested to see the film. I do hope you will give me another chance when the next opportunity presents itself.

Yours sincerely,

Dear Mr Thomas,

It was kind of you to invite me to the BACIE Conference on April 11.

I know I would have enjoyed and profited by it. However, a previous engagement, which I cannot now change, claims me on that evening and I must therefore ask you to excuse me.

May I hope you will ask me again another time? Meanwhile, I wish you a very enjoyable evening.

Yours sincerely,

Of lunch or dinner invitation

Dear Fred,

I have just received your friendly letter asking me to have lunch with you during my fleeting visit to town next week.

There is nothing I would have enjoyed more than a nice long chat with you – not to mention lunch. Unfortunately, however, I'm afraid we'll have to postpone it. My visit this time will be a dash and nothing more. I shall be attending meetings all day long and lunch will, no doubt, consist of a sandwich in the conference room – if that.

I hope you will understand. I look forward to seeing you either on my next visit or when you come up to the Midlands.

Sincerely,

Dear Mr Sanford,

I have just received your kind letter of May 21 asking me to join you and your wife for dinner during my brief visit to Harrogate next month.

There is nothing I would enjoy more, I assure you, and I very much appreciate your thoughtfulness. However, I have found from past experience that it is impossible for me to arrange anything of a social nature during our Annual Sales Conference. Every minute of my time seems to be taken up with meetings and business luncheons, cocktail parties and dinners.

I am sorry indeed about this and hope you will understand. I will certainly give you a ring while I'm in Harrogate and I hope the opportunity for a get-together will present itself before too long. Will you kindly convey my regrets to your wife?

With kindest regards.

Yours sincerely,

Dear Ms Willis,

Many thanks for your kind invitation to join you for lunch on April 17 during your brief trip to London.

I would have been delighted to do so, but unfortunately your visit happens to coincide with my own brief buying trip to the Continent. This really is a most regrettable coincidence, as I would have very much enjoyed exchanging notes with you.

I hope you have a fruitful stay in London and that you will be back again soon.

Sincerely yours,

Dear Bill,

I was delighted to learn from your letter of April 21 that you will be in London early in May and am most appreciative of your invitation to dinner. Nothing would have pleased me more than to spend an evening with you.

I'm afraid I won't be able to manage it this time, however, since Joyce and I are taking an early holiday this year and May 2 will probably find us basking in the Algarve sunshine.

I'm very sorry indeed to miss you and hope you will be back in town again soon.

I hope you have a successful trip and I'll be thinking of you on May 2.

Sincerely,

Dear Miss Peters,

Thank you for your letter of May 30 asking me to join you and the other members of your creative team at lunch on June 20.

I would have been happy to do so, but unfortunately we have an Executive Committee meeting scheduled for that morning and one never can tell just how long it will last. Quite often it goes on all through lunch-time and sandwiches are brought in when everyone is near collapse!

I am afraid, therefore, that I shall be unable to accept your kind invitation. Please accept my apologies and my best wishes for a very successful luncheon meeting.

Yours sincerely,

Of invitation to spend night at home or club

Dear Mr Manfredi,

Many thanks for your cordial letter of October 2, asking me to spend the week-end at your villa on Lake Como during my fleeting visit to Italy next month.

It is indeed kind and thoughtful of you and your wife and it would have been very pleasant to accept your invitation. My business trip to Italy will be rather hectic, however, and I fear it will not leave me time for such a pleasant interlude as you suggest. I must leave Milan on Friday evening, November 15, to be on hand in Rome on Saturday morning for a conference.

I very much regret, therefore, that I am unable to accept your gracious invitation. Will you kindly express my regrets to your wife and tell her that I hope to meet her on my next visit?

Very sincerely yours,

Dear John,

It was thoughtful of you to offer me the hospitality of your club during my overnight visit to town next week.

However, Professor Hawkins made me promise a long time ago that I would spend the night at his home and I accepted.

I greatly appreciate your kind thought and look forward to seeing you at the lecture, in any event.

Sincerely,

Dear Mr. Lewis,

Thank you very much for your kind invitation to spend the night at your home after my lecture in Oxford on November 7.

I greatly appreciate your kind thought and would have been delighted to enjoy the hospitality of your home. Regretfully, however, I have to return to London the same night, as an important meeting is scheduled for the following morning.

I shall look forward to a nice long chat with you on another occasion and am sorry indeed that my visit this time is such a hurried one.

Yours sincerely,

Dear Jack,

It was good to get your letter and I much appreciated your suggestion that I spend the night at your club after our Western Area meeting next month.

I would have been delighted to accept, but I am taking Joan with me and we have decided to make a week-end of it after the meeting.

Thanks all the same and I very much look forward to seeing you at the meeting.

Sincerely,

Dear Herr Braun,

I was delighted to receive your charming letter inviting me to spend a night at your country house during my visit to the Leipzig Fair.

Nothing would have pleased me more than to relax in the warm atmosphere of your home and if it were possible for me to change my schedule around in order to do so, I would gladly do it.

Unfortunately, however, I must leave Leipzig that very evening and press on to Dresden and thence to Switzerland.

The leisurely business trip seems to be a thing of the past and speed is now of the essence all round, alas.

I do hope you will understand and we shall certainly meet at the Fair in any event.

Please present my compliments to your wife and I hope to meet her on my next visit. Perhaps she will accompany you to England on your next trip. I certainly hope so.

Yours sincerely,

Of invitation to make speech or give talk

Dear Ms Stone,

I very much appreciate your inviting me to speak before the Kingston Chamber of Commerce at next Wednesday's luncheon meeting, and I would have been only too pleased to do so.

However, I have a Board meeting on Wednesday morning and one never knows just how long it will last. In any event, I am sure you will understand that I could not possibly undertake a speaking engagement and luncheon on that day.

Perhaps you will give me an opportunity of speaking at one of your later meetings.

Yours sincerely,

Dear Jim,

I am quite flattered that you should feel I am just the man to address your sales team at your next meeting. I would have been delighted to do so, unequal though I feel to the task.

The date of your meeting is, however, most unfortunate as far as I am concerned. I shall be in Scotland most of that week, then slowly making my way back via Yorkshire and the Midlands the week following.

It looks therefore as if I shall have to forego the pleasure of addressing your 'reps' this time, but do ask me again when you plan your next sales meeting.

I wish you a most successful gathering – even without the benefit of my 'pearls of wisdom'.

Sincerely,

Dear Mr Greenhouse,

Thank you for your letter of the 14th. It is indeed kind of you to ask me to speak at the banquet in honour of Mr Symmonds next month. It would have been a privilege to do so, for it would not be difficult to sing his praises.

Unfortunately a previous engagement, which I cannot change, prevents me from accepting and I must regretfully ask to be excused.

I shall be thinking of you all on the evening of December 5 and really am grieved that I shall not be with you.

Yours sincerely,

Dear Mr Soames,

I was quite flattered to get your letter of November 22, asking me to speak at the next meeting of the Heat and Power Club.

I would have been very pleased to do so, had circumstances permitted it. Regrettably, however, an important personal commitment prevents me from attending on that evening.

Do feel free to ask me again, as I would very much like to come.

Yours sincerely,

Dear Clarence,

Thank you for your kind letter of September 11. I would have been very glad to address the Leicester Businessmen's Club on October 3, but unfortunately I cannot leave the office that day, as we have a regional sales meeting.

I'm very sorry I cannot fit it in this time, but perhaps another opportunity will present itself later on. Will you be this way soon? We really ought to get together.

Sincerely,

Of invitation to attend meeting or conference

Dear Ms Sanders,

Thank you for your letter giving me details of the Annual Advertising Association Conference at Brighton next month.

Obviously, it would have been both a duty and a pleasure for me to attend, but it looks very much as if I shall be unable to accept your kind invitation this time because of a most important and long-standing plan to visit the United States just about that time.

Let me assure you that nothing short of an extremely important commitment would keep me away from the Conference. It really is most unfortunate that my U.S. trip should coincide with the Ad Conference, but I am afraid there is absolutely nothing I can do about it.

Do please therefore excuse me this time. The programme sounds interesting indeed and I shall be looking forward to hearing all about it from my more fortunate colleagues. Please accept my very best wishes for its success.

Yours sincerely,

Dear Ms Forster,

Thank you for your letter of March 16, inviting me to attend the April 15 meeting of the Marketing and Promotion Association.

The programme sounds an interesting one and I would very much have enjoyed attending. However, we are expecting a group of buyers from the Continent on April 15 and I shall be tied up with them for most of the day.

This means, unfortunately, that I am unable to accept your kind invitation, much as I would like to.

With best personal regards,

Yours sincerely,

Dear Carole,

The programme for the annual general meeting of the Institute, as organized by you, sounds excellent and I would be delighted to attend.

However, I am still rather weak on my pins and working only a half day. Any extra-curricular activities, so to speak, are definitely out for me for some months yet, so please excuse me, and accept my best wishes for a very successful meeting.

Sincerely,

Dear Miss Green,

Thank you for inviting me to attend the first marketing conference of the Textile Distributors Association next July.

I would very much have liked to attend and had I known about it beforehand, I would have re-organized my plans accordingly. As it is, however, I have booked my annual holiday for mid-July and it is too late to switch my reservations around at this late date.

Please accept my apologies and thank you again for asking me.

Yours sincerely,

Dear Allen,

I was surprised and delighted to get your letter, as I had been wondering what had become of you. It certainly is a splended idea for some of the Old Boys to get together and have a post-mortem on the 'good old days'. There is nothing I would have enjoyed more, but I am afraid you're going to have to count me out, none the less.

This is the busiest time of the year for my Company and it will be absolutely impossible for me to get away any time next month.

Please remember me to the others and if you decide to make this a regular event, for goodness sake don't have it in the spring, for I'd love to join you next time.

Sincerely,

Of invitation to join professional or civic bodies

Dear Mr Holloway,

Many thanks for your letter of April 21.

I am highly honoured by your invitation to me to join the Institute of Administrators.

At the moment, however, our Company is in the throes of heavy expansion abroad and I am all too frequently out of the country. For this reason, I do not feel that I could undertake the responsibilities of membership in the Institute.

I am sure you will understand my position and thank you again most sincerely for your kind invitation.

Yours sincerely,

Dear Mr White,

There is nothing I would enjoy more than to be able to join the Concrete Society and I thank you sincerely for your kind invitation.

When I join an organization, I like to do so in the knowledge that I will be able to devote to it a fair portion of my time and make a worthwhile contribution. In this instance, unfortunately, I am not in this position, because the demands on my time are increasing apace and I cannot in all fairness add to my outside commitments.

Your kind thought is very much appreciated, none the less.

Yours sincerely,

Dear Dr Clarke,

Thank you for your courteous note inviting me to become a member of the Heat and Power Club.

I would certainly like to do so, but my work takes me out of town a good deal, sometimes for long stretches at a time. This means that I would frequently be unable to attend meetings. I don't think this is fair on other people who would very much like to join the Club and have ample time to devote to meetings. I do not therefore feel that I should accept your kind invitation.

Yours sincerely,

Dear Ms Fisher,

I very much appreciate your kind invitation to join the University Club and I know it is the kind of club I would very much enjoy.

Unfortunately, however, I have not yet quite recovered from my long illness and the doctor recommends as much rest as possible. This means just work and bed for me at the moment.

Later on, perhaps, when I am really and truly back in the saddle, I may be able to reconsider taking up again some outside activities.

Many thanks, none the less, for your kind thought.

Yours sincerely,

Dear Mr Kelly,

I am flattered indeed by your kind invitation to join the Heating and Ventilating Research Association.

I would be happy to do so, but a glance through my diary tells me that, alas, I have rather overdone the joining of professional organizations and the like, and my weekly programme resembles one of those American 'See-Europe-in-a-Week' tours! I just don't see how I could fit in one single thing more and do it justice.

I am sure you will understand, therefore, why I cannot take advantage of your kind invitation just now, much as I appreciate it.

Sincerely yours,

Of invitation to serve on committees or boards

Dear Mrs Cunningham,

I am honoured indeed that the members of the Grange Estate Residents Association should feel they would like to have me on the Association's Executive Committee.

I wish I could undertake the task, but unfortunately my business commitments are so heavy these days that I feel I must not devote much time to personal matters, however important.

I hope therefore that you will excuse me and do please thank the other members for their confidence in me.

Yours sincerely,

Dear Ms Price,

Thank you for your interesting letter of March 21 acquainting me with the aims and activities of your Association and inviting me to serve on your Research Committee.

Mindful as I am of the need for co-operation between associations such as yours and the universities, I do feel that my accepting your kind invitation would serve a useful purpose and I only wish I were in a position to do so.

However, my very crowded schedule would not permit me to give the undertaking the time and attention it deserves and I must therefore ask you to excuse me.

I hope you will understand, and I extend to you my very best wishes for the continued success of the Association.

Yours sincerely,

Dear Ross,

Your invitation to join the Editorial Board of your group of journals is flattering indeed and there really is nothing I would be more keen to do.

Unfortunately, however, my days are becoming more and more crowded owing to the terrific expansion plans my Company has launched. For this reason, any activity even bordering on the 'extra-curricular' must be avoided, however reluctantly.

I really am sorry to have to say 'no', but it would not be fair to undertake the commitment lightly and you know, of course, that I could not do so.

Do continue to call on me for comment and suggestions informally, as in the past, and thank you very much for the thought.

Sincerely,

Dear Stella,

Thank you for your letter of May 30, inviting me to serve on the Association's Membership Committee.

I sincerely wish I were in a position to accept your invitation, but unfortunately I do not think I would be able to manage it. Since my last promotion I do a great deal of travelling for the Company and sometimes spend several weeks at a time abroad. This would inevitably clash with any commitments I might make to serve on a committee and I feel, therefore, that it would be safer to excuse myself.

I really am sorry and I do appreciate your asking me.

          Sincerely,

Dear Miss McKinley,

Thank you for your letter in which you ask me to serve on the Society's Finance Committee.

I wish I could accept your invitation, which I greatly appreciate, but frankly I am not really quite myself again since my severe operation and feel compelled to follow the doctor's advice and take things easy. By this, I mean, doing all essential work and cutting out anything bordering on to the avocational, however important.

Later on, unquestionably, things will be back to normal, but for the moment, at least, I feel I cannot accept.

I hope you will understand and thank you again for asking me.

          Yours sincerely,

7

Letters of Welcome

A letter of welcome is a gracious gesture which costs very little effort to write and is much appreciated by the recipient. It is one of those thoughtful gestures which builds goodwill and starts off a new relationship on a happy, friendly footing.

There are many occasions which might prompt you to write a letter of welcome. They include letters to prospective customers newly arrived in your district or town; to new customers, either retail or wholesale; to owners or executives of new businesses moving into your district and to new members of your staff.

Obviously, the content of your letter will depend on the individual circumstances, but brevity, friendliness and sincerity should be the hallmark of all of them.

In writing to new retail customers you will want to stress your pleasure in serving them and your desire to offer them excellent merchandise and service. Your new agents or wholesale customers will be pleased to know that you plan to co-operate with them in every way and look forward to a pleasant and mutually profitable relationship. Your welcome letter to a new member of your staff would do well to stress the qualities and background which got him or her the job, assure him or her of the opportunities for advancement which the new position offers, and reiterate your conviction that your relationship will be mutually pleasant.

To prospective customers

Dear Mr and Mrs Wayne,

We have just heard that you have recently taken up residence in Leicester and we hasten to send you this note of welcome. We are sure you will like it here. It is a happy, friendly town.

Please accept our cordial invitation to visit and become acquainted with our store. We have a very extensive and well-stocked men's department, as well as our ladies' fashion departments and, of course, a home furnishing department and many others.

You will find us friendly people, eager and happy to serve you. Won't you come in soon?

Yours sincerely,

Dear Mr Goodwyn,

We have just learned from our well-trained grapevine that you have moved into town from the North. May we wish you a very successful transfer into the Big City?

In addition, we feel you ought to know about The House of Gilroy, for its sole raison d'être is to serve the rising executive such as yourself. Men's wear, accessories, smoking requisites, sports equipment, men's toiletries, a gift department – even a gentleman's hairdressing department is included for your convenience. We like to feel we can take care of all your personal shopping needs at The House of Gilroy, saving you both time and wear and tear.

Do come in and see us soon. We'd be happy to serve you.

Yours sincerely,

Dear Mrs Jones,

Welcome to Oxford! We are sure you will enjoy living in this pleasant town.

Once you have settled down we hope you will pay us a visit at Harmond's to see our various departments and the fine, up-to-date merchandise we have to offer both for your home and for your own consumption.

We pride ourselves on our friendly service and we hope you will give us an opportunity of welcoming you in person soon.

Yours sincerely,

Dear Mrs Pierce,

We are very happy to learn that you have recently moved into our town and we are writing to extend a warm welcome to you.

We should also like to invite you to visit our store soon. You will find the merchandise well displayed, the fashions reflecting the latest trends, and the staff eager to be of service.

To make your shopping easier, we have taken the liberty of opening a charge account in your name. It is ready for use now. All you have to do when you have decided on your first purchase is to say 'Charge it'. We will do the rest. A single cheque at the end of the month will take care of all your purchases.

We look forward to seeing you soon and making your personal acquaintance.

Yours sincerely,

Dear Mrs Fleet,

Welcome to Slough! It is a bustling town, alive with activity and we know that you will like it here.

It is our hope that you will include our store in your 'get acquainted' trips to the shopping district. Please make yourself at home in the store. You will find our assistants and buyers eager to serve you in every way they can.

We are sure you will enjoy your shopping here and look forward to seeing you frequently.

Yours sincerely,

Dear Miss Acock,

It is a pleasure to welcome you to Birmingham.

Like most people, you will, we are sure, find the Bull Ring an exciting place in which to shop. As you may already know, parking facilities are provided and everything is done to permit you to shop at leisure, free from traffic and transport worries.

May we extend to you a cordial invitation to call in at White's and make the acquaintance of our store? The enclosed guide, 'Welcome to White's', will help you to find the various departments and also gives you the names of the buyers. Please do not hesitate to ask for the buyer personally should you experience any difficulty at all in finding just the item you want.

You will find White's staff imbued with the spirit of service and we know you will enjoy every visit here.

Yours sincerely,

Dear Mrs McGill,

We were delighted to learn that you had moved to our town and feel sure you will like it here. Everybody does!

We hope you will visit our store soon and become acquainted with its many interesting departments. You will find our gift department a mine of unusual ideas, while our furnishing department will be happy to serve you with any item you may need to complete your new home.

Should you be interested in opening a charge account, your request will be given prompt and courteous attention. But do come in anyway, either to shop or to browse. You may be sure of a warm welcome.

Yours sincerely,

Dear Ms Lester,

We are happy to welcome you to Edinburgh and to our store. If you haven't yet visited us, we certainly hope you will call soon, because we know you will enjoy browsing around and getting to know every department.

We are noted for our friendliness and service and we have been doing business in Edinburgh since 1871. When a lady in this city plans a shopping expedition, the first name that springs to mind is Eton's. We like to feel that before long it will be the same with you.

We wish you every happiness in our town and look forward to meeting you soon.

Yours sincerely,

Dear Mrs Wilson,

It is a pleasure to welcome another gourmet to our town. We have not wasted a minute in letting you know about our shop because we know full well that, as a gourmet, you will not settle down happily until you know where to get your Parmesan cheese, your fresh Emmenthal and Gruyère, your plover's eggs, Italian, French or Spanish olive oil, wine vinegar and your various exotic spices.

The answer is: at 'Le Petit Coin des Gourmets', 122 Queen Street. You will find all you need here.

We look forward to welcoming you and wish you many exquisite dinners in your new home.

Yours sincerely,

Dear Miss Levy,

Welcome to our town! It is a very friendly community and we feel sure you will like it here.

We know you will be anxious to keep abreast of fashion trends and for this reason we hasten to send you this note of welcome and introduction to our small exclusive Fashion Salon. Our buyer attends all the fashion shows and we can, without boasting, claim that our Salon is the spear head of fashion in the community.

Do come in and see us soon. All the spring numbers have arrived and we know you will be thrilled with them.

Yours sincerely,

To retail customers

Dear Ms Bradley,

This is just a note to say 'Thank you' for shopping at our store yesterday.

We are delighted to welcome you as a customer and will do everything we can to deserve the confidence you have expressed in us and our merchandise. Do return soon.

Yours sincerely,

Dear Mr Grant,

Thank you very much for making your first purchase in our store yesterday. We know you will get a great deal of satisfaction from the suit you bought and that it will wear well.

We look forward to serving you again and feel confident that you will become a regular patron of ours.

Yours sincerely,

Dear Miss Freeman,

It was a pleasure to welcome you to our store yesterday and we want you to know how much we appreciate your support.

We hope you will make it a regular practice to call in whenever you are in the vicinity and we look forward to seeing you.

Yours sincerely,

Dear Mrs Stone,

One of the duties I enjoy most is to welcome a new customer to White's.

I heard that you had called at our Millinery Department yesterday and wish to say 'Thank you' for coming in.

If there is anything we can do to make your shopping more convenient or pleasurable, please do not hesitate to let me know personally. We pride ourselves in our store and frequently make use of new ideas from our customers in order to improve our service.

We look forward to seeing you again soon.

Yours sincerely,

Dear Mrs Simpson,

We wish to thank you most sincerely for placing a regular order with the Golden Dairy and Creamery.

You will find our dairy products always fresh and delectable and deliveries reliable. Our dairy is, in fact, one of the most up-to-date in the country. We are very proud of it and are always glad to welcome any of our customers who would care to look over it. Do let us know if you would like to be shown round.

Yours sincerely,

Dear Mrs Wilson,

Welcome as a new customer of 'Le Petit Coin des Gourmets'! I was delighted to meet you yesterday and to share your pleasure in finding all the gourmet items you wanted.

I know you will be entirely satisfied with your purchases and am confident of counting you among our customers for many years to come.

Yours sincerely,

Dear Mr Ford,

Thank you for making your first purchase on our Stag Floor yesterday. We hope you found the experience satisfactory, for, as you know, our aim on the Stag Floor is to cater for the hurried, harried male in quest of a gift, a shirt, a tie for his new suit, or indeed the suit itself – all within easy walking distance.

If you require the added convenience of a charge account, please let us know and your request will be attended to without tiresome delays.

Sincerely yours,

Dear Ms Grant,

I am happy to welcome you as a Greenley customer and to thank you for your recent purchase in our shoe department.

We hope you will visit us frequently. You will always find a friendly welcome in our store.

Yours sincerely,

Dear Mrs Fisher,

It was a pleasure indeed to welcome you to our store yesterday. We hope you will enjoy for many years the purchase you made in our furniture department.

We take your patronage as a token of your confidence in our store and our merchandise and we shall certainly do all we can to deserve such trust.

We look forward to seeing you again soon and sincerely hope you are settling down happily in our town.

Yours sincerely,

Dear Miss King,

May I extend to you my personal thanks for visiting our store yesterday?

In welcoming you as a new customer, I would like to wish you many happy shopping hours at Tipping's. We shall always be pleased to see you and eager to serve you.

Yours sincerely,

To agents and wholesale customers

Dear Ms Shepherd,

It is a pleasure to welcome you as a Cosmos agent and to assure you of our utmost co-operation in making the sale of our products a source of profit to you.

We hope that this is the beginning of a pleasant, profitable, and lasting business relationship between us.

Yours sincerely,

Dear Mr Fitzroy,

Very many thanks for your initial order.

Let me assure you personally that we greatly appreciate the confidence you have placed in us and that we shall do everything in our power to deserve it.

Sincerely yours,

Dear Miss Jenkins,

We are happy to welcome you to the exclusive family of Bernall agents.

Please be assured that we shall do everything we can to support your marketing efforts and to co-operate with you in every way possible.

We sincerely believe that our products will be a very lucrative line for you and we wish you every success in this new venture.

Yours sincerely,

Dear Mr Amish,

Our sincere thanks for your opening order. Your interest in our products is very much appreciated.

Shortly after shipment is made you will receive our invoice showing our terms of sale. From this you will note that we offer a cash discount of two per cent if paid within 15 days, one per cent if paid within 30 days, with the invoice net in 30 days. The date of invoice is the date of shipment and the cash discount is based on this invoice date. We trust that you will take advantage of this opportunity of additional profit on our line.

We are certain that you will find our products the finest available and an important addition to your merchandising efforts, plus an opportunity for increased earnings. We welcome you to our organization and look forward to a long and satisfactory business relationship.

Yours sincerely,

Dear Ms Smith,

It is a pleasure to welcome you to the growing network of Knox agents and to thank you for your initial order.

Please be assured that we shall do all we can to give you our best co-operation and to help you in every way to establish our line in your territory.

If there is any specific assistance which you would like, please let us know and we shall be only too delighted to oblige.

Yours sincerely,

Dear Mrs Greenley,

I have just heard that you recently placed your first order with us and hasten to welcome you personally to our circle of customer friends.

I am convinced that you will find our products a very suitable addition to your line and that they will prove a valuable source of new business for you.

Thank you for the confidence you have placed in us and please be assured that we shall do everything we can to merit it.

Yours sincerely,

Dear Mr Shipley,

This is just a brief note to say 'Thank you' for your initial order and to welcome you to our circle of customers.

We like to do all we can for our wholesale customers, not merely by supplying first-class goods at reasonable prices, but also by helping them with their merchandising. Our merchandising man will be calling on you early next month to help you in launching our line of goods.

We feel confident that this will be the beginning of a pleasant and profitable business relationship between our two companies.

Yours sincerely,

Dear Mr Schneider,

Enclosed is your copy of the signed dealership agreement between us. I should like to take this opportunity of welcoming you into our dealer-family and wishing you the best of success with our line.

For our part, we shall do everything we can to help you to this end.

Yours sincerely,

Dear Miss Stevens,

Welcome to our large and successful company of beauty counsellors!

You will find this work brings you into contact with a great number of people, many of whom will become your friends. We are sure you will enjoy it and that you will find it a good money spinner.

Yours sincerely,

To business and professional associates

Dear Mr Sterling,

I am happy to welcome you to Slough. It is a thriving industrial centre and I am sure you will do well here.

Your industry will be a useful one to the community and I look forward to co-operating with you in any way I can.

Yours sincerely,

Dear Mr Swift,

I was pleased to learn that you are joining Smith, Watson and Keyes as Chief Accountant and look forward to having you in Worcester.

They are a fine firm and Worcester a pleasant town to live in. I am quite convinced that the move you have made was a happy one. I wish you all the very best and look forward to seeing more of you from now on.

Yours sincerely,

Dear Mr Duncan,

As you prepare for the Grand Opening of your new store, let me welcome you to our town and wish you the very best of luck.

It is a most attractive building and will make a worthy contribution to the shopping centre.

I look forward to having you as a neighbour.

Yours sincerely,

Dear Miss Jones,

Welcome to Milton Keynes! I'm sure you will find it a very pleasant place to live in, as well as a very active business centre.

Your new business will make an excellent addition to the town's facilities and I wish you every success in it.

Please do not hesitate to let me know if we at Fraser's can do anything to help.

Yours sincerely,

Dear Mr Flotohor,

I understand that you will be taking over the management of the Waterloo Branch of the Bank upon the retirement of Mr Poole and I wish to congratulate you on your appointment and welcome you to our business community.

I look forward to meeting you personally and hope to be in to see you sometime next week. Meanwhile, please accept my good wishes for success in your new appointment.

Yours sincerely,

Dear George,

I am happy indeed to learn that you are joining the company on the production side. The firm will be acquiring a very able man and I will be given opportunity to see more of an old friend.

You will find the Phoenix Metal Company an excellent place at which to work and we have a very fine management team. I know you will make a valuable contribution to it and I am delighted that you are joining us.

Sincerely,

Dear Ms Hyde,

Welcome to the Poyle Trading Estate! We are a very small and tightly-knit community – an industrial centre in the heart of the country – and when we acquire a new neighbour we like to send a note of welcome in the good old-fashioned style.

We hope you will settle down happily among us and wish you every success.

Yours sincerely,

Dear Mr Moore,

It is a pleasure to welcome you to our village.

Bourne End has grown considerably over the past three or four years and the need for another Bank to serve the community was very sorely felt by many local shopkeepers and businessmen.

In opening your sub-branch you have therefore rendered a very useful service to us all. My Company, for one, looks forward to doing business with you.

Yours sincerely,

Dear Mr Blood,

All my colleagues at Fuller's join me in welcoming you to our town and wishing you the very best of success in your new business.

We look forward to co-operating with you in maintaining a high standard of business ethics in our community, and hope you will not hesitate to get in touch with us if there is any matter you would like to discuss or if we can help you in any way.

Yours sincerely,

Dear Jane,

I was very pleased to learn that you are moving to Nottingham to join the firm of Barrie, Barrie and Weeks.

I'm sure you will find Nottingham a pleasant place in which to live and B B & W is, of course, a very distinguished and old-established firm. In fact you may talk me into transferring my legal work to you once you are established!

Meanwhile do let me know if there is anything I can do to help you settle in. Good luck!

Yours,

To staff

Dear Will,

I was delighted to learn from Mr Symmonds that negotiations have finally been concluded and you are to join our staff on June 1.

I really look forward to having you as a colleague and want to wish you every success in your career with us.

You will find Hyperion a first-class firm to work for and, as I have told you from the beginning, I'm sure you will do very well here.

I look forward to seeing you on June 1.

Sincerely,

Dear Miss Jones,

This is just a note to welcome you to our organization.

The fact that you succeeded in the face of the very heavy competition for the position is certainly a measure of your ability and qualities of mind.

Let me assure you that at Leigh and Company you will have every opportunity to continue to grow. There will be plenty more responsibility for you as soon as you are ready to handle it, and I, for one, am convinced that you will go far in the Company.

Yours sincerely,

Dear Mr Weston,

I am happy to welcome you to our growing organization.

With you at the helm, I feel convinced that our Book Division is in good hands and its expansion assured. Your qualities of leadership, enthusiasm, and industry give me confidence that the consolidation and expansion of the Division has finally left the drawing-board stage and entered the road to realization.

The task you have undertaken to carry out is a challenging one, but it is also full of promise and rich rewards. I know you are equal to the combat and worthy of the rewards.

Yours sincerely,

Dear Miss East,

It is my pleasant task to welcome you to our Company.

A young lady with your charm, poise, and good fashion sense is the kind of person most likely to succeed at Goodall's. All our buyers begin on the sales counters and, in fact, our Chairman, Miss Lena Flower, began as an assistant in the haberdashery department.

This means, of course, that opportunities for ambitious and gifted people are almost unlimited at Goodall's. We are convinced that you are the kind of person most apt to seize them as they arise, yet work patiently on in the meantime.

Yours sincerely,

Dear Sims,

It is a pleasure to welcome you to the sales team of Norris Engineering.

A young man with your sound technical background, pleasant personality and persuasive manner should go far in our Company and I certainly wish you a very successful career with us.

Our Company demands great effort and dedication, but in return offers unexcelled opportunities to those who accept the challenge. We are pleased that you should have done so.

Sincerely,

Dear Miss Willis,

It is a pleasure to welcome you to the Association's staff.

The lively mind, organizing ability, zest for work and technical knowledge which you bring with you give us confidence that under your leadership our four publications will soon acquire an attractive new look, both inside and out, not to mention a new breath of life.

We are sure you will have a successful and, we hope, a very happy career with the Association.

Sincerely yours,

Dear Ms Carruthers,

I have just learned from our Personnel Department that you are joining the Company as Technical Librarian, and as Company Chairman I am anxious to extend to you my personal welcome.

I have made it my business to acquaint myself with your background and consider that our Company is to be congratulated on its acquisition. I feel that in your capable hands our library will grow in usefulness and comprehensiveness and will indeed be that source of valuable and readily available up-to-date information I intend it to be.

You will find our Company a friendly place to work in and your new position an absorbing one. We are a growing concern, which means there is ample opportunity for all our staff to grow with us and make progress in their careers.

Yours sincerely,

Dear Mr Dalrymple,

I am happy to welcome you to Schneider and Co.

The extensive background in the export field which you bring with you will unquestionably serve you in good stead here and you will find that your numerous talents will be amply made use of.

In addition, we pride ourselves on our promotion-from-within policy and opportunities for talented and ambitious people like yourself are, we feel, unlimited at Schneider's.

I therefore wish you the very best of luck as you embark on this new phase of your career. We shall all enjoy working with you, I'm sure.

Yours sincerely,

Dear Finch,

Welcome to the Bank of Commerce and Trade!

When a young man starts work at the Bank we like him to feel – as we do – that he is beginning a career in banking and though the climb ahead may be a long one, the top is not only in sight, but attainable to all who have the right qualifications of mind and character.

We are firmly convinced that you are such a young man and it is a pleasure to wish you a happy and successful career with us.

Yours sincerely,

Dear Miss Fisher,

This is just a brief note to tell you how happy I am that you are joining us at Morgan's.

Your background is really an outstanding one and I'm convinced it will mean that I am lucky enough to have acquired that rare pearl, the perfect secretary.

You will not find us ungrateful at Morgan's and we like to see our best people get ahead.

I sincerely hope this will be the beginning of a pleasant association and welcome you to Morgan's also on behalf of the Company in general.

Yours sincerely,

Dear Lorna,

It is a pleasure to welcome you to our specialized sales force.

Unquestionably, a young woman of your pleasant appearance, savoir faire, and exceptional contacts should do well selling our travel services.

You will find that a career in the travel business is both rewarding and stimulating. There is an abundance of opportunity for ambitious, hard-working people and we are sure you count yourself as one of them. You will find that 'the sky's the limit' at The House of Travel.

I wish you a successful and happy career with us.

Sincerely yours,

8

Letters of Seasonal Greetings

Letters of seasonal greetings can do a lot to cultivate and maintain a happy business relationship and to keep a contact alive. It is a pity that so few such letters are actually written, for they are simple enough to write and need only be quite short. In fact once you have expressed your appreciation for your reader's co-operation, friendship or business over the past year and wished him or her the best for the holiday season, there is nothing more you should or can say without being repetitious and cumbersome.

Occasionally a successful longer letter is written and one or two such examples are included in the specimens that follow.

As with most other letters, a letter of seasonal greetings will vary in its degree of informality according to the relationship between the correspondents, but friendliness, sincerity, and, with few exceptions, brevity, should be common to all of them.

The examples that follow include letters to retail customers, agents or wholesale customers, business or professional associates, and staff.

To retail customers

Dear Mrs Waring,

As the bells ring out the Old Year we would be ungrateful if we failed to turn our thoughts back to the year that has gone by and to the valued support you have given us during that time. We sincerely appreciate your loyalty as a customer and we feel this is the time of year to express our thanks and send you our very best wishes for the coming year. May it be a happy and prosperous one for you and your family.

Sincerely yours,

Dear Miss Gibbs,

All the staff of Willis' join me in wishing you a very Merry Christmas and a Happy New Year.

Thank you for your support during the past year. We have enjoyed serving you and greatly look forward to doing so in the New Year and for many years to come.

Yours sincerely,

Dear Mr Gregg,

As the year draws to a close we should like to pause briefly to thank you for past patronage and wish you the compliments of the season.

We hope you have had a very successful sporting year and wish you even better angling with bigger catches in the year ahead.

Yours sincerely,

Dear Ms Braithwaite,

At this time of year we like to look back and reflect on how lucky we are to have so many loyal customers such as yourself. We truly appreciate the confidence you have placed in us and want to thank you sincerely for your support.

We hope you will have a very Merry Christmas and a New Year full of happiness and success.

Sincerely yours,

Dear Mrs Stanley,

All of us at Hoyle's would like you to know how much we have enjoyed serving you during the past year and how much we appreciate your loyalty.

We hope to have even more exciting fashions for you next year and have quite a few interesting events lined up for your enjoyment.

All of us wish you a Merry Christmas and a Happy New Year.

Yours sincerely,

Dear Mrs Jones,

I am writing to you quite simply to wish you and your family a Merry Christmas and a Happy and Prosperous New Year.

We frequently have occasion to write to our customers during the course of the year and our letters are usually concerned with a sale, an account, or some specific business matter between us. At this time of the year, however, we like to write just to thank our customers for the business they have given us and to wish them a happy holiday season.

All my buyers and their staff join me in sending you this greeting.

Sincerely yours,

Dear Ms Tippett,

This is just a note to wish you a wonderful holiday season and all the best in 1986.

We also would like you to know how much we have appreciated your support during the past year. We shall endeavour to serve you even better in the coming year and do all we can to deserve the confidence you have placed in us.

Yours sincerely,

Dear Miss Turner,

We never have sleepless nights at Harvey's, so we like to count our blessings once a year, as the holiday season approaches. You, as one of our most valued customers, are one of our blessings, and we want you to know how very much we appreciate your loyalty.

We hope you have a wonderful Christmas and a happy and successful New Year.

Yours sincerely,

Dear Mr Drummond,

A Merry Christmas to you! And a Happy New Year, too.

You may imagine that we never give you a thought except to send you your monthly bill and a stiff letter if you don't pay up. Nothing, in fact, could be further from the truth. We <u>do</u> think of you and we appreciate your support very much indeed.

We have enjoyed serving you over the past year and will do everthing we can to continue to deserve the trust you have put in us.

We hope you have a very happy holiday season.

Yours sincerely,

Dear Mrs Philips,

It has been a pleasure to have you as a customer throughout the past year and we want you to know how much we appreciate your loyalty.

It has been a very successful year for us and our success has been due in no small measure to the confidence you have placed in us. Please accept our grateful thanks, together with our sincere good wishes for Christmas and the coming year.

Yours sincerely,

To agents and wholesale customers

Dear Mr Fenn,

As the festive season approaches we would like to tell you how much we have appreciated your business during the past year and extend to you our very best wishes for Christmas and the New Year.

It has been a pleasure working with you and we look forward to an even better year in 1986.

Yours sincerely,

Dear Mr Smither,

Though this world is ever changing, we still have with us the never changing spirit of the holiday season, again prompting us to set aside our worldly problems – pausing to remember our cherished old friends, our valued new friends, and to reflect upon the fortunes of the year now quickly passing into history.

As we look back we are reminded of our pleasant association with your firm – of our appreciation of the opportunity and privilege of serving you. We will endeavour to continue to merit your friendship and confidence in our product in the year ahead.

May we add our best wishes for your happiness at this holiday season and your continued prosperity in the New Year ahead.

Cordially yours,

Dear Mrs Reynolds,

All my colleagues at Gregg's join me in sending you sincere Christmas greetings and very best wishes for an excellent business year in 1986.

It has been a pleasure to do business with you over the past year and we look forward to our pleasant association continuing not only over the year that is to come, but for many years ahead.

Yours sincerely,

Dear Arnold,

As Christmas comes round once again I want to thank you for all the hard work you have put into the Black Lion agency during the past year. Your efforts on behalf of our products have been very much appreciated and we would like you to know this.

I wish you a very happy Christmas and a busy and prosperous New Year.

Sincerely,

Dear Mr White,

The year now ending has been an excellent one for the Arrow car and I want to thank you most sincerely for the part you have played in pushing sales to such records.

I hope you have a very good Christmas and a prosperous New Year.

Yours sincerely,

Dear Mr Pitt,

As the Christmas season approaches it is a pleasure to think back with gratitude on the fine business relationship we have enjoyed with your firm throughout the past year. We truly appreciate your splendid co-operation and want to take this opportunity of thanking you for your business and goodwill. Companies such as yours make the wheels of business turn smoothly and pleasantly and we feel fortunate indeed to have you as a customer.

May all the joys and blessings of Christmas be yours and may the coming year bring you prosperity and happiness.

Yours sincerely,

Dear Mrs Soames,

I wish I could climb aboard my sledge and make a bee-line for your doorstep, there to wish you a Merry Christmas and a Happy New Year and shake you by the hand.

Alas, chained to my office desk as always, I must content myself with writing to you. First of all, I want to say it has been a great pleasure doing business with you over the past year. I realize full well how much your business has contributed to our excellent sales figures and want you to know how greatly we appreciate it.

I hope the Christmas holiday will find you happy and contented with your family and that the New Year brings you new success and ever greater prosperity.

Yours sincerely,

Dear Miss Graham,

It is a pleasure to write to you, just once a year, not to sell you anything or to ask for payment, but simply to wish you a Merry Christmas and a Prosperous New Year.

The year that has gone by has been one of consolidation. The one that lies before us will surely be a year of expansion and increased sales. We are certainly firm in our resolution to send you an excellent product that you will be proud to sell to your customers, at a price which will allow you a good profit margin.

We very much appreciate the confidence you have placed in us and in our product in the past and we will continue to do our best to be worthy of it.

Once again, my very best wishes for the holiday season.

Yours sincerely,

Dear Mr Whyte,

A Merry Christmas to you! It is an old, old wish, yet full of meaning, of good fellowship, of cheerfulness, of joy and goodwill.

I wish I could come down and bring you my good wishes in person, but, alas, I must content myself once again with writing. It has been a pleasure to enjoy your friendship and confidence through the past year and I want to thank you most sincerely for your support.

May you enjoy all the blessings and joys of Christmas and may 1986 prove even more successful and prosperous than the year that has gone by.

Sincerely yours,

Dear Ms Smedley,

The entire Phoenix family joins me in wishing you a very Merry Christmas and a most prosperous New Year.

The past year has been an excellent one for us and we realize how much you have contributed to our success. Please accept our sincere thanks and deep appreciation. Certainly, we shall do all we can to continue to merit your loyal support and you may count upon us to co-operate with you in every way possible.

Yours sincerely,

To business and professional associates

Dear Mr Watson,

It is almost a year since we began doing business together and I would like you to know how much I have appreciated your straight dealing, prompt payments, and wonderful co-operation.

The holiday season will soon be with us and I hope you have an excellent Christmas and much well-deserved prosperity throughout the coming year.

Sincerely yours,

Dear Joyce,

As the current year draws to a close, I am anxious that you should know how much I have appreciated your cheerful and enthusiastic support on the club committee. As you well know, many people are only too keen to enjoy the club's many benefits, but few care to shoulder some of the responsibilities of running it. I am therefore most grateful for all you have done and are doing to lighten my burden.

May the joys and blessings of Christmas be abundantly yours and the New Year bring you fresh successes and, above all, happiness in the service to others.

Sincerely,

Dear Bob,

I'd like you to know how much I've enjoyed working with you over the past year and to thank you for your help and encouragement, not to mention your unflagging cheerfulness.

I hope you find your parents in excellent health and that you spend a very pleasant Christmas with them. For the coming year I wish you health and prosperity, as well as continued success in your career.

Sincerely,

Dear Tracy,

I don't want you to leave for your Christmas in Switzerland before I have written to say how much I have appreciated your co-operation during the past year. I realize that if things have moved swiftly and smoothly it has been thanks, in great measure, to your unflagging efforts. It has been a pleasure to work with you.

Have a wonderful Christmas in Switzerland. You certainly deserve it, and may the New Year be a bountiful one.

Sincerely,

Dear Fred,

Having retrieved your tobacco pouch twice during the past year and offered you my shoulder whereon to weep for its loss another twice – or was it three times? – I feel that the gift of a tobacco pouch would be both appropriate and welcome.

So here it is with my blessings and very best wishes for a Merry Christmas and a Happy New Year.

Yours,

Dear Pat,

As a prelude to making my New Year's resolutions I usually think back on the year gone by and count my blessings, sparing a thought for all those wonderful people who have helped me on my way. First among them I must certainly count you and I want you to know how much I have appreciated your invaluable help with my books over the past year.

Ever patient and constructive, never yielding to the temptation to excoriate me for my inattention to detail and cavalier attitude to the language of Shakespeare, you have truly been my Maxwell Perkins – and how little I deserve it, alas! I do assure you that I appreciate it the more.

I hope you have an absolutely splendid Christmas and many far worthier authors than me in the year that lies ahead.

Most sincerely,

Dear Mr Stephens,

On behalf of the whole Radiola organization I am happy to extend to you hearty greeetings for Christmas and best wishes for the New Year.

We are convinced that the coming year will be an even better one for us all and we look forward to doing a great deal more business with you.

Yours sincerely,

Dear Mrs Charlton,

One of the highlights of the year about to end was certainly the interesting work we began together following our meeting at the March Symposium.

It has been a very pleasant association and I greatly look forward to continuing it, not only in the coming year, but for many years to come.

I hope you have a very pleasant Christmas and a fruitful 1986.

Sincerely yours,

Dear Ms Hawkins,

Before we close our books on 1985, I would like you to know how much I have appreciated our pleasant association during the past year.

May the New Year be bountiful in its gifts to you.

Sincerely yours,

Dear Peters,

I hope you will not think it rather rash of me if I take advantage of the coming Christmas season to let you know how much I have enjoyed working with you since you joined the College staff. Your enthusiastic co-operation, flexibility, and constant good humour have been of great comfort to me and I want you to know how very appreciative I am.

I hope you thoroughly enjoy the Christmas holidays and wish you the very best for the coming year.

Sincerely,

Dear Mr Fredriks,

My wife joins me in wishing you and your wife a very happy Christmas and a most successful New Year.

We both frequently think of the enjoyable hours we spent together during your extended visit to Cambridge early in the year and I hope the coming year will bring further opportunities for us to work together.

With very best wishes.

Sincerely yours,

Dear Dr Brugnoni,

As the festive season approaches I hasten to send you my very best wishes for Christmas and the New Year.

I often recall with great nostalgia the happy period spent both working with you at the lab. and enjoying the dolce vita of Italy. Certainly my own fondest New Year wish is for another opportunity to work with you and enjoy the warmth and friendliness of the Italian scene.

Please convey my kindest regards and best wishes also to your wife. How well I recall her graciousness and cordiality.

Yours sincerely,

To staff

Dear Joe,

Another year has gone by – a new year is but a few days away.

Fortunately these annual events give us an opportunity to stop and look back – a chance to express our thanks and appreciation to our fellow workers for their help in making our jobs more pleasant – and we are certain, more successful.

The privilege of working with and for you during these past 12 months has been ours – our appreciation for your help we want now to express.

To you and your family our wishes for a very Merry Christmas and a Happy and Prosperous New Year.*

To: All Sales Representatives

THANK YOU!

Those who are credited with speaking words of wisdom tell us never to look back – for if we do, we will not move ahead.

We cannot completely agree with this philosophy because we <u>have</u> been looking back during these last few days of 1985 and find that the recollection of past experiences has much in its favour.

We are reminded of the many times we have needed help and have come to you for assistance – of the splendid response and co-operation you have cheerfully given on these and other occasions – of the reliance we place in our representatives to help us do our job more effectively.

It would certainly be most unfortunate if we were not to look back – not to take this opportunity to remind ourselves of the many good friends we have in the Sales Division and to express our appreciation to all of you for your help during these past 12 months.

Our sincere thanks to you all and our wishes for continued success in the year ahead.

        Cordially,
        CREDIT DEPARTMENT
        (Signed by all members)

---

* This letter was signed by all members of the Company's Credit Department.

Dear Phil,

The year that has gone by has been a most successful one for our Company and I want you to know how much I have appreciated the hard work you have put into welding your department into the effective team that it now is.

You have done a splendid job and contributed in full measure to our increased turnover for the year.

I hope you spend a very happy Christmas with your family and that the New Year brings you much deserved success and prosperity.

Yours sincerely,

Dear Jim,

It is a fairly well acknowledged fact that none of us is a success by our individual efforts alone and that success is the result of the endeavours on our behalf of those with whom we are associated.

As we look back over this past year we are reminded of the assistance cheerfully given to us by you and the other members of our sales organization. This help has contributed greatly to whatever small degree of success we may have attained in serving the needs of our customers and fulfilling our obligations to our Company.

We sincerely appreciate this co-operation and take this opportunity to thank you and to wish you and your family a very Merry Christmas and a Happy and Prosperous New Year.

Cordially yours,
CREDIT DEPARTMENT.
(Signed by all members)

Dear Miss Wilkins,

     This is simply a note to wish you and your family a very happy Christmas and the best of good fortune in the New Year.

     It has been an extremely busy and successful year and I am very much aware of the fact that without the wholehearted co-operation of every member of the staff the Company could not be as successful as it is. I want you to know how much I appreciate your efforts over the past year.

     I like to feel we are building the Company together, for even as it grows, so do we grow with it.

     It is in this spirit, therefore, that I wish you renewed vigorous growth in the coming year.

                Yours sincerely,

Dear Mr Smiles,

     Just as many companies, including our own, draw up a balance sheet and close their books at the end of the calendar year, I am accustomed at this time of the year to look back and make a mental balance sheet of my human assets. I treasure these every bit as much as the other kind and, in fact, I consider the people who work for the organization to be our greatest assets.

     My balance sheet tells me that you have all worked extremely hard over the past year and this hard work is reflected in the sales figures, which are up 20 per cent on last year's.

     I should like to thank you most sincerely for your efforts during the past year and to wish you an enjoyable Christmas. May the New Year bring you health and happiness, as well as a good measure of prosperity.

                Yours sincerely,

Dear Jeff,

Once again it is time to lay down our shovels – figuratively speaking – and join our families over Christmas festivities. I wish you a very joyous Christmas, full of merriment and good cheer.

You have worked hard over the past year and you can truly make merry in the satisfaction of a job well done.

For my part, it is a real pleasure to reflect upon the number of years it has been my good fortune to send you my personal Christmas greetings. Loyal, long-term employees are the backbone of the Company and I want you to know how much I appreciate the contribution you have made to the Company's growth.

May the coming year be full of happiness for you.

Sincerely yours,

9

Congratulations and Good Wishes

We all like to be congratulated on our achievements and are pleased when the milestones in our career are suitably noticed by friends and associates. Yet how often do you pause during the day's business to write a short note to a friend or business connection who has achieved recognition of some sort? It is easy enough to do, takes but a few minutes, and brings a glow of pleasure to the recipient.

Occasions for writing such messages are innumerable. Why not make a point of seizing such opportunities from now on? Make your message short, crisp, friendly and, above all, sincere. As with all other letters, you will naturally match your degree of informality and the tone of your message to the age of the recipient and the relationship between you, but, generally speaking, you will do well to write in a natural, informal, chatty style, tingeing your message with the enthusiasm of true sincerity.

The specimen letters that follow cover most occasions frequently encountered in the course of business life.

To business and professional associates

On receiving a new business or professional appointment

Dear Mr Harrison,

      I was delighted to learn that you are moving to Birmingham to take charge of the new Branch in the Bull Ring.

      Please accept my most sincere congratulations and my very best wishes for success in your new position.

              Yours sincerely,

141

Dear Haynes,

I have just heard from Ernest that you have been appointed a full professor of history at North-Western University. I hasten to send you my congratulations and to wish you a very successful academic career.

It is truly an achievement in one so young, for I know full well that few universities can boast of so youthful – and so pretty, I may add – a professor. But one comes to expect the outstanding from you and I cannot say that I am really surprised.

No doubt everyone will be rushing to take history next term and you will have a full and successful class.

All the best.

Sincerely,

Dear Mr Little,

I was very interested to hear that you had left the Small Business Administration to take up the editorship of Learning.

Unquestionably the quarterly will benefit greatly from your insight and deep knowledge of the subject and I feel that your employers have made a splendid acquisition.

In offering you my warmest congratulations, I send you also my best wishes for success and satisfaction in your work.

Sincerely yours,

Dear Steve,

I have just read in Campaign that you have been appointed Advertising Manager to Marlex Foods.

It is a fine opportunity for you and you have worked hard for it. I know you will make good and I hasten to send you my hearty congratulations together with my very best wishes for your success.

Sincerely,

Dear Susan,

I have just returned to town after one of my jaunts North. I called, as usual, at Fennicks hoping to see you, but to my astonishment was informed that you had left to take up a position as Purchasing Manager with Finnigans.

My disappointment at not seeing you was mitigated by my delight at your good fortune and I am writing to let you know how happy I am for you and to wish you all the best.

Certainly Finnigans couldn't have picked a better person and I know you will make a go of it.

Congratulations and best wishes. Do let me hear how you are getting along.

Yours sincerely,

Dear Mr Spry,

I called at Halls this morning to deliver the manuscript of my new book and was surprised to learn that you had left the Company to take up a new position as General Manager for Flowers & Son.

I shall greatly miss working with you, as we have enjoyed such a pleasant relationship for several years. At the same time I am very happy for you, since Flowers is one of the leading British publishers and this must be a splendid opportunity for you.

Please accept my sincere congratulations and warmest wishes for success in your new post.

Yours sincerely,

Dear Ms Farringdon,

I have just read in the trade press that you have been appointed Public Relations Officer for UK Spinning Mills Limited and hasten to offer you my congratulations and good wishes.

Unquestionably the Company will benefit from your drive and enthusiasm and I confidently expect to hear more about UK Spinning Mills from now on.

I hope your new position will give you a great deal of satisfaction and stimulation.

Sincerely yours,

Dear Fred,

This is just a note to wish you all the very best in your new job. I'm sure you will like it up North; the atmosphere is so friendly and hospitable, and I know you will be given a hearty welcome.

Congratulations on your appointment! It means that we'll be working even more closely together from now on and I greatly look forward to this.

Sincerely,

Dear Mr Scott,

I was very pleased to learn that you have been appointed Secretary of the Kingston Chamber of Commerce.

I know you will do an outstanding job and look forward to co-operating with you in any way I can. If I personally or my Company can help, please let me know.

Meanwhile, I hope you will accept my heartiest congratulations and good wishes.

Yours sincerely,

Dear Joan,

I have just learned that you are joining Jerrolds and Co. as Personnel Officer and hasten to send you my sincere congratulations and best wishes for success in your new post.

I know you will make a resounding success of it, as you do of all your undertakings. Don't forget to let me know whether you like it there and how you are getting along. I'll be keeping my fingers crossed for you. Good luck.

As ever,

Dear Ms Weston,

I was delighted to learn that you had been appointed Managing Editor of Women at Work. You certainly have worked hard to earn this recognition and I am especially pleased to send you my congratulations and best wishes.

I'm sure this new and greater challenge will find you more than equal to the task and that you will throw yourself into it with your usual drive, enthusiasm and persistence.

I'll be watching the next issues with added interest.

Yours sincerely,

On being promoted

Dear Joe,

I have just learned of your promotion to Sales Manager upon the retirement of Mr Wood, and would like to congratulate you most sincerely.

No one has worked harder than you over the past several years and I, for one, am delighted to see your efforts rewarded.

Unquestionably, under your enthusiastic leadership our sales team will rise to still greater efforts and achieve even more outstanding sales records.

Sincerely,

Dear Joy,

I was delighted to learn that you have been promoted to Editor of <u>Executive Management and Methods</u>. You have certainly worked hard and fully deserve this opportunity.

I am always especially delighted when a woman achieves recognition, for a person of our sex invariably has to work twice as hard and be twice as efficient as a man before she is given her due.

Congratulations, therefore, and the very best of luck in your new post.

Sincerely,

Dear John,

You are a very modest chap, so the news of your election to the Board of Constructix Limited has only just trickled down to my far less exalted level.

Congratulations on a well-deserved appointment. If hard work and dedication are ingredients of success, then you undoubtedly deserve success in full and overflowing measure. I am very happy for you.

Sincerely,

Dear Len,

I have just read in <u>Campaign</u> about your appointment to a directorship at Haywoods and hasten to send you my hearty congratulations. I cannot think of anyone more deserving of the honour, for you have worked hard and diligently.

When next we meet we must celebrate at 'The Printer's Devil'.

Sincerely,

Dear Mr Sydney,

I was pleased to read in this morning's <u>Financial Times</u> of your appointment as Managing Director of Roxton and Company Limited.

This is certainly a fitting recognition of the outstanding work you have done for your Company over the years and it is with great pleasure that my partners and I send you our warmest congratulations.

Yours sincerely,

Dear Mr Sladden,

All of us at Whiting's were delighted to hear of your promotion to Manager of the London Chamber of Commerce.

This is indeed excellent news and we all send you our sincere congratulations.

We know from past experience that you will do an excellent job and you may count on our co-operation and assistance at all times.

Sincerely yours,

Dear Mr Stone,

I was pleased indeed to learn that you have been promoted to Branch Manager and will be moving to Bracknell to open the new Branch there.

It is always a pleasure to see merit rewarded and I know how long and how diligently you have worked for this opportunity. At last it is yours and I am especially happy to offer you my warmest congratulations, together with my very best wishes for your success in your new post.

Yours sincerely,

Dear Mr Skinner,

I heard only the other day that you were back from your long trip to the Near East and now suddenly I hear that you have been made Export Director of Bridie & Son Ltd! This is fast work indeed and I feel I must rush in with equal swiftness to offer you my congratulations and best wishes.

You have certainly gone a long way in a short time, both figuratively speaking and in fact, and it has been an exhilarating experience to watch your progress. Here's wishing you God speed on your further climb up the executive ladder!

Sincerely yours,

Dear Peter,

It's nice to hear of a friend making good! Congratulations! Now you are Manager of Mark's I expect you'll get a swollen head and cut all your friends dead! There – you see how your good fortune has gone to my head!

Best of luck, old friend. I'm as pleased as Punch!

As ever,

Dear Mrs Fields,

It is with great satisfaction that I write to congratulate you on your promotion to Manager of the Salford Castle Hotel.

I have followed your career in the catering line for many years and have always admired the diligent, conscientious and energetic way in which you tackled the job at hand. You have quite obviously enjoyed your work and I wish you much happiness and personal fulfilment in your new post.

Sincerely yours,

Dear Ernest,

I have just read in the European edition of the New York Herald Tribune – of all papers! – that you have become a partner of Preece, Fennimore and Broom.

Hearty congratulations on this most important achievement! You are a very influential man now and when next I phone to ask your advice on my small investment problems, I shall do so with some trepidation!

Joking apart, I am very happy for you and hope your new status with the firm brings you much personal satisfaction – not to mention financial rewards!

Sincerely,

Dear Marion,

Congratulations! It couldn't have happened to a better gal! I mean your promotion to Personnel Manager of Christie's, of course.

You are more than qualified for the job and I know you'll make an outstanding success of it! All the best.

Sincerely,

Dear 'L',

I have just learned that you have been promoted to producer of the BBC Italian Programme and I am wasting not one moment in sending you my most sincere congratulations.

Such an important promotion is a splendid recognition of your ability and should give you ample opportunity to spread your wings.

Good luck to you and best wishes.

Sincerely,

Dear Mr Mortimer,

It is a pleasure indeed to congratulate you on your advancement to Managing Director of the Quixset Company Ltd. The company reins have certainly passed to firm and knowledgeable hands, for no one, I imagine, could be more intimately acquainted than you with all the facets and ramifications of your business.

This appointment is the crowning achievement of your career to date and my fellow-executives and I send you our most sincere wishes for the arduous yet rewarding task that lies ahead of you.

Yours sincerely,

Dear Mr Warren,

I have just read in The Factory Manager that you have been promoted to Production Manager of Seymour Engineering Co.

This is certainly a fine tribute to your ability and devotion to the service of the Company. Everyone in the Howard organization joins me in sending you sincere congratulations and good wishes.

Yours sincerely,

Dear Ms Jones,

I have just heard that you have recently been promoted to be Chief Librarian of your organization.

Please accept my most sincere congratulations and best wishes. May you find ever greater satisfaction in your new post, which you so richly deserve.

Sincerely yours,

Dear Mr McGregor,

I was glad to read in this week's Campaign that you have been promoted to the post of Public Relations Officer for The Wayland Motor Company.

I very much look forward to working with you in your new capacity and wish you every success and happiness in this new phase of your career.

Yours sincerely,

Dear Bob,

It's always a satisfaction to see a friend make good, but when the friend is as hard-working and well-deserving as you, the pleasure is doubled.

Congratulations and best wishes on your recent promotion. I shall be following your career with renewed interest from now on and mentally spurring you on all the way to the top.

Sincerely,

On business anniversary or special business achievement

Dear Mr Whitlock,

On the occasion of your Golden Anniversary my partners join me in sending you hearty congratulations and very best wishes for the second half of your first century in business.

The fact that your department store has not merely survived but prospered and expanded through both a world war and the recession is a sure sign that your policies have included good service, fine merchandise and fair dealing.

May the next 50 years of service to the community bring you fresh successes and even greater satisfaction.

Yours sincerely,

Dear Ms Matthews,

One million blinds is a lot of blinds! As you set out to celebrate this milestone in the RUNWAY marathon of blinds, my congratulations and good wishes go to you.

May RUNWAY'S future be just as sunny as its past.

Sincerely yours,

Dear Mr Strall,

Many thanks for your kind invitation to join in your celebrations on manufacturing your one millionth Venetian blind.

I am happy to accept and in doing so, send you my most sincere congratulations. Leadership in your field could not have been achieved without a good deal of business acumen, industry, and, above all, a product and service which commend themselves to the consumer.

Best wishes for the continued success of Runway blinds.

Yours sincerely,

Dear Mr Ross

After months of planning and frustration your magnificent new building is completed. It is handsome indeed and, without doubt, it will become the pride of the community.

Please accept my hearty congratulations, together with my sincere good wishes for your company. May it continue to grow and prosper in our community as it has done in the past.

Yours sincerely,

Dear Herr Schwarz,

As you complete your first year as our German licensed manufacturer, I would like to congratulate you on your splendid record and fine achievement in this first year's work.

It really is a pleasure to work with a firm such as yours: prompt in meeting its obligations, clear and courteous in its requests and instructions, effective in its sales effort.

We look forward to many years of fruitful and pleasant co-operation.

Yours sincerely,

Dear Dr White,

Five years ago today you came in to see us with your first manuscript. You were still doing post-graduate work at London University and when we decided to go ahead and publish your book I recall that you were as happy as a sandboy.

You have come a long way since then and it has been our privilege to publish several more of your books.

May we seize the opportunity afforded by this fifth anniversary of our association, to congratulate you on your achievements? It has been a pleasure to work with you and we look forward to doing so for many years to come.

Yours sincerely,

Dear Mark,

I have just heard that you are opening a branch office in the North and hasten to send you my warmest congratulations. May this new expansion of your business be every bit as successful as your last move to the West.

Sincerely,

Dear Mr Simpson,

Please accept my warmest congratulations on this tenth anniversary of the founding of your business. Your record since that time is one you may well be proud of, for your reputation and standing in the community are second to none.

May continued success and prosperity be yours.

Yours sincerely,

Dear Ms Jenkins,

On the eve of the opening of your new shop I wish to send you my most hearty congratulations and good wishes.

Tomorrow will be a big day for you, one towards which you have worked hard for many years. May the fulfilment of your long-cherished dream bring you much happiness and satisfaction.

Yours sincerely,

Dear Mr Montgomery,

May I, as a fellow practitioner, warmly congratulate you on your recent butter advertising campaign. The copy is witty, sophisticated, and delightfully understated. Only an Englishman could have written it! As for the art work, it achieves a perfect marriage with the copy.

Yours sincerely,

Dear Mr Benson,

This must be a happy day for you. Exactly 25 years ago you founded Benson's, a small shop selling tea and coffee. Today Benson's supplies these commodities to the whole country and the tiny shop has blossomed into an elegant meeting place for tea and coffee lovers from all over London.

Please accept my hearty congratulations on your anniversary, together with my warmest wishes for your continued success.

Sincerely yours,

Dear Mr Glasser,

My partners and I send you our warmest congratulations on the occasion of your Golden Anniversary.

Over the years your fairness and spirit of service to the community have earned you an enviable reputation, of which you are fully justified in being proud.

Our best wishes for continued success go with you as you enter your second half-century in business.

Sincerely yours,

Dear Bridget,

Your bright new shop is not merely handsome, it is a credit to your perseverance, faith and courage.

I could not let this important milestone in your career pass by without sending you my hearty congratulations. I know just how much it means to you and this makes me the more keenly happy for you. Good luck, Bridget, you truly deserve it.

Sincerely,

On retirement from business

Dear Mr Wheelock,

I have just read in the <u>Financial Times</u> that you are to retire as Chairman of Foster and Wheelock Ltd.

Thirty-five years of service to the textile industry is certainly a record to be proud of and I'm sure all your business associates will agree that you have earned your leisure.

I wish you many more years of health and happiness.

Yours sincerely,

Dear 'Fin',

As you prepare to retire from business and enjoy your well-earned leisure, I should like to add my warmest wishes to the many you will have received.

Your record in the service of our community has been a splendid one and unquestionably you will be sorely missed by your loyal customers for a long time.

Sincerely,

Dear Ms Franklin,

I have just heard that you are taking early retirement from Leeland and Company Limited and should like to congratulate you on your long and outstanding career.

Your enthusiastic leadership has been a spur and an inspiration to many. Your record will unquestionably be a pattern on which others will build. I wish you every happiness in your retirement and continuing good health in which to enjoy it.

Sincerely yours,

Dear Mrs Gillmore,

No words of mine can do justice to the valuable contribution you have made to the publishing business during your life-time of service to it.

All I can do is to express my immense admiration of your achievements and the wish that your retirement – reluctant though it may be – will be a very happy one.

Sincerely yours,

Dear Mr Hendrick,

I read in <u>The Times</u> that you are retiring as Managing Director of Harvey's and will devote your time to writing and gardening.

Any man with a record of service to industry such as yours has more than earned his leisure and I am most anxious to send you my very best wishes for a happy and healthy retirement. Both the steel industry and the country have reasons to be grateful to you and proud of you and I would like to add my congratulations on a job well done to the many you are no doubt receiving.

Sincerely yours,

Dear Mr Knight,

News of your retirement from busines has just reached me and I would like to congratulate you on a long and honourable career.

Few men have contributed as much to the field of retailing as you have and your record of devotion to the highest business ethics is known to all.

May your retirement bring you contentment and happiness.

Yours sincerely,

Dear Mr Bradley,

Fifty years of service to the building industry is a record of which few men can boast. You have given this and more: you have devoted your whole energy, leadership and positive business genius to our industry and for this we owe you a very real debt of gratitude.

May I add my warmest congratulations and sincere best wishes for a happy and healthy retirement? Your name will long be remembered in the industry – of that you may be sure.

Yours sincerely,

On receiving professional or civic honour

Dear Ms Quinton,

Hearty congratulations upon your splendid victory at the polls on October 15. Your election is great news to me, for I know that we now have on the Council one who is determined that inefficiency shall cease in our borough and be replaced by constructive, purposeful activity.

I sincerely hope that your efforts will bring about the results you have at heart.

Yours sincerely,

Dear Mr Poulson,

I am delighted that you have been elected President of the Manchester Chamber of Commerce and write to offer you my most sincere congratulations.

With you at the helm, we can expect a very lively year and I look forward to serving under you.

Yours sincerely,

Dear Mr Wilson,

I write to offer you my warmest congratulations on your election as Chairman of the Council of the Institute of Industrial Designers.

Your election is a fitting recognition of the unstinted effort you have put into the Institute's affairs for the past ten years and I can think of no member more deserving of the honour. The coming year promises to be a very interesting and active one and your leadership at such a crucial period will be invaluable to the Institute.

Yours sincerely,

Dear Peter,

Congratulations!

I have just read a very impressive paragraph in the Financial Times to the effect that you have been elected President of the F.R.E.M.A. Council.

It really is a pleasure to watch a friend move into more and more influential positions and I feel very proud of you.

All good wishes and the best of luck to you.

Sincerely,

Dear Cavaliere,

I have only just heard that you have been made a Cavaliere del Lavoro and I wish to extend to you my most sincere congratulations, and also those of my fellow-executives here at Freeman's.

Your career has certainly been one long dedication to the industrial life of Turin and it is gratifying indeed to see your tireless efforts so splendidly rewarded.

I look forward to shaking you by the hand and congratulating you personally when next we meet.

Sincerely yours,

Dear Jim – or perhaps I should say 'Dear Doc',

I got a real kick out of seeing your photograph in the local paper as you stepped up gingerly to receive your Degree Honoris Causa. You looked a picture of legal dignity and wisdom and I felt like dashing out and telling everyone 'That's my friend Jim'.

So congratulations, Jim. I'm truly happy for you and no one has ever better deserved the honour.

Hope to see you soon.

As ever,

Dear Phil,

Imagine my pleasure when, scanning the Birthday Honours List in this morning's <u>Times</u>, my eyes fell upon your name.

This really is splendid news and I hasten to send you my most sincere congratulations. It is always good to see merit rewarded, but when the person honoured is a close and long-standing associate, then the satisfaction is two-fold.

I look forward to seeing you in the autumn and we must have a real celebration then.

Sincerely,

Dear Mr Lyon,

It is a great pleasure to send you my heartfelt congratulations on your award of the OBE.

I can think of no one in the community who more richly merits the honour, for your dynamic leadership and unfaltering sense of mission have made the name of our town a household word almost throughout the entire world.

As a fellow industrialist who takes great pride in our community, I am delighted at the recognition that has come to you.

Sincerely yours,

Dear Miss Matthews,

I was delighted to read in the paper this morning that one of your chairs had won the Duke of Edinburgh Good Design Award. This is an honour indeed and, certainly, congratulations are in order.

You must be very proud of your award-winning chair and deservedly so. I wish you the greatest of selling success with it.

Yours sincerely,

Dear Anne,

Congratulations!

I can't tell you how pleased I was to hear that your journal had won first prize in the best House Magazine contest.

You truly deserve this recognition, for I know how hard you have worked since taking over the editorship last year.

May this timely recognition of your talents spur you on to even greater efforts.

Sincerely,

Dear Al,

Transatlantic news sometimes travels but slowly, especially when its protagonists are as modest as you. So it is that I have only just heard that you have been elected President of the New York Bar Association.

This is truly great news and I hasten to send you my hearty congratulations and very best wishes for a successful administation.

Sincerely,

Dear Mr Fields,

I am writing to congratulate you on your election as Chairman of the Council of the N.A.A.P.I.

Your brilliant business record assures members of a capable and dynamic Chairman and we all look forward to an interesting year's work under your leadership.

Yours sincerely,

Dear Mr Griffiths,

I have just heard over the radio that you have been elected Mayor of Stanton and hasten to congratulate both you and your town. Certainly your outstanding business record augurs well for the ability and decisiveness you will bring to the office.

Please accept my best wishes for a most successful term of office.

Sincerely yours,

Dear Mrs Skelton,

It came as no surprise to me to learn that you had been awarded an MBE for your outstanding work in the fields of politics and public service in Windsor and Maidenhead.

It is a great pleasure to offer you my congratulations as well as my thanks as a fellow-resident of Berkshire.

Yours sincerely,

Dear Mr Wilkins,

Warmest congratulations on your election as Chairman of the Brompton branch of the Agents' Society.

If there is any way in which I can help during your term of office, do let me know. Meanwhile I wish you a very successful year.

Sincerely yours,

Dear Mr Johnson,

It is a pleasure to congratulate you on your election as President of the Rotary Club of London for the coming year.

Under your genial and expert leadership the members of your club will undoubtedly enjoy a lively and interesting year.

Yours sincerely,

Dear June,

I was very pleased to hear that one of your spring ads won the Leyton Award. This is a splended feather in your cap and you have my hearty congratulations.

Keep up the good work!

Sincerely,

Dear Mr Cox,

Joseph Clayton joins me in congratulating you on your election as President of the Institute of Administrators.

Your election is a sure sign of the esteem in which you are held by your fellow-members of the Institute and, indeed, they are to be congratulated on the wisdom of their choice.

I wish you a very fruitful term of office.

Yours sincerely,

Dear Sir John,

News of your election to the presidency of The Law Society has just reached me.

Your election to this high office is a fitting tribute to your long and outstanding career and to your devoted service to the cause of justice.

Unquestionably the Society will benefit greatly from your wisdom and knowledge in the Presidential chair. I wish you health and success and send you my heartfelt congratulations on an honour well deserved.

Sincerely yours,

Dear Peter,

The news that you have been awarded a knighthood has just reached me and I hasten to send you my most sincere congratulations.

This high honour is a fitting tribute to your untiring efforts in the service of the business community and your unswerving devotion to the highest business ethics.

My warmest regards to you.

Sincerely,

Dear Mr Spencer,

Warmest congratulations to you on your election as President of the Confederation of British Industry! This is indeed a tribute to your outstanding ability and qualities of leadership. Quite obviously CBI members know how to choose the right man.

Very best wishes for a fruitful and interesting term of office.

Yours sincerely,

My dear Griffiths,

Your election as Secretary to the Institute of Works Managers is really good news! You have my hearty congratulations and best wishes for a successful term of office.

You certainly have what it takes to keep the Institute in good working order and members are to be congratulated on the wisdom of their choice.

Sincerely,

Dear Bill,

Congratulations to the British Institute of Management and to you! To you goes the honour of presiding over their Council during the coming year and to them the satisfaction of having chosen the best man for the job.

I was really glad to hear the news, and wish you great success and every satisfaction in the office.

Sincerely,

Dear Mr Ferris,

It is a great pleasure to congratulate you on your election as Chairman of the Building Societies Association.

Because of our close association with you over the past ten years, we at Farmers' Building Society know how well qualified you are for this important office. We feel sure that you will make it a year of real progress and achievement.

Sincerely yours,

On speech, article or book

My dear Sanders,

It isn't often nowadays that one takes the time to write to congratulate a friend for 'saying a few words'. Your talk at the Sales Conference, however, was so outstanding that I feel compelled to put pen to paper.

It really was a masterful job and, to judge by the way everyone was hanging on your words, I'd say it had a salutary and lasting effect on the audience.

Sincerely,

Dear Ms Kinney,

I have just finished reading your article 'Are Your Business Letters Dated?' which appeared in the current issue of Business and found myself nodding in agreement all the way through it. Your points are well taken and I only hope your readers take them to heart.

Please accept my congratulations for a timely and well-written article. I shall certainly look forward to your further contributions.

Yours sincerely,

Dear Miss Andrews,

I am writing to tell you how very interesting I found the short paper you wrote under the title of 'Is Worker Fatigue Costing you Dollars?' It contains a good deal of information which is quite unknown to the ordinary business executive and which he would be wise to apply in his own company.

The Small Business Administration is to be congratulated on putting out this remarkably interesting series and I very much hope you will be making further contributions to it.

Sincerely yours,

Dear Mr Mitchell,

I want you to know how useful and revealing I have found your book, The Businessman's Lawyer and Legal Lexicon. I am planning to go into business for myself and, realizing how little I know about the legal aspects involved, I decided to get your book.

It was the best possible thing I could have done, for here, in plain everyday language, was all the information I needed. I know I shall dip into the book many times in years to come and would like to congratulate you on putting together such an eminently practical and easy-to-read volume.

Sincerely yours,

Dear Mr Brown,

Your new book, <u>Effective Sales Letter Composition,</u> is a gem. You really have brought sales letter writing to a fine art and no serious student of the subject should fail to read your book and to keep it nearby for frequent reference.

We do just that in our direct-mail selling department and I am confidently expecting sales to improve as a result.

Yours sincerely,

Dear Ms Fothergill,

I should like to congratulate you on the painstaking research job which resulted in your book, <u>Decorations, Initials and Abbreviations.</u>

Certainly we should not want to be without it in our editorial department and we look forward to a new and enlarged edition in the not-too-distant future.

Meanwhile, all of us at Cygnet Press send you our grateful thanks.

Yours sincerely,

Dear Dr Fields,

So many of the members have commented favourably on your talk at our last meeting that I felt I ought to let you know how very much it was appreciated.

We all hope you will soon return to the Rotary Club of London.

Yours sincerely,

Dear Mrs Smith,

Many thanks for sending me the booklet, <u>Investors' Guide to Growth Stock.</u> It really is an extremely well-put-together publication and I would like you to pass on my congratulations to the person responsible for it.

Yours sincerely,

Dear Ms Porter,

I have just read your article 'Enter – the Next Boom' in the Wall Street Journal and would like you to know how much I appreciated your penetrating analysis of the situation, as well as the clear, concise way in which you put it into words.

I have been following your financial articles for a number of years and am always very much impressed by your grasp of the subject and by the shrewdness of your 'educated guesses'.

Congratulations to you!

Sincerely yours,

Dear Allen,

When it was decided to entrust you with the job of editing the proposed booklet, Advertising Ethics, on behalf of the advertising profession as a whole, I felt they had the right man for the job. Now I have see the finished product, I know I was right.

It is a splendid effort, and one that does great credit to you You must have received a host of congratulations from some of the biggest names in advertising. I should like to add my small voice to theirs.

Sincerely,

Dear Mr Weeks,

Fred Lindley brought me a copy of your latest book with him from America and I must confess that I devoured it in one long session, ending well into the small hours.

It is truly a fine work and I want you to know how much I enjoyed it. I certainly hope English readers are not to be deprived of it and that plans are already afoot for an English edition. Meanwhile I feel privileged at having had a chance to read it.

Every good wish,

Yours sincerely,

Dear Ms Bradley,

Every business executive should have a copy of your article 'Do your Business Letters Pass Muster?'. I read it myself with a great deal of pleasure and satisfaction and found several of my own quaint usages getting the treatment they deserved!

Stereotyped 'commercial' English seems to be a sacred cow in many quarters and few are the business letter writers, particularly at the more junior executive levels, who dare to throw out the old clichés.

I thoroughly enjoyed the way you ripped them to pieces and showed them up as the meaningless mumbo-jumbo they are!

Is there any way in which I can get reprints for the people in my Company?

Sincerely yours,

Dear Dr White,

Your talk on 'Getting More Capital into the Business' at the Institute of Directors last night was very instructive and of vital interest to almost every member of the audience.

My hearty congratulations on your thorough grasp of the subject and clear, attention-holding delivery.

Yours sincerely,

My dear Harris,

Your talk last night at the Advertising Club certainly hit the spot. I really envied the way you kept the audience listening in rapt attention and the enthusiastic roar of applause which greeted you at the end.

Hope you'll come back soon.

Sincerely,

Dear Ms Crane,

May I congratulate you on an excellent job? I mean your book, The Sophisticated Investor. Not only have I read it from cover to cover, but I find myself constantly referring to it as I ponder on my next investment move.

Years of experience have gone into the writing of this book and it is indeed generous of you to share your knowledge and experience with thousands of readers. I'm sure all of us will be better investors if we heed your advice.

Sincerely yours,

Dear Miss Wentworth,

Your little pamphlet on forms of address is an absolute godsend! Congratulations on a tricky, time-consuming job well done. Hardly a day passes without someone coming into my office to borrow your pamphlet and I can see already that the only solution will be to order half a dozen copies, so that everyone has one handy on his or her desk.

Yours sincerely,

Dear Jim,

Congratulations, old friend!

Last night's speech at the Chairman's farewell banquet was a veritable tour de force. Only you could have carried it off so well and I doff my cap to you. At the same time, I must warn you that, having proved yourself such a masterful speech-maker you can expect to be called upon more frequently in future!

Sincerely,

Dear Ms Hardy,

Your article in Personnel Management on the Employment Bill is most lucid and helpful.

There is always a certain amount of apprehension when new Bills are introduced and one is not quite sure what effect they will have. Your timely article comes to dispel all doubts, clear up misconceptions and answer most questions. I, for one, am very grateful for it.

Yours sincerely,

On outstanding community service

Dear Mr Kinney,

As your term of office as President of the Kingston Chamber of Commerce draws to a close, we should like to thank you for the untiring efforts you have put into the Chamber's affairs and for the dynamic and enthusiastic leadership you have given us.

We all feel that our Chamber of Commerce has made great strides during your term of office. You have indeed performed a worthwhile community service and we all owe you a vote of thanks.

Sincerely yours,

Dear Mr Spencer,

I was delighted to read in The Bucks Free Press that the Bourne End Community Centre Fund Drive has reached its target three months ahead of the time allotted.

This is indeed a splendid achievement, due, in no small measure, to your tireless efforts and enthusiasm.

All of us in the village send you our grateful thanks and sincere congratulations.

Yours sincerely,

Dear Mr Mayor,

News of your premature retirement due to ill-health has come as a great shock to me, as it doubtless was to a great many other members of this community, which you have served so well.

As you prepare to leave us for a more benign climate, I should like to express my sincere appreciation for all you have done to make our town a better place to live in. May the knowledge of a difficult job well done be of solace to you and help you to a speedy recovery.

Very best wishes for your health and happiness.

Sincerely yours,

Dear Mrs Smedley,

I should like to congratulate you on the splendid way you organized and led the 'Save the Wye' Committee. Thanks to you, a motorway will not now cut right through our beloved 'green' and we can all look forward once again to our picnics and frolics, free from this ugly threat.

May I add my thanks to the many you must have received?

Yours sincerely,

Dear Mac,

This is just a note of congratulations on the outstanding way you organized and M.C.'d the Spring Gardens Estate Residents' Association Dance last night.

You are rendering our small community a fine service and I, for one, am most grateful to you.

Let me know if there is any other way in which I can help.

Sincerely,

Dear Mr Bradley,

I have just read the report on our Chamber of Commerce's first year. It makes very pleasant reading indeed and I wish to congratulate you on your fine achievement as its first President.

You have given generously of your time and talents to our growing community and all of us who do business here owe you a debt of thanks.

I wish you continuing success in the coming year.

Yours sincerely,

Dear Mr Skinner,

Reading can well be proud of having you as Chairman of its Town Planning Committee! I have studied the plans for the modernization of the town centre and must congratulate you on their originality, beauty, and functional qualities. Rarely are these three united and so often we have to sacrifice one for the other. You, however, have succeeded in blending them to give us a beautiful yet functional town.

You may be sure of my full support when plans leave the drawing-board stage and the usual implementation problems begin to emerge.

Sincerely yours,

Dear Mr Clarke,

My hearty congratulations for the outstanding success of the first High Wycombe Arts Festival!

No one knows better than I how much work and energy you have put into the project from its inception last summer, nor how much the festival's success owes to your enthusiastic leadership and determination.

The festival has brought a considerable amount of new business to High Wycombe and many local businessmen have reason to be grateful, quite apart from the cultural aspects involved.

You may certainly count on my renewed support when next year's programme gets under way.

Yours sincerely,

Dear Mr Crispin,

This is just a note to congratulate you on the able way in which you led the Civic Improvement Forum last night. You did a fine job and the programme was one of the best we have had.

Sincerely yours,

Dear Mr Jenkins,

The Festival of the City of London was an inspired idea which has aroused a good deal of interest in the City, among tourists and Britons alike.

On behalf of the whole management team of Baxter's Limited, I should like to congratulate you on the leading part you have played in this excellent venture, assure you of our wholehearted support in next year's event, and wish you continued success with this most happy conception.

Yours sincerely,

Dear Major Harrison,

I was very pleased to read the fine tribute paid to you in the current issue of the <u>Maidenhead Advertiser</u> and would like to add my small voice of thanks and congratulations for your life-long service to our community.

We are indeed fortunate in having you as a resident, for your public-spirited work has touched almost all of us, from business people to pensioners.

I wish you many more years of health and happiness in the service of our town.

Yours sincerely,

For son's or daughter's achievement

Dear Jim,

I have just learned that your son John has obtained a First Class Honours Degree at Oxford. You must be very proud of him and I hasten to send my sincere congratulations to you both.

Sincerely,

Dear Mr Bates,

I was delighted to read in the local paper that your twin daughters, Margaret and Mary, both passed their Oxford Entrance Examination on the same day.

You must be a proud father indeed, for your pleasures come in pairs. Please extend my hearty congratulations to the two young ladies, together with my best wishes for their continued success.

Sincerely yours,

Dear Mr Spires,

You must be a proud and happy man today and rightly so, for it is not given to many to have an Olympic star for a daughter.

I was really moved to see your little Sheila, not yet a woman, pitting herself so valiantly against the world's greatest swimmers and coming out on top every time. Yet in victory she was modest and unassuming.

Do please extend my warmest congratulations to her, and my very best wishes for her future.

Sincerely yours,

Dear Eric,

I have just heard that your son Peter has got his Oxford Blue for rowing. This is indeed a fine achievement and proves conclusively what we have suspected all along, namely, that Peter is a chip off the old block in every sphere.

The best of luck to him and congratulations to you both.

Sincerely,

Dear Allen,

One of my well-trained spies has informed me that your daughter Carole has graduated with Honours from Reading University.

You must be a proud father indeed and rightly so. Please give her my very best wishes for her future career, as well as my heartfelt congratulations on her success.

Sincerely,

Dear Mr Higgins,

Thank you for your announcement that your son Paul is to become a partner in your firm. All of us at Hale's are delighted with the news. We realize how much this means to you and send you our hearty congratulations and sincere wishes for his continued success.

Sincerely yours,

Dear Mrs Burton,

I was delighted to learn that your son Edward has won a scholarship which will take him all the way to Yale.

This is a splendid achievement and you must be very proud of him. Congratulations to you both and very best wishes for Edward's American studies.

Sincerely yours,

To staff

On special personal occasion

Dear Ted,

It is a pleasure to send you my hearty congratulations on your forthcoming wedding.

May it be the beginning of a long and happy marriage for you and Joan.

Sincerely,

Dear Hugh,

Congratulations! I've just heard that it's a bouncing boy, as you and Joyce wanted, and I'm very happy for you.

My very best wishes to you both, and for a long, happy and successful life for your son and heir!

Sincerely,

Dear Mr Skinner,

Tomorrow you reach one of life's milestones and it is a special pleasure for me to wish you many happy returns of the day and to congratulate you on your seventieth birthday.

May you have a very happy day and many more years of good health, good cheer and good companionship.

Sincerely yours,

Dear Mr Fenmore,

I have just read about your engagement in the Daily Telegraph and hasten to send you my sincere congratulations and best wishes for many years of happy marriage.

Yours sincerely,

Dear Alec,

I always knew that ballroom dancing was your form of relaxation, but I did not realize that we actually harboured a potential champion in our midst. Well, now I know! I must say, you really looked slick on television last night and I felt proud of you.

Hearty congratulations to you and your lovely partner and best wishes for your continued success.

Sincerely,

Dear Miss Whitmore,

I have just learned that after several years of evening study you have obtained your BA degree, which you are to receive next week.

This is indeed a splendid achievement, and one which speaks volumes for your persistence, diligence, and intelligence. Hearty congratulations to you. I'm very proud to have people like you on our staff.

Sincerely yours,

Dear Fred,

News has just reached me that it's a bonny eight-pound girl! Hearty congratulations to you and Paula and very best wishes to the baby. With parents like you she will assuredly make a splendid start in life.

Sincerely,

Dear Miss Wynn,

This is just a note, on the occasion of your engagement to Mr John West to send you the best of good wishes.

May you enjoy many years of shared happiness.

Sincerely yours,

For outstanding work

Dear Liz,

Congratulations!

The half-year sales figures have just appeared on my desk
and I find that your sales are way ahead of any other person's in
the Company. This is great going!

At the Annual Sales Conference later this year you will see
the Company's appreciation take a more tangible form, but
meanwhile, I want you to know how pleased I am with your
efforts. Keep it up, Liz, this is the kind of thing we like!

Sincerely,

Dear Ivor,

Congratulations on landing the Brooke's account! I know it
was a tough nut to crack and your success is a measure of your
skill and singleness of purpose. Jolly good show!

Sincerely,

Dear Joan,

The little book, Furnishing Your Home, is a gem.
Congratulations on a job well done. I'm convinced that it will do a
lot for us.

Sincerely,

Dear Chris,

Ten years ago today you joined Evans and Day as a hopeful
lad. Your career with us can be described as little short of
brilliant. You quickly showed a remarkable grasp of the business
and gradually built up a reputation for reliability, dependability
and, above all, a love of work which is nowadays so rare.

I did not wish this anniversary to pass without your knowing how much we appreciate your contribution to the Company's success.

Sincerely,

Dear Philip,

We have almost come to expect you to bring home the biggest side of bacon, yet every year you surprise us even more.

This year you have broken all existing records: you have chalked up the biggest slice of sales for the company, you have sold more hardware than ever before, and you have landed the biggest order in the history of the Company.

This is splendid work, Philip! We are planning for you to play a star role in our next sales conference, so that you can inspire the other sales reps. to follow in your footsteps. Meanwhile, a very warm and personal 'Thank you'.

Sincerely,

Dear Carole,

When I asked you to put out a book list in about two minutes flat I realized I was asking for the moon. Yet you came across most handsomely and produced a very well-designed, attractive, and crisply-worded folder.

Many thanks for a difficult assignment admirably carried out.

Sincerely,

My dear Coleman,

This is just a note to tell how very much the Company appreciated the outstanding effort which your whole department put into getting the Baxter order out on time.

Without everyone's wholehearted effort it could not have been done and I want you to convey my sincere thanks to every one of your staff. It was a splendid effort.

Sincerely,

Dear Jean,

You will be pleased to learn that our spring line has sold outstandingly well. I attribute this success in no small measure to the series of direct-mail letters which you composed for our last campaign. I thought at the time that they were remarkably good and contained all the necessary ingredients to make a sale. Now I know they are good and would like to congratulate you on an outstanding job.

Keep up the good work!

Sincerely,

Dear Bill,

You will be happy to know that you are the man to carry off First Prize in our annual sales contest! As you know, this will mean £500, plus the satisfaction of knowing that you are the Company's No. 1 sales person.

Congratulations to you and every best wish for an equally good year in 1986.

Sincerely,

On promotion or other advancement

Dear Jack,

I am sorry indeed that you will soon be leaving us. You have done excellent work for the Company and we had come to rely on your judgement and dependability. However, I am delighted that such a splendid opportunity should have come your way and I know you will do well in your new position.

My very best wishes go with you.

Sincerely,

Dear June,

This is just a note to congratulate you on your promotion to Assistant Sales Manager.

Since you joined our sales force three years ago your sales volume has increased every year and we have found you to be an enthusiastic, reliable, and knowledgeable sales person. Your qualities of leadership definitely put you in line for promotion and we know your presence will give added zest to the sales management team.

Sincerely,

Dear Bert,

Congratulations on your promotion to board level!

Your outstanding record as Production Manager has earned you this important advancement and we are all confident that you'll be a signal success as a company director.

Sincerely,

Dear Mr Hyde,

As you prepare to leave our Company to take up your new position as Chief Accountant with Dearborne and Son, I want you to know that you take with you our very best wishes for a successful and satisfying career.

You know already how sorry we all are to see you go, yet we appreciate full well what a splendid opportunity this is for you and we feel sure you have made the right decision.

The very best of luck to you!

Sincerely yours,

Dear Brown,

My heartfelt congratulations on your promotion to Chief Export Clerk. As you know, this gesture is intended as a recognition and reward for your conscientious and efficient work in the Export Department since you joined the Company two years ago.

My best wishes for your continued success.

Sincerely,

Dear Joseph,

This is the kind of letter I very much enjoy writing, for I know it will bring you pleasure.

The Board has decided to grant you a substantial rise, bringing your annual salary to £15,000, as from January 1 next. This is in recognition of your outstanding performance since you joined the Company as General Manager three years ago.

Hearty congratulations and sincere best wishes for your continued success.

Sincerely,

Dear Julian,

I am happy indeed about your promotion to Branch Manager and my only regret is that we shall no longer have you around at Head Office.

This is a very important step forward for you, the culmination of many years of devoted service to the Bank.

As you prepare to take up your new responsibilities in your own branch, my warm congratulations and sincere best wishes for your continued success go with you.

Sincerely,

Dear Max,

The only trouble with having a good man in the team is that, sooner or later, someone snaps him up and he is off to pastures new. And so it is with you. I'm sorry to see you go, and my regret is but a reflection of the esteem in which I hold you and of my appreciation for the splendid job you have done for me since you joined the Johnston sales team five years ago.

The opportunity offered you is a handsome one indeed and I know you will make a resounding success of it. You take with you my very best wishes and sincere congratulations. I know you will go far.

Sincerely,

Dear Miss Wasey,

I have just learned that you are leaving our Company to take up a position as Public Relations Officer with Dobson and Co.

The opportunity offered you is unquestionably an excellent one and I am always pleased to see members of my staff forge ahead in the business world.

You must not think, however, that you will not be missed – you most certainly will be. Your sound judgement and perception, as well as your unquestionable writing ability, were much appreciated by all those who had occasion to work with you, within and outside your department and I know they are all sorry to see you go.

You take with you my sincere congratulations and warmest wishes for success in your new post.

Yours sincerely,

Dear Marguerite,

Congratulations on your promotion to Editor of <u>Office Management</u>! It is an achievement which gives me particular pleasure, inasmuch as I have followed your career with the Company since you joined us as a hopeful and very lively lass of 18. I didn't really believe at the time that you would one day be editor of one of our leading journals. It is a splendid achievement which you richly deserve.

Warmest wishes for your continued success.

Sincerely,

For special professional achievement or honour

Dear Ralph

I was greatly pleased by your election as President of the Nottingham Advertising Club and send you my hearty congratulations on an honour well deserved.

You have given a tremendous amount of spare time and energy to the Club and your election shows just how very much your fellow members appreciate your efforts.

Good going, Ralph!

Sincerely,

Dear Jane,

I have just finished reading your excellent article in this week's <u>Business</u> and must congratulate you on its cogency, lucidity, and vitality.

You certainly know how to combine useful information with a lively style and as I read the article I felt proud to have you on the staff.

Let me know when further articles of yours are due to appear.

Sincerely,

My dear Wilson,

I was surprised and delighted to see your name on the roster of speakers at next month's course at the Chamber of Commerce. It is an honour indeed to figure in the company of such renowned speakers and I'd like to bet you'll be the youngest expert present.

Congratulations! I feel very proud of you and unless something very unforeseen happens, I'll be there applauding you.

Sincerely,

Dear Ms Cooper,

It was kind of you to present me with a copy of your first book and you may be sure I'll treasure it.

I spent part of the weekend reading it and found it most interesting, practical, and well-written.

My sincere congratulations to you on a really worthwhile achievement.

Sincerely yours,

Dear Basil,

Mr Fenwick has just told me that you have completed two 'A' levels at night school and I want you to know how proud of you we all are at Wrexham's.

It is a fine thing for a young man to continue his education by devoting some of his spare time to evening study and it is very gratifying to have such young men within our Company.

Congratulations on your fine achievement and best wishes for your future.

Yours sincerely,

Dear Rex,

Congratulations on your election to the responsible office of Secretary of the Reading Chamber of Commerce.

I know how hard you have worked for the business community and you certainly deserve the honour which is now yours. Quite obviously many others in the community agree with me.

Best wishes for a very satisfying and successful term of office.

Sincerely,

Dear Emma,

Your book, Why Public Relations?, is an excellent piece of work. I spent the best part of yesterday evening reading it and, while I have not yet finished it, I am very much impressed by the sound, practical advice it gives, its clear and friendly style, and the loftiness of its philosophy.

Congratulations on a truly fine achievement. It must have been a great satisfaction to you to write it and I hope the financial rewards will also prove worth while.

Sincerely,

My dear Fletcher,

Your election as President of the Cold Rolled Sections Association is one which calls for congratulations. I was delighted when you first joined the Association and it gives me a great deal of satisfaction to see how much progress you have made and how well-thought-of you are by your fellow-members.

It is an excellent thing for our Company that one of its youngest members should so distinguish himself and I wish you a very successful and satisfying term of office.

Yours sincerely,

Dear Peter,

Thank you for sending me a reprint of your article 'Cutting Corners with Conveyors' from the January issue of <u>Materials Handling</u>.

It is an excellent article and covers the subject very thoroughly and expertly. You have my most sincere congratulations on an outstanding piece of work.

Sincerely,

Dear Bill,

I was very happy to learn of your election as President of Rotary International. This is an impressive recognition of your talent for leadership and I am very proud that you should represent our industry at the Club.

I'm sure that members have a very lively year before them under your able guidance.

Congratulations on an honour richly deserved.

Sincerely,

10

'Thank You' Letters

The letter of appreciation can take many forms. It is as varied, in fact, as there are reasons for our gratitude. If it is to be effective it should be written at once, for nothing creates a worse impression than a 'Thank You' letter which begins with an apology.

If you have time to write the note by hand, so much the better, but in any event, make it brief. No good purpose is served in going on and on. Simply say your piece and close.

The informal approach is the best one for a note of thanks, but several factors must be taken into consideration in deciding just how informal to be. You should bear in mind how personal the favour was, the degree of friendship between you and your correspondent and, finally, the age and character of your addressee.

Above all, a note of thanks should be sincere. If you are just 'going through the motions' because you think it is the right thing to do, it will be quite obvious to your correspondent.

In these days of constant haste, it is the minority that finds time to drop a note of thanks for a favour received or a pleasant evening. Yet no letter gives more pleasure to the recipient and does more to cement a friendship, either inside or out of the business circle.

To retail customers

For opening charge account

Dear Ms Collins,

> Thank you for opening a charge account with John Ferris.
>
> We greatly welcome this opportunity of including you in our large circle of special customers and will do all we can to make your shopping at our store a pleasurable experience.
>
> Sincerely yours,

189

Dear Mr Allen,

It is a pleasure to write you this personal note to say 'Thank you' for opening a charge account with our store. We take it as an expression of confidence in Wills and Son Limited, our goods and our service.

We look forward to serving you and will do our very best to make each one of your visits to our store an enjoyable experience.

Yours sincerely,

Dear Mrs Watson,

I have just learned from our Credit Manager that you have opened a credit account with us and hasten to send you this note of thanks.

It is the policy of our organization to sell quality merchandise at competitive prices. We also pride ourselves on our efficient, courteous service aimed at making your shopping expeditions here easy and pleasant.

Please let us know if ever there is anything we can do to make our service even better.

We look forward to welcoming you to our store.

Yours sincerely,

Dear Mrs Armstrong,

This is just to say 'Thank you' for opening a charge account at our store.

As an account customer you will be kept informed of our sales and other special events. In fact the first day of both our winter and summer sales is exclusively for our charge account customers, who can come and shop at their leisure before the crowds surge in.

All of us at the store will do our best to make you welcome always. Should you occasionally prefer to phone your order, however, just ask for the Special Service Department. They will be delighted to serve you.

We very much appreciate having you as a charge customer.

Yours sincerely,

Dear Mr Thompson,

It is a pleasure to welcome you as an account customer. We appreciate this token of your confidence and all of us at the store will strive to deserve it.

Enclosed is a list of the buyer's name in each department. If you have any difficulty in finding the exact item you are looking for, do please ask for the buyer by name, for she will be delighted to help you.

As a charge account customer your name will go on our special mailing list and you will be sent prior notification of special purchases, sales and other events.

We hope you will enjoy shopping in our store as much as we shall enjoy serving you.

Yours sincerely,

Dear Miss Jones,

Enclosed is your brand-new credit card.

Your opening of a personal charge account with our store is a measure of your confidence in us which we shall do everything we can to justify.

There is absolutely no charge for the credit service we offer. Merchandise will be billed to you at regular list price and accounts are sent out on the 10th of each month for purchases made the previous month. We would appreciate your letting us have your cheque as soon thereafter as convenient, in order to help our accounts department.

We hope you will enjoy your every visit to our store and that we shall have the pleasure of counting you as our customer for many years to come.

Yours sincerely,

Dear Mrs Holland,

I have just learned that you have opened a charge account with us and want you to know how much I appreciate your confidence in us.

Enclosed is a little booklet which I hope you will find both interesting and useful. It gives a short history of Wannaker's, location of the various departments, names of the individual buyers, and our terms of sale.

Do please make yourself at home in our store and be assured that we consider it a privilege to serve you.

Yours sincerely,

Dear Ms Green,

Welcome to the large family of Greer's special customers!

No doubt you are already familiar with our Career Woman Department, which was specially planned for the busy executive who cannot spare the time to wander all over the store co-ordinating suits with accessories or selecting gifts.

Everything in this department has been specially bought and co-ordinated with the career woman in mind. If you are too busy even to make a selection from the many alternatives available, our fashion consultant, Lorna Horn, will be happy to assemble a complete outfit for your approval.

We look forward to serving you and would welcome any suggestion on how we can further improve any facet of our service.

Yours sincerely,

Dear Miss Beer,

I was delighted indeed to learn that you had opened a charge account with us. We shall certainly do our best to deserve this expression of your confidence in The House of Fashion.

I hope this will be the beginning of a long and mutually pleasurable connection.

Sincerely yours,

Dear Mrs Mathews,

Thank you for opening a charge account with us.

There are many advantages in shopping at White's. Perhaps all of them have not occurred to you. The enclosed booklet, 'Shopping at White's' makes many useful suggestions and we hope it will help you to enjoy your visits to our store.

Certainly we shall enjoy serving you and our whole selling staff will do everything in its power to deserve the confidence you have placed in us.

Yours sincerely,

For first use of charge account

Dear Mrs Jennings,

This is to thank you for making the first use of your charge account. We appreciate this first opportunity to serve you as an account customer and will make every effort to merit the confidence you have placed in us.

Should you have any suggestion on ways to improve our service, please do not hesitate to let us know.

Yours sincerely,

Dear Ms Jones,

Many thanks for your first order since you became one of our special customers.

We sincerely hope that all your dealings with us will be a source of satisfaction to you and look forward to serving you for many years to come.

Yours sincerely,

Dear Mr Stewart,

Thank you for calling in at Harrison's the other day and making your first 'charge' purchase.

We hope you will visit us again soon. You will always find us happy to see you and eager to serve you.

Yours sincerely,

Dear Miss Smith,

Enclosed is our first account for purchases made by you since you became one of our valued charge customers.

We welcome this opportunity to thank you for your patronage and to assure you once again of our willingness to serve you in every way possible.

If you have any suggestions on how we can improve either the service or the displays in our store, do please let us know.

Yours sincerely,

Dear Mrs Sampson,

This is just a note to say 'Thank you' for coming into the store yesterday and making your first purchase on your new charge account.

We want you to feel quite at home in our store and hope you will visit us frequently, even if only for a browse.

Thank you again for your support.

Yours sincerely,

Dear Mr Quinn,

Our first statement for purchases made since you became one of our account customers is enclosed. For your convenience it is sent to you in a special envelope which can be re-used to send us your cheque.

May we take this opportunity to thank you for your purchases? We hope you are thoroughly satisfied with every one of them and look forward to seeing you in our store frequently.

Yours sincerely,

Dear Ms Hammond,

Thank you for coming into our store yesterday and making your first purchase on your new charge account.

Please come in again soon. We are always happy to see you and will do everything possible to make each of your visits enjoyable.

Yours sincerely,

Dear Ms Brown,

Ms Guinness, in our Career Woman Department, told me you were in yesterday to select a few gifts, which you charged to your new account. May I say 'Thank you' for calling in? I do hope you found this special department as convenient as we believe it to be.

Yours sincerely,

Dear Mrs Reynolds,

Thank you for visiting us yesterday and for making your first purchase on your credit account.

I hope the article you bought will give you lasting satisfaction and that you will come in and see us again soon. A sincere welcome awaits you always.

Yours sincerely,

Dear Mr Myers,

We recently had the pleasure of serving you for the first time as an account customer in our Ready-to-Wear Department, and we sincerely hope that you were completely satisfied.

The purpose of this letter is to ask what you think of the suit now that you have had the opportunity of wearing it. If, as we hope, you are satisfied, we should appreciate knowing it, but if for any reason you are not, we should equally like to know.

Needless to say, your reply will be treated in strict confidence, and no publicity use will be made of it at any time.

Just jot down your reply on the back of this letter and post to us in the enclosed envelope which needs no stamp. Thank you.

Yours sincerely,

Dear Mrs Dow,

I was delighted to learn from Ms Jones, our buyer in the Millinery Department, that you were in yesterday to make your first purchase since you became one of our valued account customers.

It is a pleasure to serve you as an account customer and we all look forward to seeing you again soon.

Yours sincerely,

For prompt payment

Dear Mrs Higgins,

This is just note to tell you how much we appreciate the splendid way in which you always deal with your account.

If all our customers were like you, life in the Credit Department would be an absolute paradise.

Do let us know if there is any way in which we can make your account with us even more convenient for you.

Yours sincerely,

Dear Miss Gibbons,

Since you opened your account with us last May you have always sent us your cheque promptly and without a single reminder.

We should like you to know how much we appreciate this and how happy we are to have you as a customer.

Please be assured that we shall continue to do all we can to merit your loyalty and confidence.

Sincerely yours,

Dear Mrs Fields,

Your cheque arrived this morning, right on the dot, as it has been ever since you opened your account with us almost a year ago.

It is certainly a pleasure to have customers like you who meet their obligations promptly, thereby saving our Credit Department a lot of detail work.

Please accept our grateful thanks.

Yours sincerely,

Dear Mr Giles,

You are one of those customers who seldom, if ever, gets a letter from the Credit Department. You are always so prompt in paying your account that we have no cause to write and remind you.

Perhaps it has never occurred to you, but we do appreciate your prompt payments. It makes the work of the department so much more pleasant and saves us endless time.

Our grateful thanks to you, and may you long remain a much valued customer.

Yours sincerely,

Dear Miss Collins,

Many thanks for your cheque for £23.50 in settlement of your November account.

I should like to take this opportunity of telling you how very much we appreciate the promptness with which you always settle your account with us.

We shall try in every way to demonstrate our appreciation by giving you the best and most courteous service every time you come to Marshall's.

Sincerely yours,

Dear Mrs Freeman,

Letters we send from our Credit Department are usually quite different from this one, yet this is the kind we most enjoy writing.

Its pleasant purpose is to thank you for the fine way in which you handle your account with Simpson's.

We greatly appreciate your co-operation and you can count on our doing our best to merit your continued loyalty and confidence.

Yours sincerely,

Dear Mr Hill,

In all the years we have had the pleasure of having you as a credit customer, it has never been necessary to remind you of an overdue payment.

This is a splendid record, of which you may well be proud. Certainly, we appreciate having customers like you and the sole purpose of this letter is to tell you so.

Many thanks for your co-operation. We shall continue to do all we can to deserve your confidence and loyalty.

Sincerely yours,

Dear Mrs King,

Your charge account with us is just one year old this month. During this whole period you have always paid your account promptly, never once have we had to remind you.

We greatly appreciate your co-operation and would like you to know it has not passed unnoticed. Accounts such as yours make the work of the department so much more pleasant.

May we therefore say 'Thank you'? We enjoy having you as a customer.

Yours sincerely,

Dear Mrs Wayne,

As the year draws to a close we like to count our blessings and certainly one of the greatest blessings a store can have is customers like you, who are so prompt in settling their credit account.

Never once during the past year have we had to remind you of an overdue account. Your cheques come in as regularly as clockwork, making our task so simple and pleasant.

Thank you for your co-operation and best wishes for the coming year.

Yours sincerely,

Dear Ms Hawkins,

This is just a note to say 'Thank you' for the business-like way in which you always settle your Benson's monthly account.

We should like you to know how much we appreciate your continued co-operation and how much we like having you as a customer.

If there is anything we can do to make your charge account with us even more useful to you, please do not hesitate to let us know.

Yours sincerely,

Dear Mrs Jenkins,

Customers like you make the wheels of business run very smoothly and pleasantly indeed.

We very much appreciate the prompt way in which you settle your monthly account with us and are writing to send you our sincere thanks.

Your credit record is an enviable one and we are proud to have you as a customer.

Sincerely yours,

Dear Mr Austin,

This note brings you a very special 'Thank you' for your wonderful record of prompt payment of your Benson's account.

We very much appreciate customers like you and would be happy to recommend you as a charge customer if ever you wished to use our name as a reference.

Please let us know if there is anything we can do at any time to make shopping at Benson's even more pleasant and practical.

Yours sincerely,

For loyal patronage

Dear Mrs Burnett,

It is a long time since you first opened a charge account with Fennimore's! To be exact, it is ten years this month. I wonder if you had realized it was an anniversary?

We feel this is an unequalled opportunity to let you know how much we appreciate your custom and to say what a pleasure it has been to serve you for so long.

Please let us know if there is anything we can do to make your visits to Fennimore's even more rewarding than they have been in the past.

Sincerely yours,

Dear Ms Swanson,

As the year draws to a close we would like you to know how much we appreciate your loyal patronage and to thank you for your support and co-operation during the past year.

You have been an account customer of The House of Fashion for a number of years and it is a source of deep satisfaction to us to have enjoyed your confidence and friendship for so long.

We hope this pleasant relationship will continue for many years to come.

Yours sincerely,

Dear Miss Kimble,

This is just a note to say 'Thank you' for your support over the past year and to tell you how much we appreciate having you for a customer.

We know you have visited the store frequently since opening your account with us a year ago and we are very pleased that you enjoy shopping at Hodder's. It is a pleasure to serve you and we look forward to many more opportunities of doing so.

Yours sincerely,

Dear Mrs Fox,

Your charge account is one year old today! We should like to celebrate this first anniversary by thanking you for your continued support and confidence and telling you how happy we are to count you among our most valued customers.

We look forward to continuing this pleasant association for many years to come.

Yours sincerely,

Dear Mr Green,

Department stores are growing bigger and bigger and size brings with it a certain remoteness. The first Mr Coleridge no longer stands at the door, greeting almost every customer by name. We do not wish you to think, however, that this means we no longer care for our customers. Nothing could be further from the truth. We not only care, but appreciate them highly and keep careful track of each one of them.

This is how we know that you opened your charge account with The House of Coleridge exactly five years ago and have been a regular and frequent patron ever since.

On this fifth anniversary we should like to thank you for your loyalty and support over the years and assure you that we shall continue to do all we can to make your shopping at our store a pleasure.

Sincerely yours,

Dear Ms Smithers,

It is my pleasant task to write and thank you for your loyal patronage over the past year.

It has been a great pleasure to serve you and we look forward to doing so for many more years.

Yours sincerely,

Dear Mrs Fenton,

The year's end is a good time to take stock and among our assets we can certainly include loyal customers such as you.

We should like you to know how much we appreciate your support and how proud we are to have had you as an account customer for so long.

We hope the New Year brings you many blessings and look forward to seeing you at Mayer's as frequently as in the past.

Yours sincerely,

Dear Miss Gibbs,

I expect you had no idea that your charge account with Brendan's was one year old today! We always keep track of such things because our faithful customers are very important to us.

May we mark the first anniversary by thanking you most sincerely for your support during the past year? We would like your second year as a charge customer to be even more convenient and pleasurable than the first. Do please, therefore, let us know how we can make this so.

Yours sincerely,

Dear Mrs Lawson,

At the dawn of the New Year we should like to thank you for your support in the past year and let you know how much we appreciate having you as a customer.

If there is any way in which we can serve you better in the New Year, please let us know. We hope it is a very happy one for you and your family.

Yours sincerely,

Dear Ms Moore,

There are times when I wish Maitland's were a small shop, as it was early in this century, so that I could get to know each of our customers personally and tell them how much I value their loyal support.

I hope, however, that you will accept this poor substitute for a personal 'Thank you'. We really have enjoyed serving you during the past year and sincerely hope that you have enjoyed shopping at our store every bit as much.

Yours sincerely,

Dear Mr Wentworth,

We were very pleased to note how frequently you have made use of your account with our store since you opened it several months ago.

We have greatly enjoyed serving you and will do everything we can to continue deserving your confidence and support for many years.

Yours sincerely,

Dear Mrs O'Grady,

I don't suppose you've ever before received a Valentine from a department store. Yet this being the time of year to let friends know how highly you think of them, we too would like you to know how much we have appreciated your support and friendly custom throughout the past year, and indeed, for many years now.

Loyal customers such as you are greatly valued by department store managers like myself and I am most anxious that you should know this.

We look forward to counting you as our customer for a long time to come and meanwhile send you our very best wishes.

Yours sincerely,

Dear Mrs Scott,

You may not have given it a thought, but your charge account with our store is ten years old this month.

We are proud indeed of this wonderful record and would like to thank you for your loyal support over the years. We have always tried to do everything to deserve it and will re-double our efforts so that our association in the years ahead may be even more pleasant than it has been in the past.

Very sincerely yours,

Dear Miss Scudder,

I should like to begin the New Year by thanking you for your patronage and friendly custom throughout 1985. It has been a pleasure and a privilege to serve you and your frequent purchases are proof that you, too, have enjoyed your visits to Freeman's.

We all look forward to seeing you as frequently during 1986 and I hope you will let me know personally if there is anything we can do to improve our service in any way.

Yours sincerely,

Dear Mr Graham,

You have been a loyal customer of The Man's Shop for almost five years and I am writing to thank you for your patronage and to let you know that it is highly appreciated.

Do please let me have your comments or suggestions on any aspect of our service or merchandise at any time, as we are most anxious to keep abreast of the times and constantly improve both the selection of goods we offer and their display.

Sincerely yours,

For renewed patronage

Dear Miss Wentworth,

Welcome back! I was delighted to learn that you had made a purchase in the dress department, after a prolonged absence.

It was a pleasure to serve you and we much appreciate your patronage.

We hope you will come in to see us again soon and that the pleasant relationship we enjoyed in the past will be renewed.

Yours sincerely,

Dear Mrs Bridges,

It was a pleasure to serve you yesterday in the soft furnishings department and we are happy indeed to welcome you back to the large family of loyal Barking customers.

I should be most grateful if you would let me know if there is any way in which we can make your visits to our store even more of a pleasure and convenience.

Yours sincerely,

Dear Mr Dorking,

We very much appreciated the opportunity of serving you again in the men's accessories department yesterday.

It had been a long time since you used your credit account with our store and we had missed you.

We hope you will come in again soon and look forward to welcoming you.

Yours sincerely,

Dear Mrs Fisher,

I am writing to tell you how pleased I am that you have started using your charge account with us again.

It was a pleasure indeed to serve you and we all hope you will be back soon.

If there is anything we can do to improve our service, or otherwise make your account more convenient to you, we hope you will let us know.

Yours sincerely,

Dear Ms Butler,

I was delighted to learn that you were in the store yesterday after so long an absence and I am writing this note of appreciation.

You had not used your Wahring's charge account for so long that we had missed you. It is a pleasure to welcome you back and I very much hope you will now resume your frequent visits.

Sincerely yours,

Dear Mrs Brunning,

It is always sad to lose a friend and you had not been in for so long that we were beginning to fear we had lost your friendship. But yesterday at last you returned and I am writing to tell you how happy we were to see you.

Please pay us another visit soon and we shall do all we can to merit your confidence and friendship.

Yours sincerely,

Dear Ms King,

I am writing to thank you for making a purchase in our Coats and Suits Department yesterday, after a long absence from our store.

We had missed you and are happy to have you back again.

Do come in again soon. A welcome always awaits you.

Yours sincerely,

Dear Mr Billings,

Welcome back to Bollard's!

We had missed you during your long absence and are very pleased to count you once more among our regular customers.

Do come in again soon. We are all eager to serve you.

Yours sincerely,

Dear Miss Collins,

I notice from our books that you made use of your charge account again last week, after a prolonged absence from our store. I am delighted about this and write to tell you how much we appreciate your patronage.

If there is anything at all we can do to make your visits to Benson's even more convenient or if there is anything else we can do for you, do please let us know.

Sincerely yours,

For recommending firm to others

Dear Mrs Barrett,

Mrs Williams was in the store yesterday on your recommendation, and I should like to thank you most sincerely for your kindness in recommending us to her.

We will certainly do all we can to serve Mrs Williams well and live up to the good report you were kind enough to give her about us.

Yours sincerely,

Dear Miss Manders,

When Miss Smythe called in on Wednesday to open a charge account with us she mentioned that you had recommended the store to her.

This was extremely kind and thoughtful of you and we appreciate it very much indeed. It is most gratifying that you should think so highly of Kimbel's and you may be sure that we shall take special pride in serving Miss Smythe well and continuing to deserve the confidence you have placed in us.

Sincerely yours,

Dear Mr Giffiths,

I had a visit from Mr Charles M. Greenock yesterday during the course of which he opened a current account at our Bank and told me of his decision to put his banking business in our hands. Your glowing recommendation of our services had, it appears, decided him to take the step.

I very much appreciate the friendship and loyalty which prompted you to speak so well of our Bank and you may rest assured that we shall endeavour in every way to merit your continued confidence.

Yours sincerely,

Dear Mrs Manders,

It was very kind of you to come in with Mrs Saunders yesterday afternoon and I want you to know how much we appreciate your loyalty and thoughtfulness in doing so.

I feel quite sure that Mrs Saunders will find as much pleasure and satisfaction in shopping at Clayton's as you do. Certainly we shall enjoy serving her and will take special pride in doing all we can to deserve the confidence she has placed in us at your recommendation.

Yours sincerely,

Dear Mr Quinton,

We feel flattered! Yes, indeed. When one of our valued customers recommends our firm to one of his friends, that's just how we feel about it.

It was very thoughtful of you to send Mr Hunter to us and I want you to know how very much your gesture was appreciated. We shall certainly spare no effort to meet his requirements in every way.

Yours sincerely,

Dear Ms Cramer,

I am writing to thank you for your courtesy in recommending Hartley's to your friend, Ms Curtis.

It was a friendly gesture, which was sincerely appreciated. Do be assured that we shall continue to do all we can to merit your confidence.

Yours sincerely,

Dear Mrs Horn,

Yesterday afternoon Mrs Fisher called in to select some curtain material and mentioned that you had recommended Goodall's to her.

This was indeed kind of you and I am sending you this personal note to let you know how much we appreciate it.

Mrs Fisher left very satisfied with her purchase and now plans to open an account with us.

Our sincere thanks for your recommendation.

Yours sincerely,

Dear Mrs North,

It was kind of you to recommend our service to Ms Gilmore and we would like you to know how much we appreciate it.

You may be assured that we shall do everything we can to serve your friend well.

Yours sincerely,

Dear Mrs Moore,

Our sincere thanks for recommending our store to your neighbour, Mrs Wilkins.

She happened to mention this when she came in to open a charge account last week and we would like you to know how much we appreciate this expression of your friendly goodwill.

We shall certainly do all we can to serve Mrs Wilkins well.

Yours sincerely,

For help in rectifying error

Dear Ms Jenkins,

Thank you for calling our attention to the error in your October account.

Try as we may to be accurate always, we do occasionally slip up – but then perhaps that's what makes us human! Thank you for being so thoughtful and understanding about it.

Sincerely yours,

Dear Mr Whitworth,

This is both to apologize for the confusion which occurred in delivering your parcel to you and to thank you for the good humour with which you bore the incident.

Such things do not happen very often and we shall certainly do our best to avoid such inconvenient mix-ups in future.

Thank you again for your forbearance.

Yours sincerely,

Dear Mr O'Brien,

Many thanks for your cheque for the amount of £15 and for your understanding and co-operation in clearing up our unfortunate mistake.

Without your courteous assistance no doubt we should still be wondering why our ledger didn't balance! Thank you again.

Yours sincerely,

Dear Mrs Collins,

Many thanks for calling into my office this morning to straighten out the unfortunate error which occurred in your account.

Your kind assistance was very much appreciated. Do be assured that we shall continue to do all we can to merit your friendly support.

Sincerely yours,

To wholesale customers

For special courtesy or service

Dear Mr Mortimer,

I wish to thank you most sincerely for your splendid and wholehearted help when our delivery van broke down early this week.

Without your invaluable assistance not only would we have been unable to deliver your order on time, but other customers would have been disappointed as well.

Your friendly co-operation was most appreciated.

Yours sincerely,

Dear Mr Jones,

Thank you for your kind words and good wishes for 1986.

I, too, have much enjoyed our long association and it is my sincere wish that our two companies continue to do business together for many years to come.

May the New Year be a happy and prosperous one for you.

Sincerely yours,

Dear Mr Skinner,

It was kind of you to send Mr Harold Jenkins in to see us. It so happened that we had a suitable vacancy in the storeroom and were very pleased for him to join our staff.

Many thanks for your friendly co-operation.

Very sincerely yours,

Dear Mr Hayden,

We had a letter this morning from Mr Stone of Wilkins and Sons Limited in which he inquires about our steel brackets and mentions that our firm had been recommended to him by you.

This was very kind of you and your courteous gesture is much appreciated.

We shall certainly do our best to live up to the good things you said to Mr Stone about our Company and hope that your introduction results in a pleasant association between Wilkins and Sons and our firm.

Thank you again.

Yours sincerely,

Dear Mr Finney,

I wish to thank you most sincerely for all your kindness to Allan Goodey since he became Area Manager for the West of England in rather trying circumstances.

He has told me how helpful you have been and I am just as grateful to you as he is.

Thanks in great measure to your support and co-operation, he seems to be settling down well now. I expect to be in Cornwall myself early next month and it will be a pleasure to call and thank you personally.

Very sincerely yours,

Dear Mr Ingham,

I wish to thank you most sincerely for the many courtesies extended to me during my brief visit to Glasgow.

Your kindness and wholehearted co-operation, not to mention your true Northern hospitality, made my trip not only a most successful, but also an extremely pleasant one.

Please let me know if there is anything I can do for you down here, either personal or otherwise.

Yours sincerely,

Dear Mr Tirrell,

Many thanks for your friendly letter of September 22, telling me how much you enjoyed meeting our new sales representative for your area, Mr Fred Arnold, and how helpful he was.

Mr Arnold is indeed one of our best men. He made a signal success of our Northern Area before moving down to London and we expect great things of him.

I'm delighted that you should have hit it off so well together and thank you for the courteous reception you gave him.

Sincerely yours,

Dear Mr Owens,

It was indeed kind of you to write me such a charming letter. I most heartily reciprocate your good wishes for 1986 and hope your business has a bumper year.

I have always found Owens and Sons an extremely helpful and co-operative company to work with and look forward to many opportunities of doing business with you during the coming year.

Do let me know if there is anything at any time that I can do for you.

Yours sincerely,

Dear Mr Spencer,

I am returning to you in a separate registered parcel the marketing report you so kindly lent me.

It is a most interesting and revealing study and I am most grateful for your courtesy in allowing me to see it.

I look forward to seeing you again during my next trip North, some time in February.

Yours sincerely,

For reliability in meeting obligations

Dear Mr Walker,

We owe you a special word of thanks. Normally we are so busy with our problems that we seldom find time to express our appreciation to customers such as you who pay their account, month after month, year after year, quietly and regularly, with no effort on our part.

It has been said, and it is true, that a credit man is so busy saying 'Please remit', that he overlooks the opportunity to say 'Thank you'. So we are forgetting our problems for the moment to express our gratitude to you and your entire organization for your acceptance of our product and for the manner in which you are consistently maintaining your account.

The success of our efforts depends entirely upon the co-operation of our customers, so it is to you that we feel most indebted. Our appreciation is great – our thanks genuine.

Yours sincerely,

Dear Mr Henderson,

Occasionally a credit man has an opportunity of writing the kind of letter he really enjoys – and this is one of them. Its object, quite simply, is to thank you for your splendid credit record since our two companies began doing business together almost five years ago.

We very much appreciate the promptness with which you settle your accounts and we should like you to know it.

It is a pleasure indeed to do business with you and our greatest wish is for this relationship to continue for many years.

Yours sincerely,

Dear Ms Stanley,

It is with great pleasure that I write to tell you how much we appreciate the business-like way in which you handle your account with us.

The fact that you never fail to discount your invoices is a tangible sign of the careful way in which you run your business and the high regard you have for your fine reputation.

Please accept our sincere thanks, together with our best wishes for the continued success of your business.

Yours sincerely,

Dear Mr Lyon,

The credit manager's lot includes writing many letters reminding people of overdue accounts. This, however, is the kind of letter I prefer to write. It is quite simply to thank you for the punctual way in which you always pay your invoices.

If all the companies on our books were like Lyon and Son Limited, the credit manager's life would be a bed of roses.

Your thoughtfulness and consideration are highly appreciated.

Yours sincerely,

Dear Mr Sampson,

It is the wheel that squeaks that gets the most attention, so they tell us. And the squeaky wheels of a credit manager's life are companies which are slow in settling their accounts. In our preoccupation with chasing them up, we sometimes forget – or appear to forget – those splendid companies such as yours who always meet their obligations promptly without the slightest prodding from us.

Do be assured that your fine credit record has not passed unnoticed and that we appreciate your co-operation and consideration a great deal.

Doing business with you is a pleasure which we hope to enjoy for many more years.

Sincerely yours,

Dear Mrs Murphy,

The promptness with which you settle your bills helps our accounts department to run so much more smoothly and pleasantly that we want you to know how very much we appreciate your splendid co-operation.

Our sincere thanks to you. It is a great pleasure to have you as a customer.

Yours sincerely,

Dear Miss Skinner,

I seldom have occasion to write to you, since you always pay your bills so promptly, making the work in our department that much simpler and pleasanter.

We do not want you to feel neglected, however, nor do we want you to feel that your excellent credit record has passed unnoticed. Quite the contrary, we count you as one of our most valuable customers.

The sole purpose of this letter, in fact, is to say 'Thank you' for your promptness in settling your invoices. We appreciate it greatly.

Yours sincerely,

Dear Ms Whitworth,

In the rush and hurry of business it is frequently easy to forget to give a word of appreciation where it is due. I am most anxious that this should not happen in your case.

Ever since our two companies began doing business together two years ago you have settled your invoices punctually and without the slightest prodding on my part. This is indeed an enviable record of which you may well be proud.

Certainly I am proud to have customers like you and I want you to know how much you are appreciated at Jackson's.

Sincerely yours,

For long standing patronage

Dear Mr Fuller,

You are the most important part of our business. Without customers such as you, not a wheel would turn in our plant – we just could not exist.

Many times I have wished for the opportunity to meet you and thank you personally. Since this cannot be done frequently enough, I am writing this letter as a token of our gratitude to you for just being a good customer. As you grow and prosper, I would like to feel that the products of Fulton Sylphon Division have contributed a small but important part to your prosperity.

In the future, I hope we can serve you better and more often. To this end, Robertshaw-Fulton Controls Co. continues to expand its plants, to enlarge its engineering and research facilities – all to produce more and better products to enable industry to broaden its margin of profit. The accompanying brochure is presented in evidence.

Again I say 'Thanks' for the opportunity to serve you.

Yours sincerely,

Dear Ms Mortimer,

Just 12 years ago you gave us your first small order for Venetian blinds. Since that day both your Company and ours have grown beyond all recognition.

I am sending you this personal note to thank you for the confidence and loyalty you have shown us throughout these years.

We greatly value the fine relationship which exists between our two companies and look forward to doing business with you for many more years.

Yours sincerely,

Dear Mr Hamilton,

At the end of their financial year most companies take stock, and our Company has just completed that operation. In so doing it has occurred to me that it is only fitting and proper that we should also take stock of the goodwill of our clients, for without it, we would have no business.

I would therefore like to thank you most sincerely for the business you have given us, not only during the past year, but for many years.

Unquestionably, your valuable support has helped to make 1985 a very successful year for us. We earnestly hope it has been an equally good one for your Company.

Please accept our very best wishes for a most successful 1986. We shall certainly do all we can to continue to merit your loyal support and confidence and should welcome any suggestion you may have on how we can improve our products, service, packaging or other aspects of our business.

Sincerely yours,

Dear Mr Livermore,

There is nothing more satisfying than the bond of friendship that develops between two companies which have been doing business together for a number of years, in mutual trust and co-operation.

Such a relationship has existed between our two companies since 1957 – since March of that year, to be exact – when you sent us your first order for Sleepwell Mattresses. Since that time your orders have become larger every time and both our firms have grown and prospered.

We would like to take advantage of this anniversary to thank you for your loyal patronage and friendly co-operation over the years and tell you how much we have enjoyed doing business with you.

Our fondest wish is that this pleasant relationship will continue to prosper for many years.

Yours sincerely,

Dear Mr Springer,

We should like to celebrate our Silver Jubilee by first thanking all the customers who have helped to make our Company what it is today. Without you and many others like you, we never could have grown from a small workshop to a sizeable factory within the short span of 25 years.

Our thanks and gratitude therefore go first of all to you. We have greatly valued your loyalty and friendly support over the years and intend to continue doing all we can to deserve it in the future.

It has been a great pleasure to do business with you. Thank you again.

Yours sincerely,

Dear Mr Smedley,

I am writing to thank you most sincerely for the business you have given us during the past years. Your loyalty and support have been greatly appreciated even though we seldom pause to tell you so.

Normally we feel that our efforts to serve you well speak of our appreciation of you as a customer. Every now and again, however, it is good to pause to say 'Thank you' for your business.

It is indeed a pleasure to deal with so businesslike, reliable, and reputable a firm as yourselves, and it is a source of pride to us that you represent us in Scotland.

Yours sincerely,

Dear Miss Hunter,

On this our 15th birthday we want you to know how much we have valued your friendship and loyal support over the years.

It is good and loyal customers such as you who have helped to build our business and make it flourish and we want you to know how much we appreciate you.

We have always done our best to serve you well and hope that in this we have succeeded. In the years that lie ahead we are pledged to do even more to supply you with the highest quality product at the lowest feasible price, and the best service ever.

Sincerely yours,

For special sales effort or achievement

Dear Ms Waring,

Thank you for the splendid order for Quigley Pens.

Ever since you took over the distribution of our pens for the West of England your orders have grown steadily larger. This is indeed a fine achievement and we are very pleased with the active way in which you are tackling your section of the market.

We are most anxious to support your sales effort in any way we can and hope you will let us know if there is anything further we can do.

Best wishes for your continued success.

Yours sincerely,

Dear Mr Smedley,

It is not every day that a company has the good fortune to find an agent such as Smedley and Sons Limited. Since you took on our lines just a year ago, your orders have steadily increased and you celebrated your first anniversary by chalking up a very fine record indeed.

I would like you to know how very much I appreciate the efforts you have made over the past year and the splendid results you have achieved.

We certainly owe you a vote of thanks and as you embark upon your second year as a Robbins agent we send you our very best wishes for an even more successful year. You may count on our wholehearted support and co-operation in every respect.

Yours sincerely,

Dear Mrs Geddy,

To secure the corner window at Halston's for a week is no mean feat and I would like both to congratulate you and to thank you most heartily for your splendid achievement.

Unquestionably, this excellent bit of promotion will have a noticeable effect on sales in your area and we shall be watching your future order forms with great interest.

Best wishes for your continued success with our line.

Yours sincerely,

Dear Mr Greenley,

As we close our books on 1985 we should be ungrateful indeed if we did not pause to thank you for your splendid sales record during the year.

Your ever-increasing orders during the past year have been very much appreciated by us and we are grateful indeed for your continued loyal support.

In wishing you every success in 1986 and thereafter, we also pledge you our continued co-operation and the best service we can possibly give.

Yours sincerely,

Dear Miss Murray,

Thank you for your splendid order, just received.

We really are most happy to see that each of your orders is larger than the last. At this rate you will have a record year.

We very much appreciate the excellent work you are doing in expanding the market for Windrex products in your area and are most anxious to give you all the sales support we can.

Do please let us know if you are well supplied with literature, displays and point of sale material, or if there is any other way in which we can help you in your good work.

Our very best wishes for your continued success.

Yours sincerely,

Dear Mr Fennimore,

You've done it again! Yes, your 1985 sales have topped those of 1984, just as your 1984 sales were well ahead of your 1983 figures.

We are delighted with your efforts and want to thank you and congratulate you on a splendid performance. We know full well that results such as these are not achieved easily. You have worked hard and to good purpose and you have our gratitude and appreciation.

Best wishes for 1986 and – remember – we here at Head Office are always ready to back you with all the assistance and co-operation you need.

Yours sincerely,

Dear Mr Gilmore,

Five years ago today you became our wholesale distributor for the North of England. Since that time you have done a splendid job in developing the market in your area and your orders have increased steadily, reaching record proportions this year.

I would like you to know how much I have appreciated your splendid efforts on behalf of our products and what a pleasure it has been to do business with you. The enthusiastic, progressive and methodical way in which you have developed your market has been a source of admiration and satisfaction to us all.

We are proud of your achievement and look forward to co-operating with you during the next five years of your distributorship.

Sincerely yours,

To business and professional associates

For special favour or service

Dear Mr Hayne,

Please accept my sincere thanks for your warm welcome and your generous assistance in my writing project.

It was a great pleasure to meet you, Ms Bennett, and your enthusiastic training staff. Please thank them all on my behalf for being so kind and helpful.

Yours sincerely,

Dear Mr Metcalfe,

Many thanks for your most useful letter of March 18 and the material sent to me separately. All this material will be invaluable to me in preparing my book.

Would you kindly extend my thanks also to your father, who write to me on March 20?

Yours sincerely,

Dear Herr Porzig,

Many thanks for your letters of May 6 and May 27. The announced material arrived safely yesterday and I really don't know how to thank you for your thoughtfulness and generosity.

You may be assured that I shall take great care of all the material and return the three 'on loan' books to you in due course.

The two Okulare Skizzen are absolutely beautiful and I shall be very proud to place them on my bookshelves when I move into my new home two months from now.

Thank you again, and with every good wish to the Carl Zeiss company, I remain,

Yours sincerely,

Dear Dr McMurry,

Many thanks for your letter of June 11 enclosing a reprint from <u>Scope</u> and granting me permission to reproduce your standard Patterned Interview form.

All this material will be most useful to me in my work on the book. Thank you again.

Yours sincerely,

Dear Mr Howard,

I wish to thank you most sincerely for your welcome last Tuesday.

My visit was most interesting and, what is more, extremely useful and informative as far as my research is concerned.

Thank you again. I wish you the best of success in your future endeavours to improve work methods at Halex.

Yours sincerely,

Dear Jim,

Thank you for speaking to Mr Davies about my qualifications for the job I am hoping to fill on his journal. If I'm lucky enough to land it I'll do all I can to live up to the fine things you said about me.

Thanks again. I really do appreciate your kindness.

Sincerely,

Dear John,

When Don got back from Edinburgh he told me how much
he had enjoyed visiting your plant and how helpful you were to
him. I gather that he learned a lot from you and I thank you most
sincerely for spending so much of your valuable time with him
and helping to steer him in the right direction.

Do let me know if I can be of any service to you from this
end.

Sincerely,

Dear Mrs Ashton,

Safely back at home-base, I am writing to thank you for
your kindness to me during my brief visit to your city. I enjoyed
every moment of it and only hope you will give me an opportunity
of reciprocating before long.

Sincerely yours,

Dear Mr Akuma,

I wish to thank you most sincerely for your invaluable help
during the recent visit of our Japanese friends. I really don't know
what we should have done without you. They too appreciated your
valuable assistance, I know, and I thank you also on their behalf.

I'm sure they enjoyed their visit to our country and no
doubt we shall be hearing from them upon their return to Tokyo.

Thank you again.

Yours sincerely,

Dear Jack,

I was absolutely delighted to receive an autographed copy of your latest book, Investments for Capital Gain. How very kind of you to reward me in this way for the slight help I gave you with it.

I have already dipped into it and can see right away that it is an excellent book both for the small and the not-so-small investor. In fact, I quite expect to learn a few things from it myself.

Congratulations on a splendid job, best wishes for its deserved success, and thanks again for thinking of me.

Sincerely,

Dear Mrs Short,

Many thanks for the author's copies of my book. It is a splendid production job and I am most pleased with it. Do please extend my grateful thanks to everyone on your production team. I certainly hope to be in some time next week to thank all of you personally.

It really is a great satisfaction to me to see my book so beautifully turned out.

Yours sincerely,

Dear Sir Charles,

I have just received the copy for the Foreword to my book which you have so kindly written. It reads very well indeed and I am convinced that it will help sales enormously.

It is most kind of you to do this for me and I am truly grateful.

An autographed complimentary copy of the book will be on its way to you as soon as it is off the press. Thanks again.

Yours sincerely,

Dear Mr Avery,

Many thanks for returning the draft of my book, together with your useful comments. I have been all through the typescript again, working in the suggestions you made, and I am very grateful indeed for your help.

The typescript should be with the publisher by next week and it is quite a relief to have finally completed the work.

Again, very many thanks for your valuable suggestions and comments.

Yours sincerely,

Dear Jane,

How thoughtful of you to send me a ticket for the Marketing Symposium. I very much enjoyed attending the meetings and learned a great deal from them.

Thank you for thinking of me.

Yours,

Dear Vince,

You are a rare bird indeed! I had almost reached the stage of refusing to lend a book to anyone, having found that lending a book is tantamount to saying goodbye to it. But not you – you borrow a book and return it. Thanks a lot. Glad you enjoyed it.

Sincerely,

Dear Mrs Stone,

Thank you for all the help you gave me in securing my re-election to the Council.

You may rely upon me to do everything in my power to serve you well.

Yours sincerely,

Dear Joe,

I am writing to you from the beautiful Villa Fiorita, which you so highly recommended and with good reason. We found everything taken care of and in apple pie order, thanks to you.

It really was most kind of you to undertake to fix the reservations and everything else for us. It was just like coming home, and our Italian hosts acted as if they had known us for years.

I'm sure we are going to enjoy our stay here every bit as much as you did. As the Italians say, a thousand thanks.

Yours,

Dear Steve,

It was good to see you again after such a long time and I want to thank you for making my visit to your factory so enjoyable. The discussions with you and the members of your management team were extremely helpful to me in crystallizing my plans.

Thank you again for making my trip so pleasant and fruitful.

Sincerely,

Dear Mr Halperin,

This is to thank you once again for so kindly making your plant available to our team of visiting engineers. I know they were very impressed with your works, as well as by the hospitality shown to them.

I am most appreciative and hope to have the opportunity of reciprocating in the not too distant future.

Yours sincerely,

Dear Bill,

I wish to thank you most sincerely for the loan you have so kindly made me. You are truly a friend in need and I appreciate it immensely.

I should be over the hump by the end of next month and I'm sure I'll be able to repay you then. Thank you again, Bill.

Sincerely,

Dear Señor Garcia,

Many thanks for your gracious letter and the two charming little Spanish dolls. My daughter, Julie, was thrilled with them and we all had a wonderful time finding Spanish names for them.

We enjoyed your visit to London immensely and were only too delighted to do what we could to make your stay a pleasant one. We hope you will return soon.

Yours sincerely,

Dear Herr Winkler,

Upon my return to London my first thought is to write and thank you and the other people at Winkler's for all your kindnesses to me during my stay in your city. I enjoyed every minute of it and I feel that this personal meeting will be most beneficial to our future business dealings.

I will write to you again shortly about the concrete proposals we discussed.

Yours sincerely,

For help to company, club or other organization

Dear Mrs Bayley,

I wish to thank you most sincerely for your valuable assistance in the committee room during the by-election. We'd certainly be lost without volunteer workers like you. I am really most appreciative.

Yours sincerely,

Dear Mr Haynes,

Many thanks for your generous contribution to the Bourne End Community Centre Association. I am enclosing a receipt and a special certificate for founder members. Your name will be inscribed in the founder members' book and you will be invited to attend all planning meetings.

Your valuable support is much appreciated by the whole community.

Yours sincerely,

Dear Mr Jones,

May I, on behalf of the whole club, thank you heartily for the wonderful work you and your busy team have put into the club grounds? They really look a picture and no professional – which the club cannot afford – could have done a better job.

I'm sure that every one of us, as we admire the flowering shrubs and the velvety well-kept lawns, thinks of all the work you and your team have put into them and sends you a blessing and a 'Thank you'.

Most sincerely,

Dear Miss Mills,

It was extremely generous of you to give so much of your time to help us get together a useful nucleus of foreign language dictionaries for our export department. May I extend our grateful thanks to you, also on behalf of our export manager?

Selecting the <u>right</u> dictionary is half the battle and it takes an expert such as yourself to do the job properly.

Thank you again.

Yours sincerely,

Dear Mr Granger,

I wish to thank you on behalf of my marketing team for attending our workshop yesterday. It was generous indeed of you to give so much of your time to make our meeting a success. The consultants were extremely keen on having one or two outside people at the workshop and they are also grateful for your contribution.

I hope you enjoyed the rather unusual meeting. We were all somewhat staggered and are keeping our fingers crossed on results. Certainly it made a pleasant change from the usual conference where one or two people hold the floor the whole time.

Kindest regards.

Yours sincerely,

Dear Philip,

Many thanks for standing in for me at such short notice at the Sales Conference. It really was noble of you and I am most grateful, both on the Company's behalf and on my own.

I understand that you were excellent and I shall now know what to do with you at our next conference. They won't let me out of here for quite a while, but luckily I know the 'shop' is in good hands.

Thanks for everything.

Sincerely,

Dear John,

How kind of you to send us a small supply of your excellent 'secretary booklets'. I have distributed them to all the secretaries in our department and we're expecting tremendous improvements in performance.

Joking apart – they are very well-produced and well-written booklets and I much appreciate your kind thought in sending them along.

Best wishes.

Sincerely,

Dear Mr Taylor,

Your thoughtfulness and generosity in offering us the use of your delivery van are very much appreciated. However, we have managed to organize deliveries by private car for the next few days and it looks as though we shall manage all right until our own shattered van is in good order again.

None the less we are most grateful for your generous offer of help.

Yours sincerely,

Dear Harding,

I'd like you to know how grateful I am for your valuable assistance at the Christmas Party. I never knew you had such hidden talents. I'm convinced that, but for your expert and witty M.C.-ing, the dance would not have been anything like the success it was. You certainly 'went down well', as the saying goes.

Thank you.

Yours sincerely,

Dear Miss Whiting,

Thank you for taking the French class at such short notice yesterday. I know it is not an easy task to step into the breach unwarned and unprepared and I greatly appreciate the readiness with which you rose so successfully to the occasion.

I understand Mr Gaillard is a little better already and no doubt he will be back at his post next week.

Yours sincerely,

Dear Mrs Sperry,

I'd like to take this opportunity of thanking you most sincerely on behalf of all club members for the excellent work you have done during your tenure of office as club treasurer. You have done a splendid job and we all appreciate the time, effort, and devotion you have put into club work during the past year.

We are really sorry to see you relinquish the responsibility, but it is only fair for such tasks to be rotated frequently among us all.

Yours sincerely,

Dear Mr Simpson,

Please accept my warmest thanks for your very generous donation to our Association. Ours is a cause which is so often neglected because other claims seem more urgent. None the less we are doing vital work and very badly need funds if we are to succeed. You quite obviously realize this and we greatly appreciate your support.

Yours sincerely,

Dear Cliff,

It was most kind of you to lend me a copy of your Sales Manual. It is, indeed, an excellent one, and will be most useful to us in compiling our own. I could not agree with you more about bringing the sales representatives in at the planning stage and that is exactly what we are going to do.

When our draft manual is complete, I will send you a copy for your comments and suggestions, if you would be so good.

Your valuable help is greatly appreciated both by the Company and by me personally.

Sincerely,

Dear Mr Stone,

May I thank you most sincerely for your generous donation to the Bank's Opera Society? We feel the Society fufils a very useful service in giving our staff an opportunity to express themselves either creatively or interpretatively and consequently welcome your support most warmly.

As a Friend of the Orpheus Opera Society you will receive complimentary tickets for every performance and we greatly look forward to seeing you in the audience at next Friday's performance of 'La Traviata'.

All the Society's members join me in saying 'Thank you'.

Yours sincerely,

Dear Mr Harwell,

This is just a note to tell you how much I appreciated your sparing me some time during your busy morning. Your suggestions were most constructive and helped me a lot in getting the programme worked out.

Thank you for your unstinted co-operation.

Yours sincerely,

For lunch or dinner at home or club

Dear Mr Stevens,

Just a note to tell you how much I enjoyed having lunch with you at the Sixty-Six Club yesterday and hearing Sir Alan's talk. How thoughtful of you to ask me. Many, many thanks. I greatly look forward to reciprocating soon.

Yours sincerely,

Dear Judd,

Muriel joins me in thanking you and Edna for a delightful evening of pleasant company, delicious food, good music, and intelligent conversation. It is not often that all four are united in one and the same evening. When it <u>does</u> happen the occasion is a memorable one.

We liked your new home immensely. I don't blame you for being so proud of it.

Thank you both once more.

Sincerely,

Dear Mr Springer,

It was indeed kind of you to take me along to your Rotary Club luncheon when I visited your city last week. I thoroughly enjoyed it and greatly appreciated your thoughtfulness in asking me.

I look forward to your next trip to London in the spring when I shall do all I can to return your kindness.

Yours sincerely,

Dear Fred,

I very much enjoyed seeing you again in Glasgow after such a long time. It was most thoughtful of you to ask me to lunch with you at the club and I enjoyed every moment of it.

Thank you again and do remember that a warm welcome awaits you in London. We really must not let another five years go by before we meet again.

Sincerely,

Dear Signora Gigli,

Back in London after my whirlwind trip to Italy I wish to thank you warmly for the kind hospitality extended to me during my stay in Florence. I was delighted to meet you and your husband, and I am most appreciative of your charming welcome and the exquisite dinner you served.

The trouble with these trips to Italy is that one hates to leave and when one is back in our English climate, one longs to return. All the warmth seems to remain behind.

I look forward to seeing you again soon.

Yours sincerely,

Dear George,

Thank you for the rare pleasure of a leisurely lunch in your good company. In these days of constant mad rush such an event is memorable. I must say you haven't lost your flair for picking out the good eating places and I congratulate you on your choice and thank you for taking me along.

Don't forget – the next lunch is on me. Let's make it soon!

Sincerely,

Dear Mrs Smythe,

My wife and I wish to thank you and your husband for the delightful evening at your home. It was most kind of you to ask us and we enjoyed every minute of it.

When the new wing to our home is completed sometime next month, we very much look forward to asking you over to dinner.

Yours sincerely,

Dear Walter,

It was very kind of your wife to suffer an old man like me to dinner. Do please thank her again on my behalf and thank you too, old friend. It was a thoroughly enjoyable evening and I only have one thing on my conscience – we were tempted into talking rather a lot of 'shop' over coffee. I do hope your wife has forgiven us. We really are incorrigible.

Thank you again. You <u>are</u> a lucky man, you know!

Sincerely,

Dear Ray,

I have only just returned to London after my trek across the Continent and I want to take this opportunity of thanking you once again for all your kindnesses to me during my visit to your 'outpost'. The delightful lunch we had at your club stands out particularly in my mind. You certainly know how to do things down there.

I look forward to seeing you here for the Sales Conference and we'll have another talk then.

Sincerely,

For invitation to spend night at home or club

Dear Mr and Mrs Swift,

Back in London after our refreshing trip to Cornwall, Pauline and I wish to thank you warmly for the wonderful hospitality extended to us at 'The Haven'. We enjoyed every moment of our stay and feel much refreshed, invigorated and re-charged.

It was kind indeed of you to have us, and our most cherished wish is that you will soon give us an opportunity of reciprocating. Certainly a welcome is always waiting for you at 'The Oasis' and we hope it won't be too long before you visit us.

With every best wish,

Yours sincerely,

Dear Charles,

I couldn't rest easily if I didn't drop you a line just to say once again 'Thank you' for the wonderful weekend at the hunting lodge. There is no better antidote to a harassed week in the City than a weekend such as that.

You are indeed a lucky man to have such a retreat. My only regret is that I cannot reciprocate with an invitation to spend a weekend on my yacht! But, there, one can only offer what one has. So please accept my thanks, my gratitude, my warmest friendship and lunch at the club, sometime this week, I hope. I'll ring you.

Sincerely,

Dear Mrs Wynn,

My trip to London was a great success, thanks, in no small measure, to you and your husband. Certainly the memory of the warm welcome you gave me, of all the little things you did to make me happy and comfortable stand out in my mind as the highlights of the trip.

Thank you both very much indeed. I shall not forget your kindness and thoughtfulness.

Very best wishes,

Yours sincerely,

Dear Tony,

It was very thoughtful of you to allow me to spend last night at your club. It certainly helped me out of a tight spot. Thanks again. I look forward to seeing you when things have settled down a bit.

Sincerely,

Dear Mr and Mrs Cavanagh,

It was a kind thought to ask me to stay at your home during the National Sales Conference. I cannot tell you how much I enjoyed it. Thank you both very much indeed. I shall long remember the warm welcome you gave me and the friendly, cheerful atmosphere of your home.

I know you very seldom come to London, but if ever you decide to do so, I hope you will not fail to let me know, for my wife and I would very much welcome the opportunity of having you with us.

Yours sincerely,

Dear Dr Perugia,

I have only just got back to London after my extended trip on the Continent. It has been a very busy and tiring trip, with a few interludes for good companionship, fine food, and conviviality. But the night I spent at the Villa Incantata stands out as a memorable one indeed and I wish to thank you for your wonderful hospitality on that occasion.

Now I know what Italian cooking really is. Before, I thought I knew, but I was labouring under a delusion. I also thought I knew Chianti wine, but it took you to put me right! Thank you for everything, I have learned so much, experienced so much – I am quite overwhelmed. What can we offer you here to compare with the gifts you lavish so generously on us, poor pilgrims from Albion?

Keep well, dear doctor.

Yours sincerely,

Dear Mr Moss,

I very much appreciate your thoughtfulness in putting me up at your club during my brief stay in London. I was extremely comfortable and well taken care of and thank you most sincerely for your kindness.

Do let me know if there is anything I can do for you in Scotland, for I'd be happy indeed to be of service to you.

Yours sincerely,

Dear Muriel,

Jean and I wish to thank you once more for your wonderful hospitality during our brief visit to Yorkshire. Our stay at your home 'made' the trip for us.

Do be assured that you have a standing invitation to 'The Brick House' for as long as you care to stay should business or pleasure bring you to these parts. We shall do our very best to reciprocate the warmth and sincerity of your welcome.

Sincerely,

For entertainment

Dear Dr Hands,

I wish to thank you most sincerely for all your kindness and hospitality during my brief trip to Zürich.

You did a magnificent job of steering a clumsy stranger, devoid of the gift of tongues, through your interesting city. I knew Switzerland was famous for its excellent food and this you proved to me most convincingly, but I did not realize how many other entertainments it had to offer. It was most kind of you to demonstrate this to me so well.

I do hope you will be in England for the technical conference, if not before, as I am most anxious to reciprocate to the best of my ability with all that London has to offer.

Yours sincerely,

Dear Jim,

Thank you once again for the excellent afternoon at your Country Club. Not only was the lunch fit for a king, but the golf course is one of the best I have ever been privileged to play on. Even losing a game seemed bearable on a course such as that!

It was very thoughtful of you to ask me, and I do appreciate it.

Sincerely,

Dear Mr Green,

I am writing to you from the quiet backwaters of Somerset to thank you once again for the wonderful hospitality extended to me during my brief trip to London. It is so seldom that I have an opportunity of seeing some really first-class theatre that our visit to the Haymarket stands out in my mind as one of the highlights of the trip. How thoughtful of you to include me in your party.

It was a visit I shall long remember. Thank you again for everything.

Yours sincerely,

Dear Frank,

It was good to see you again last weekend and I want to tell you how very much I enjoyed our day on the moors.

I so seldom have an opportunity of getting away from town nowadays that such a rare occasion is all the more enjoyable.

Thank you very much for asking me.

Sincerely,

Dear Sidney,

I very much enjoyed Sir Geoffrey's talk last night and greatly appreciate your taking me along to hear him. Don't forget you promised to join me for lunch next week and were going to let me know which day you are free.

Thanks again and let me hear from you soon.

Sincerely,

Dear Mr Wingate,

My wife joins me in thanking you warmly for our most enjoyable day on the river. The <u>Sole Mio</u> is indeed a handsome craft and I can well understand the pride you take in her.

We shall long remember that lazy sun-filled day cutting swiftly down river, the surf giving us an occasional refreshing spray.

It was very kind of you to ask us along.

Yours sincerely,

Dear Ed,

Back in the Old Country, I hasten to drop you a line of thanks for so gallantly doing the honours during my all too brief visit to America.

You really rolled out the welcome carpet and mere words seem wholly inadequate to thank you. I enjoyed everything you so thoughtfully provided, but then, you know my tastes so well, so how could you fail?

I owe you an extra special thanks for the unforgettable evening at the opera. Even for one accustomed to Covent Garden standards, it was a thrilling performance and one I shall not easily forget.

Thanks for everything, Ed. I am fortunate indeed to have a friend like you.

Sincerely,

Dear George,

I haven't enjoyed anything so much as last night's show for a long time. Not even the rather draughty run home succeeded in dampening my cheerful spirits.

Thank you for asking me. You're quite right – a dash of frivolity now and again <u>is</u> good for the soul.

Sincerely,

For making a speech

Dear Mr Dickens,

May I thank you once again, both personally and on behalf of the Rotary Club, for your splendid talk at last night's meeting?

It really was most interesting and enjoyable and I know that our members will remember it for a long time. In fact there already have been requests that you be asked to make a return visit!

Yours sincerely,

Dear Mr Falkner,

I wish to thank you most sincerely for your excellent talk, 'Bringing Home the Bacon'. It went down really well and I know that the 'reps' will profit from it.

Largely thanks to you and your enthusiastic, punchy, and pertinent talk, our sales meeting was a huge success and I feel the sales people went out on the road the following day full of renewed vigour and enthusiasm.

It was most kind of you to come along.

Sincerely yours,

Dear George,

Just a quick note to say 'Thanks' for your talk at the new community centre yesterday. It was a very good speech, both apt and amusing.

The occasion went very well indeed and gave great satisfaction to all of us who have worked so hard and so long for the centre's establishment. It was good of you to contibute so generously to the evening's success.

Sincerely,

Dear Mr Stevens,

Your talk to our members last night was one of the most outstanding we have heard at the Society for a long time and the originality of your approach to industrial accidents will give our members considerable food for thought.

Please accept my most sincere thanks, as well as those of our Board of Governors and our members, for sharing with us your unique experiences in the field of accident prevention.

I feel sure that many of our members will now decide to adopt your methods in their own factories.

Sincerely yours,

Dear Mr Swanson,

On behalf of the Association I wish to thank you once again for your enlightening presentation of the Construction Industry Training Board's safety package last night.

Many of our members have been very worried about the high accident rate in our industry and I'm sure they went away with the feeling that the CITB has now put in their hands some very effective ammunition for their constant battle for safety on site.

It was kind indeed of you to spare the time to put us in the picture.

Yours sincerely,

Dear Fred,

Congratulations and thanks once again for your excellent speech. I don't have to tell you how much everyone enjoyed it – the crowd which surged around you as you attempted an exit spoke far more eloquently than I could.

So I will simply say how grateful I am and express the hope that you will come again soon.

Sincerely,

Dear John,

What a first-class job you did last night! It is not often the Young Conservative Club is privileged to hear so well-planned and well-delivered a talk. Every point you made was cogent and amply supported by fact, and as you progressed logically from one point to another, you had your audience with you all the time. A splendid achievement!

I am now basking in the light of your triumph and am already being pressed to invite you again. Congratulations and many thanks.

Sincerely,

Dear Mrs Gibbs,

Thank you most sincerely for your splendid talk at our Youth Club last night. I very much admired the skilful way in which you tackled your subject and the subtlety and savoir faire you used in getting the audience on your side.

Talking to young people is far from being an easy task, particularly when one is trying to impress them with the responsibilities involved in marriage, rather than its romantic aspects. You succeeded admirably and I'm sure your talk went home and gave the youngsters something to think about.

All the club organizers are extremely grateful to you, and they all join me in thanking you and expressing the wish that you will make a return visit soon.

Yours sincerely,

Dear Mr Wheeler,

Your talk at the Women's Press Club last night was an excellent one and the attendance, in anticipation of it, was a record. Many many thanks on both counts.

I can't remember a more successful evening. Your witty talk was certainly the highlight of the programme and we count ourselves fortunate indeed to have had you with us.

Yours sincerely,

Dear Miss Gibson,

The rapt attention which greeted your words, as well as the many questions put to you afterwards, were proof enough of the success of your Wednesday's talk at the Institute.

Thank you again for so kindly accepting my invitation. I always enjoy your friendly informal manner and it is appreciated by audiences of all sorts. Last night's was no exception and your success is a double satisfaction to me.

Yours sincerely,

Dear Mr Grossman,

I had hoped to thank you again for your fine speech at the Conference, but you had left for Cambridge before I had a chance to do so. I hope you had a pleasant journey back.

I heard nothing but favourable comments on your talk and it certainly contributed in great measure to the success of Friday's proceedings.

On behalf of the Committee may I thank you again for giving so generously of your time to make our Conference a success?

Yours sincerely,

For mention in speech or publication

Dear Mr Lucas,

I have just read the enthusiastic review of my book in Business Methods and wish to thank you most sincerely for your kind words. I'm delighted to learn that you think so highly of my effort and only hope that the general reader shares your high opinion of it.

If the book sells well I shall feel that it is in no small part due to your excellent review.

Yours sincerely,

Dear Michael,

    While I was not fortunate enough to be there myself, I have had reports of your good words about my forthcoming book at your last night's talk at the Institute of Personnel Management. It was very kind indeed of you to praise my work before such an important audience and I appreciate it tremendously.

                Sincerely,

Dear Miss Giles,

    I am delighted to learn that you are planning to use several passages from my book, <u>Direct Mail Selling</u>, in your article for <u>Tack</u>.

    It is kind of you to make an acknowledgement to my work and I look forward to reading the article when it is published.

                Yours sincerely,

Dear Ms Marks,

    I was very pleased to read the excellent review of my book in your March issue. Praise of this kind from such an expert journal as <u>Personnel Management</u> is complimentary indeed.

    Advance sales of the book are going very well, it appears, and your good words cannot fail to have their effect. Many grateful thanks and best wishes to P M.

                Yours sincerely,

Dear Fred,

    It was good of you to mention me in your talk at the YMCA last night. I have only too willingly and gladly done what little I could for the men at the Association, yet a public word of appreciation always pleases, none the less. Thank you very much indeed.

                Sincerely,

Dear Ms Murray,

May I thank you for the splendid article in your February issue about the work of our organization? It is an excellent job of reporting and, of course we cannot but feel flattered by the kind remarks you made about us.

We will certainly do our best to live up to your generous appraisal of our work.

Yours sincerely,

Dear Ms Greenley,

How kind of you to speak so highly of my little paper 'Is Worker Fatigue Costing you Dollars?' in your house journal. I hope your readers do find my research on the subject interesting. I certainly enjoyed making the study.

Thank you for your courtesy.

Sincerely yours,

Dear Dr Copeman,

I was delighted to discover my book up at the top of the ladder of your 100 Best Books on Business Management. It really is most gratifying, since the choice is no arbitrary selection by one man, however eminent, but the considered judgement of a distinguished selection committee of experts.

Thank you very much for sending me a complimentary copy of the very attractive booklet.

Yours sincerely,

Dear Miss Chapman,

Many thanks for sending me a marked copy of Office Equipment News and for the generous review of my book.

It was kind of you to speak so well of it. I shall take your favourable comments as a good omen for future sales.

Yours sincerely,

For message of congratulations

Dear Philip,

I can't tell you how much I appreciated your warm note about my book. I'm very pleased that you like it. If all my readers feel as you do about it, I'll be lucky indeed.

As a matter of fact, I rather enjoyed writing the book. Writing for me is not a chore, but the most pleasant task in the world. Sometimes I feel I could write on any subject under the sun.

I hope to see you soon.

Sincerely,

Dear Fred,

How kind of you to take the trouble to write to me about my talk at the Rotary. I'm glad you thought it good and I was both surprised and relieved to learn that I appeared relaxed and perfectly at ease. Let me assure you I felt no such thing. I was absolutely terrified.

Thank you again for your kind words . . .

Sincerely,

Dear Ms Green,

Thank you for your letter of March 16 commenting on my article in Management Methods. I'm delighted you should feel that my technique has something to commend it and I do assure you that it works.

If you will let me know when next you plan to be in town, I'd be only too pleased for you to attend one of our workshops, if dates happen to coincide.

Meanwhile, many thanks for your kind words of appreciation.

Yours sincerely,

Dear Mr Greenway,

Thank you very much for your thoughtful letter of congratulations. I greatly appreciate your words of praise and only wish I felt more deserving of them. It is true that I have served Hoxton, Barton and Swiffen to the best of my ability these past 25 years, but that was no more than my duty.

I take up my new position as partner of the firm with utter humility, supported and encouraged, none the less, by the kind words of such friends as you.

Yours sincerely,

Dear John,

How kind of you to write! Yes, it was thrilling to have my magazine win the award, but you really must not heap all the merit on my unworthy head. It was a team effort and credit goes to the whole team. I merely did my best to inspire and motivate my staff to give their all. I have passed on your kind words to them.

Thank you, John. It's good to have friends like you.

Sincerely,

Dear Mr Hurley,

Please accept my sincere thanks for your kind words about my work for the Association. I value your letter highly and it will serve to remind me of my 15 happy years with the WFA.

It is sad indeed to part, but the years are beginning to weigh heavily on me and it is time that I bowed out.

I shall always think fondly of the Association, its officers and its members and I leave it happy in the knowledge that my efforts over the years have been well and truly appreciated, as well as being deeply satisfying to me.

Yours sincerely,

Dear Joan,

Many thanks for your good wishes and congratulations. It is a beautiful home and we are very proud indeed of it.

Once we are properly settled down, with curtains up and carpets down, you must come over and see the place.

Your kind thought in writing was much appreciated.

Sincerely,

Dear Dr Sellers,

It was good of you to write to me as you did. I greatly enjoyed attending your workshop meeting and I am pleased indeed that you should feel my small contribution to it was of some help.

I very much enjoyed meeting the other members of your management team and hope that such an opportunity will present itself again in the near future.

Yours sincerely,

Dear Mr Fillmore,

May I thank you most heartily, also on behalf of my Board of Directors, for your thoughtful good wishes on the occasion of the Company's Golden Jubilee?

Having friends like you makes our Company what it is and we sincerely hope that our pleasant business relations will continue for many years to come.

Yours sincerely,

Dear Joe,

Your letter was the very first I found sitting on my brand-new desk in my brand-new office. What a pleasure it was to read it and to know you wish me well in my new venture, for confident though we may profess to be, that little bit of extra support from a well-wishing friend is comforting indeed.

Thanks, Joe; it was kind of you to write.

Sincerely,

Dear Peter,

Thank you for your kind words about my talk at your Sales Conference last week.

It was a pleasure to address the members of your sales team and if my talk contributed in any way to the success of the Conference, then I am doubly pleased.

Sincerely,

Dear Ken,

How very nice of you to write me such a kind letter.

If I now proceed to become a conceited ass, I'll only have you to blame.

As ever,

Dear Ms Greer,

How kind of you to write to me about my booklet, The Perfect Secretary. I'm very happy that you find it so useful, although, without wishing to flatter you in any way, I would hardly have thought you needed any further advice on the subject. Could it be that you are flattering me?

Yours sincerely,

Dear Mr O'Connell,

Many thanks for your kind letter of March 15. Your high appraisal of my worth certainly gives me a great deal to live up to.

Unquestionably the years ahead will be challenging ones for our Company and my new post will call for all the energy, imagination, and acumen I can muster. It is comforting to know that at least one of my close associates believes I am blessed with these qualities.

Thank you again for writing.

Yours sincerely,

Dear Alex,

Thank you for your all-too-generous tribute to my new book. There really is no one whose approval I value more than yours. If you think it's good, then I feel it must be so.

Thank you for reassuring me. Now we shall see what the buying public has to say!

Sincerely,

For message of condolence or sympathy

Dear Bob,

Your cheery note of encouragement was like a breath of fresh air and did me a world of good.

I am now at the convalescent stage, sitting in the garden basking in the sunshine and flirting with the pretty nurses – not too bad at all, really.

Thanks for writing. Your note was a real tonic.

See you back at the old shop soon.

As ever,

Dear Mr Winslow,

On behalf of the Partners and myself, I wish to thank you most sincerely for your kind words of sympathy on the death of Mr Wilfred Sorrell.

His wise and energetic leadership will be sorely missed by the firm, and we feel we can pay our best tribute to him by continuing his policies of fair-dealing and close personal concern for the financial problems of our clients. This we intend to do.

Your friendship and support at this time means a lot to us.

Sincerely yours,

Dear Fred,

Thank you for you kind words of sympathy.

At a time of great personal sorrow such as this there is no greater solace than the knowledge that our friends are there and feel with us.

Thank you again.

Sincerely,

Dear James,

I want to thank you most sincerely for your cards and cheerful notes while I was in hospital. They were a great help and I appreciated them immensely. I would have written to thank you sooner, but I tired so quickly that writing did not come easily to me. Then, just as I thought I really <u>must</u> put pen to paper, another cheerful note from you arrived.

Thanks a million, you have been most kind.

I am back at the office now and look forward to seeing you later on in the month when I go up North.

Sincerely,

Dear Mike,

Your thoughtful note was much appreciated by Molly and me. The blow was, of course, far harder on her, but I am doing all I can to comfort her. The sympathy and support of friends like you do a lot to help. Thanks again.

As ever,

Dear Milly,

How good of you to write! Your cheerful letter was a real tonic to me as I lay in my hospital bed feeling that perhaps I'd 'had it'.

I'm very much better now and should be fighting fit again before long. Do give my regards to everyone on the team and tell them my morale is high!

Sincerely,

Dear Mr Worth,

Your kind words of sympathy on the death of our Chairman, Mr Henry Carver, were deeply appreciated.

His sudden loss has been a great shock to us and his absence from the helm will be keenly felt.

At a time such as this your friendship and kindness are a great comfort to us all.

Sincerely yours,

Dear Harry,

Your kind and thoughtful letter helped a great deal during my stay at the hospital. Thank you for thinking of me.

I have been back at the office for a couple of days, but am still 'under observation'. I should be back in full harness by the end of the month, however, and greatly look forward to seeing you at the Sales Conference in October.

Sincerely,

Dear Mr Green,

My grateful thanks for writing me such a cheerful and comforting letter while I was confined to my bed.

I am now back in full swing again and planning a business trip to the West. I will let you know exact dates as soon as my plans have crystallized and look forward to seeing you again then.

Yours sincerely,

Dear Tim,

It was just like you to write me such a cheering note while I lay on my sick bed. I was quite convinced that it was a death-bed, but apparently my hour has not yet come – thank God!

The convalescent part is rather pleasant and I am now enjoying that long rest I've been needing for years.

Thanks for writing, old pal.

As ever,

To staff

For useful suggestions

Dear Jack,

Your 'Better Business Letters' contest has been such a success that we have decided to retain it as a regular feature. Not only has it generated a good deal of interest and friendly rivalry between departments, but the quality of letters going out from the company has considerably improved.

You are therefore to be congratulated on an excellent and successful idea. We are planning to show our appreciation in a tangible way and I will let you know more about this before the next prize-giving ceremony.

Yours sincerely,

Dear Carole,

Your suggestions for the more efficient running of the Wordprocessing Centre are so constructive and promising that we have decided to put them into effect.

Thank you for taking such an interest in the efficient running of our business. We are fortunate indeed to have such thoughtful and capable women as yourself on our staff.

Yours sincerely,

My dear Wilkins,

Joy Desmond has told me that the quiz idea for the September issue was a brain-child of yours and I am writing to thank you for the interest you are taking in our journal.

Please do let us have any other ideas which may occur to you. We shall be most appreciative.

Sincerely,

My dear Simpkins,

You will be pleased to learn that Mr John Lacrosse has now agreed to write the book on Alpine Gardens for us. We are most grateful to you for having brought this potential author to our attention, and we very much appreciate your interest in our Company.

Yours sincerely,

Dear Frank,

When you suggested some time ago that Jenkins and Sons of 24 Belmont Square might be interested in our office-decorating service, we got in touch with them right away and, as a result, they have now signed a contract with us.

Thank you for your valuable lead and for your keenness and loyalty to our Company. It is very much appreciated and will not be forgotten.

Sincerely,

Dear Ms Wilkins,

This is to thank you for kindly recommending Ms Mary McGuire to us. She turned out to be just the person the Chairman was looking for and she will start work for him next Monday.

Your interest and thoughtfulness are keenly appreciated.

Yours sincerely,

Dear Conrad,

Your suggestion for a Safety Week at the works was most successful, as you undoubtedly already know. The whole work force took to it with vigour and not a single accident occurred that week.

We shall undoubtedly repeat the event some time in the future and, meanwhile, thank you for your valuable suggestion. It is most gratifying to have such keen and enthusiastic people on the staff.

Sincerely,

Dear Margaret,

Your ideas on the handling of the Company Suggestion Scheme are very constructive and show a good deal of thought. We have decided to put them into effect from January 2 of next year and wish to thank you for the interest you have taken in this very important aspect of personnel relations.

We have also decided to reward your suggestions with a prize, as is only fitting. A cheque will be presented to you at the next prize-giving event.

Thank you again.

Yours sincerely,

For loyal or outstanding service

Dear Larry,

Ten years ago today you joined our Export Department and I would like to send you my personal thanks for ten years of loyal, efficient and dependable service to the Company.

As you begin your second decade with Harrison and Co. I wish you continued success and ever-increasing satisfaction in your work.

Yours sincerely,

Dear Miss Desmond,

I should like to thank you most sincerely for the splendid way in which your department rallied round and kept working during the unprecedented Christmas rush.

Without the wholehearted co-operation of your girls we could not have coped with the situation. And I realize all too well that you were the dynamic force behind them.

Please convey to your girls my sincere thanks. Your efforts and theirs were very much appreciated.

Yours sincerely,

My dear Glover,

Since you took charge of the office six months ago the improvement has been remarkable and I want you to know how pleased I am with the effort and enthusiasm you have put into your new assignment.

We expected much of you when we decided to entrust you with this difficult task, and you have certainly come out with flying colours.

Please carry on the good work in the full knowledge that your efforts are much appreciated.

Yours sincerely,

Dear Malcolm,

Twenty-five years with one company is a long time, even when that company is as fine as ours. When this quarter of a century has been devoted consistently to hard work, cheerful co-operation, and unstinting loyalty, then it is a record anyone may be proud of. And this is just what you have done.

I know you heard all these things last night at the Celebration Dinner, but I very much wanted to tell you in my own words just how proud of you I am and how much I have appreciated your loyalty throughout the years.

My heartfelt personal thanks go with you as you begin your 26th year with the firm.

Sincerely,

Dear Mr Kidmoor,

I should like to thank you, both personally and on behalf of the Company, for your splendid work during the recent postal strike. Without your unflagging efforts and those of your splendid team of messengers, we would never have been able to 'carry on as usual'.

You have earned the Company's gratitude and you may be sure that we shall not forget your titanic struggle.

Yours sincerely,

Dear Ms Whitworth,

I write to thank you, on behalf of Mr Spencer and myself, for the kind and patient interest you have been taking in our overseas trainees.

The Company has done a great deal to make them feel at home among us, but there is nothing to equal the feminine touch which you have kindly taken upon yourself to supply.

Your action has not gone unnoticed and we want you to know how much we appreciate your good work.

Yours sincerely,

Dear Mac,

When you joined the company as a junior exactly ten years ago, neither you nor we realized how far you would go with Whinsmoore and Sons. But we certainly know now and I would like to seize this opportunity to congratulate you on your zest for work, initiative, persistence, and natural selling talent which put you where you are today.

It has been a pleasure to have you with us and all of us in the management team wish you continued success in your career with our Company.

Sincerely,

Dear Peter,

Since you started our Export Department a year ago results have been enouraging beyond expectations and I want you to know how pleased I am with your splendid efforts in this difficult field.

You have the full support of top management in your endeavours and we are confident that in your hands the new department is headed for a very fine future. Keep up the good work!

Sincerely,

11

Letters of Condolence and Sympathy

A letter of sympathy or condolence is perhaps the most difficult to write. It is the kind of letter we all keep on postponing, making our task harder the longer we leave it. Yet why should we find such letters so difficult to write? Perhaps it is because we don't know when to stop; because we feel we should go on and on weaving one beautiful phrase upon another; or because death leaves us speechless and we know not what to say of it.

Yet who would criticize a message of condolence? Who at a time of grief would pause to pull to pieces a friend's well-meant effort to give solace?

The best procedure is to write the message right away and to tailor it according to the degree of friendship between writer and recipient, the known feelings of the recipient towards the deceased, and the temperament, character and characteristics of the addressee.

Let simplicity and sincerity be your guide and you cannot go wrong. Just say your piece and be done. Long philosophical messages on the meaning of life and death, detailed dwelling on the virtues and attributes of the departed are unnecessary, in bad taste and may do more harm than good. By all means pay a suitable tribute to the departed, but resist the urge to go on and on.

When it comes to expressing sympathy for other mishaps, it is often enough simply to associate yourself with your correspondent's sorrow, to give a word of encouragement or of solace, to set the matter in the right perspective for him. Put yourself in his place, that's the secret of writing the right letter for the occasion.

The letters of condolence and sympathy which follow cover a number of different cases and varying degrees of formality or informality between the correspondents.

To business and professional associates

On family bereavement

My dear William,

I cannot tell you how upset I was to hear the sad news about your mother's passing. She was a wonderful old lady and a pleasure to be with. She enjoyed the company of the young and made them feel very much at home with her and, as you know, I spent many delightful hours in her company. I shall miss her.

I know that nothing I can say can really soften the blow for you, but if there is anything I can possibly do to be of help, please let me know.

As ever,

My dear Roger,

I was distressed indeed to hear that you had lost your mother. Mere words are such puny comforters at a time such as this, yet it can be of some solace to know that our friends are close to us and feel with us in our grief.

Do be assured that I am at hand and if there is anything at all I can do, please let me know.

Sincerely,

Dear Mr Ross,

It is with deep regret that we have just heard of the death of your wife.

Mere words seem so futile at a time such as this, yet all of us here at Freeman's want you to know that you have our deepest sympathy. We only wish there were some way in which we could lighten your grief.

Yours sincerely,

Dear Michael,

Almost the first news I heard upon my return from the Continent this afternoon was that of your father's death. This is sad news indeed and I know what a loss it is for you. Few fathers and sons were as close and as congenial as you two.

I shall not exhort you to bear up manfully, for I know how easy it is to say and how hard to do. I also happen to believe that it is far better to let grief have its season and then be gone. You will then realize that your father lived a full, happy, and useful life, earning the love and respect of many and the envy of none. Let this thought be a measure of solace to you.

As ever,

Dear Mr Skinner,

It is with deep regret that I heard of the passing of your wife.

Aware as I am of the scant solace which words can bring at such a time, I none the less want you to know that you have my heartfelt sympathy.

Yours sincerely,

Dear Mr Harriman,

It came as a great shock to all of us at Hartley's to hear of the sudden tragic death of your brother.

His loss is a great one indeed, to you personally, to Harriman Brothers, to Hartley's, and to the community in general. All of us remember very vividly his tireless efforts to put Ross on the industrial map and the unstinting generosity with which he worked, not merely for himself and his Company, but for the business community as a whole.

His work lives on and I am sure that his memory will remain green in Ross for many years to come.

You have our deepest sympathy in this great and premature loss.

Yours sincerely,

Dear Mr Fletcher,

This is just to let you know how deeply I feel for you in your sorrow.

Yours sincerely,

Dear Fred,

I was deeply shocked to hear of the death of your son.

I know full well what an irreparable loss it is to you and realize how little my words can do to soften the blow. But I do want to express my deepest sympathy in the hope that the closeness of your friends will be of some small solace to you.

Sincerely,

Dear Steve,

I was sorry indeed to learn of the death of your wife.

Knowing how close you were and what an irreparable loss it is to you, I realize what scant consolation mere words are to you.

I want you to know, none the less, that you have my heartfelt sympathy. If there is anything at all I can do, please let me know.

Sincerely,

Dear Mrs Wiseman,

Even though mere words can do little to comfort you at a time such as this, I want you to know how much I sympathize with you in your bereavement. May the kind thoughts and sympathy of your friends and associates help to give you courage and fortitude.

Yours sincerely,

Dear Tim

I have only just learned of the sudden passing of your father during my business trip on the Continent and hasten to let you know how very sorry I am.

I know full well how close you were to him and how you strove to live up to his high business ethics and ideals. His loss must have been a terrible blow to you.

Your one consoling thought must be that the Company he created lives on to keep his memory alive and you will steer it along the same straight course that he would have done.

Sincerely,

Dear Marjorie,

I cannot tell you how sorry I was to hear of the death of your husband, after such a long and lingering illness.

There will be many painful but necessary tasks for you to take care of in the days ahead and as I know you have no relatives to shoulder such burdens for you, I will gladly help you in any way I can.

Meanwhile please be assured that all your friends here at Chapman's sympathize with you in your bereavement.

Sincerely,

Dear Sandy,

There are times when even our best friends can be of little comfort and this is one of them. I want you to know, nevertheless, that you have my deepest sympathy in the irreparable loss you have suffered.

Please let me know if there is anything at all I can do to lighten your grief.

As ever,

Dear Mr Bayley,

It was with deepest regret that I learned of the passing of your wife.

How much I wish there were some way in which I could lessen your sorrow. Do be assured at least that you have my heartfelt sympathy.

Sincerely yours,

On death of company executive

Dear Kay,

It is with the deepest regret that I received the news of the death of your senior partner, Mr Richard H. Colmer. I can assure you that the partners of my firm would wish me to express their sympathy to you and to your partners on your great loss.

Sincerely yours,

My dear Roger,

I have just read in the papers that Lord Straker has died and I can guess how heavy a blow this will be to you and to all your colleagues on the Board. But I want you to know that the blow is felt almost equally by myself and others like me who had the pleasure of doing business with him over the years. It is said that a businessman's word is his bond, but alas, it is rare nowadays for this to be true. It could not have been truer, however, of your late chairman. He proved by his example that complete integrity is no bar to success in business. He will be sorely missed.

Please convey my sympathy and that of my wife to your Board. We have never had the pleasure of meeting his widow, but if you think that it would please her to know just how highly her late husband was regarded, then by all means show this letter to her. There is, after all, so little one can do to help in a time such as this.

With kind regards and best wishes,

Yours very sincerely,

Dear Mr King,

Every member of my staff joins me in this expression of heartfelt sympathy on the untimely death of your Managing Director, Mr Stephen Briggs.

His cheerful personality and fair dealing will be sorely missed, not only in your Company, but by his many friends throughout the furnishing trade.

His loss is a great one for all of us.

Sincerely yours,

Dear Mr Smith,

The entire Fairway organization joins me in expressing our deepest sympathy in the loss of your Secretary-Treasurer, Mr Robert Preston.

His sterling qualities earned him and your Company numerous friends in the profession and he will be mourned and missed by many.

I myself will feel his loss keenly, both personally and as head of my Company.

Yours sincerely,

Dear Ms Green,

The news of the fatal accident which deprived you of your Managing Director, Mr Sidney Howard, came as a great shock to me.

While his sudden passing is a crippling blow to your Company, it will also be felt by his many friends in the hardware field all over the country. It is indeed hard to believe that one so dynamic, so energetic, so full of the joy of living, is no more.

The whole of my management team join me in conveying to you our heartfelt sympathy in your tragic loss.

Yours sincerely,

Dear Mr Winter,

The passing of John Windsmore is a loss to all of us – his countless friends in every corner of England, Scotland, and Wales.

Everywhere he went John took with him a word of good cheer, a friendly joke, a hearty smile. He will be sorely missed.

Yet for you the loss is greatest of all and for this reason I want you to know how much I feel with you at this sad moment.

Yours sincerely,

On personal injury or illness

Dear George,

Philip told me yesterday that you were in hospital undergoing an emergency operation. I hope it is all over by now, bar the restful convalescing period, and I hasten to send you my very best wishes for a speedy recovery.

I will phone your home in a couple of days' time to find out how you are and whether I have the green light to pay you a visit.

All the very best to you.

Sincerely,

Dear Jim

I was delighted to learn from Muriel this morning that you were off the danger list and well on the way to recovery.

I cannot tell you how relieved I am. You gave us all quite a shock, you know. Discreet inquiries at the hospital revealed the fact that it is quite all right for you to eat fruit and I have therefore taken it upon myself to send you along a few early strawberries which I picked up specially for you at Covent Garden.

It also appears that you will very soon be able to have visits from outsiders such as me, and you can therefore expect me to drop in on you quite soon.

Meanwhile take it easy and be assured that all of us at the office are thinking of you and wishing you well.

Sincerely,

Dear Miss Springer,

I was very sorry to learn from Mr Wade that you have been home on the sick list for the past several days.

Please accept my best wishes for a speedy recovery and, indeed, I hope this note finds you much improved already.

Yours sincerely,

Dear Mr Smythe,

Word of your painful accident has just reached me and I hope that by now you are well on the way to recovery.

A man as active as you will find it difficult to sit still for many hours and I am therefore sending you a couple of books to help you pass the time pleasantly. Please accept them with my sincere best wishes for a speedy recovery.

Yours sincerely,

Dear Jean,

I was very disappointed to learn when I called to see you yesterday that you were in hospital. I'm very sorry about this and only wish I had known sooner. At any rate I want you to know that all your friends at Windsmoor's are thinking of you and hoping for your speedy recovery.

I don't know when I'll be in Reading again, but if it is soon, I will certainly drop in to see you.

Meanwhile, you have my very best wishes.

Sincerely,

Dear Mr Evans,

I was very sorry to hear of the nasty mishap which left you temporarily deprived of the use of your right hand.

I do hope the wound is making progress and that you will soon be in good working order again.

Yours sincerely,

Dear Jack,

I have just heard that you are home unwell and must remain under the doctor's care for several more weeks.

Knowing you as I do, I'm sure you are not taking too kindly to idleness and the rest in bed. On the other hand, I'm sure that you'll pull out of it far quicker than the doctors predict. They have counted without that bulldog spark in you and I know you'll fool them!

Meanwhile, to help you while away the time, I am sending you a record of one of your favourite composers and as you lie there listening to its mighty strains I know you will feel strength and fitness coursing through you once again.

Keep cheerful and get well quickly.

As ever,

Dear Mrs Peters,

News reached me this morning that you had successfully undergone your operation and were resting quietly.

This is splendid news and I feel convinced that very soon you will be ready to leave the hospital for home. Everyone at the office joins me in sending you best wishes for a speedy recovery and a pleasant convalescence.

Sincerely yours,

Dear Mrs Russell,

I am writing to tell you how much we have missed you at our meetings and that we look forward to enjoying your witty remarks and spirited sallies once again in the near future.

We are all delighted to know that you continue to make good progress and that we can expect to see you again fit and well very soon.

May our thoughts and best wishes help to speed you on towards complete recovery.

Sincerely yours,

On injury or illness of relation

Dear Mr Wilson,

I was very sorry to hear about the painful accident suffered by your wife. Please convey to her my sympathy and best wishes for a speedy recovery.

Yours sincerely,

Dear Ron,

I've just heard about your son's skiing accident and want you to know how sorry I am. I remember all too well the misgivings you had when he set out on his trip.

I certainly hope he will recover speedily and that there will be no after-effects.

Sincerely,

Dear Mr Morrow,

Fred Morrison has just told me about your wife's illness. I certainly hope it is not very serious and that she will soon be completely recovered.

Please tell her how much I sympathize and give her my best regards and good wishes for a speedy recovery.

Sincerely yours,

Dear Mr Philmore,

I was much relieved to read in the paper today that your daughter had successfully undergone her operation and could now be considered out of danger.

It must have been a tremendous relief to both you and your wife. I sincerely hope that her progress from now on will be rapid and that she will soon be well on her way to convalescence. Do remember me to her as soon as she is well enough.

Yours sincerely,

Dear Henry,

I was sorry indeed to learn of your wife's illness. Please give her my kind regards and best wishes for a quick recovery.

Sincerely,

Dear Mr Little,

I was very distressed to learn that your small son had been stricken with leukaemia. I can well imagine what anguish it has caused you and only wish there were something I could do to help.

I'm sure you do not need me to remind you that great strides have quite recently been made in the treatment of this disease. In fact, as I expect you know, the Imperial Cancer Research Fund has recently made it known that improved methods of treatment and better drug therapy were now enabling three-quarters of children to survive this once dreaded disease.

So do take heart and put your trust in the medical experts who have your little boy in their care.

If there is anything at all I can do to help, you have only to call on me.

Yours sincerely,

Dear Mrs Quentin,

I called in to see you yesterday and learned that you had been obliged to remain at home to nurse your ailing mother.

I'm very sorry to hear about this and hope that the invalid is making steady progress and will soon be fit and well again.

I look forward to seeing you at your old stand again when I make my next call, probably early in March.

Yours sincerely,

Dear Jim,

I was very sorry to hear about Mollie's fall and am most anxious to learn how she is faring. I certainly hope it was not very serious and that she is already on her way to recovery.

Do please keep me in touch and meanwhile give her my love and tell her I'm keeping my fingers crossed for her.

As ever,

Dear Mrs Carstairs,

News of your husband's illness has only just reached me and I should like you to convey to him my very best wishes for a speedy recovery.

I sincerely hope he will soon be enjoying his usual excellent health once again.

Sincerely,

On loss or damage to property

Dear Mr Perry,

I was very distressed to hear on the evening news that your wonderful shop and warehouse had been completely gutted by fire.

It was painful indeed to hear of something so dreadful happening to a friend and customer. I can well imagine what it must have done to you.

I'm sure there is some way in which my Company can help. Our warehouses, for instance, are at your complete disposal for any merchandise that may have been salvaged. Do be sure to let us know what we can do and meanwhile courage and faith, I'm quite convinced, will make Perry and Sons rise again from its ashes.

Very sincerely yours,

Dear Mr Longstaff,

I've just read in The Bucks Free Press that your premises were extensively damaged by the severe storm we had last week. I'm sorry I didn't know about it sooner, for I might have been able to extend a helping hand.

Do let me know if I can help in any way at this late date and I sincerely hope that the papers may have exaggerated the damage somewhat.

Yours sincerely,

Dear Mr and Mrs Reynolds,

I have just heard the distressing news about the burglary at your home. I am extremely sorry, knowing as I do, how many wonderful things it contained, all lovingly collected by you over the years.

I know there is little one can say to console you for the loss of so many precious things, but do remember that you still have the devotion of your friends, and no one can take that away from you.

Yours sincerely,

Dear Sid,

I was very distressed to learn that your home was severely damaged by fire and can well imagine what a trial it has been for you and Gail.

I want you to know how much I sympathize with you in your loss and that I stand ready to help in any way I can. Do let me know what I can do for you.

As ever,

Dear Mr Winter,

News of the extensive damage sustained by you and your family during the recent floods in Worcestershire has only just reached me and I want you to know how much I sympathize with you.

I can think of nothing more distressing than to have one's home submerged in water and no mere word of mine can do much to comfort you. Yet if there is anything at all I can do to help, I am more than ready to do it.

I know you will find the fortitude to bear with this great misfortune, strong in the knowledge that all your many friends are behind you.

Yours sincerely,

Dear Mr Waring,

All of us at the British Rubber Company were sorry to hear about the extensive fire damage which your Company has sustained.

We are wondering whether we can help in any way and hope you will feel free to call on us for any assistance we can render. We would consider it a privilege to help out a friend and customer at such a time as this.

Yours sincerely,

Dear Mr Savage,

I was horrified to read in the morning papers about the daring robbery which took place late last night at your Bank.

I want you to know how sorry I am and how much I hope that the culprits will be caught and the Bank's assets restored. It was certainly a relief to learn that none of your staff was in any way hurt.

Yours sincerely,

Dear Signor Bianchi,

I was deeply shocked to read about the terrible earthquake which struck your town and doubly so upon learning that your premises had been totally destroyed.

Such a terrible catastrophe is very much like death – it leaves us without words and what little we can find to say brings small comfort.

Coraggio, Signor Bianchi! You must pick yourself up and start afresh, like so many of your fellow-countrymen before you. As you may know, a fund has been started here in Britain to be sent to your town, but do let me know what I can do personally to help you. If you manage to find new premises, we can certainly arrange to let you have new stock without delay, at long terms, if necessary.

The important thing is to carry on, to look ahead, to have courage. Coraggio!

In great sympathy,

Dear Miss Dinsmore,

It was most unfortunate that your shop should have been so severely damaged by the disturbances which occurred last night. If ever there was an asset to the community, it was your shop and it seems so unfair that it should have suffered the fate it did.

I want you to know how much I sympathize with you. I certainly hope your premises will be in good order again very soon and that you will be fully compensated for the damage. Do let me know if I can help in any way.

Yours sincerely,

Dear Ed,

I want you to know how very sorry I was to hear about the severe hurricane damage suffered by your family – and indeed – by the whole of your city.

Such savage destruction by the forces of nature seems so unreal to us in Britain, for we seldom get anything worse than a gale or a trifling snow storm. But when a close friend and business associate suffers such damage, it suddenly seems all too real and terrifying.

Do take courage and tell Madge how much I sympathize. It is difficult to help at this great distance, but if there is anything at all I can do, please let me know. I shall be thinking of both of you.

Yours sincerely,

Dear Mr Wahring,

We were all very distressed to learn about the fire which caused such havoc to your premises.

Please feel free to call upon us if we can help in any way. You have been our loyal customer for many years and we would consider it a privilege to help you out in any way possible.

Sincerely yours,

Dear Mr Simpson,

News of the storm damage to your premises has only just reached me via Charles Kenny and I want you to know how sorry I am.

You are too far away for me to offer to store your merchandise, but if there is anything else at all I can do to help, do please let me know.

You have been our friends and suppliers for so many years that we feel very sorry indeed that something so dreadful should have happened to you.

Yours sincerely,

To staff

On family bereavement

My dear Miss Watson,

I was very sorry indeed to hear of the death of your father and I am writing at once to express not only my own sympathy, but also that of all my colleagues on the Board. I did not have the pleasure of meeting your father, but by all accounts he was a most well-loved and highly-respected gentleman. We trust that your mother is bearing up as well as possible in the circumstances and we would be glad if you would let us know if there is anything we could do to be of help at this anxious time.

Do not worry about things at the office. but do be assured that our thoughts and sympathy are with you.

Yours sincerely,

Dear Mr Simmonds,

My wife and I want you to know how much we sympathize with you in your bereavement. It was most distressing to hear of your sad loss.

Sincerely yours,

Dear Jim,

I was sorry indeed to learn of the great sorrow that has come to you.

I know mere words can be of little solace at such a time, but I do none the less want you to know how much I sympathize. If there is anything at all I can do to help you, do please let me know.

Yours sincerely,

Dear Miss Cross,

I was much distressed to learn of the sudden passing of your mother. She seemed so much better last time I saw her, but, then, there often is a slight improvement before the end.

Do please let me know if there is anything at all I can do to make this trying time a little less sad for you. I do sympathize with you deeply in your sorrow.

Yours sincerely,

Dear Jack,

There is very little I can say to you on this sad occasion, except how much I sympathize with you in your loss – and that you already know. Words – so effective on countless other occasions – are quite useless in the face of death.

If there is anything tangible I or the Company can do, please say the word.

Sincerely,

Dear Mr Atkinson,

All the members of the Board join me in sending you our deepest sympathy in the irremediable loss you have sustained.

It was sad news indeed to hear of your bereavement.

Sincerely yours,

Dear Eric,

I want you to know how much I sympathize with you in your loss.

Hard as it is to find consolation when the greatest of all losses faces us, you must try to do so in the thought that your mother lived a full and useful life, and that you did a great deal to make her happy and proud of you.

I know you have been a good son and this thought must bring you comfort.

Yours sincerely,

Dear Will,

I want you to know how very distressed I am to learn of the sadness that has come to you.

How I wish there were something I could do to give concrete expression to my sympathy. Perhaps there is some way in which I can help to lighten your sorrow. If there is, I hope you will let me know.

In deepest sympathy,

On injury to self or illness

Dear Bill,

I was very sorry to hear of the nasty accident you had yesterday. I certainly hope you will be well on the way to recovery by the time you get this note.

Don't forget to let us know how you get along at the hospital, as everyone at the works is very much concerned about you.

We all look forward to seeing you back when you are completely recovered, but no dashing back with your arm in a sling!

Best wishes from all of us,

Sincerely,

Dear Meg,

I am sorry indeed to hear that the 'bug' has really and truly got you down. There is certainly a lot of it going around and you are one of our several casualties. I realize that this is no consolation to you and I only tell you to keep you abreast of the news!

I know you are in excellent hands so I am not unduly worried about you. You, in turn, must not worry about a thing at the office. Everything is under control and I don't want you to think of coming back until you are your old self again.

Best wishes for a speedy recovery from all of us at Greendale's.

Yours sincerely,

Dear Frank,

Your mother phoned this morning to let us know that you had come out of your operation with flying colours and were now resting quietly.

This is splendid news which all of us here at Harper Brothers were delighted to hear.

Here's wishing you a speedy recovery and an early release from the hospital.

Yours sincerely,

Dear Fred,

I hope you're lying there counting your blessings! Just think of it – if it hadn't been for this illness you never would have had a rest at all this year. Seriously, Fred, I sincerely hope you're feeling very much better and that you're resigning yourself to keeping strictly to your doctor's orders.

I know how hard it is for you to rest, but you really must do so this time for everyone's sake.

I shall be coming to see you early next week and will expect to see you very much improved.

All here send their very best wishes to you.

Very sincerely yours,

Dear Miss Jones,

Everyone at the office was happy to learn that you had successfully come out of your operation and would be released from the hospital in a week to ten days.

A 'delegation' will be visiting you very soon and in fact I'm having a hard time convincing all your many friends here that even two's a crowd for a convalescent.

Meanwhile all of us send you our very best wishes for a speedy recovery.

Yours sincerely,

Dear Muriel,

I was very sorry to hear about your skiing accident and am most anxious to learn how you are.

Do please get in touch with us and let us know whether there is anything we can do at this end. I realize you have parents to take care of you, but nevertheless, it can't be much fun suddenly to find yourself in a foreign hospital. So please keep in touch, by phone if necessary, and let us know if there is anything you need.

Best wishes from us all.

Sincerely,

Dear Mrs Quartermain,

I was very sorry indeed to hear of your painful fall and its unfortunate repercussions.

I hope the surgeon has wrought his magic on you and that you are well on the way to recovery by now.

Rest is, of course, most important in such cases and you must not attempt to walk on your leg too much in an effort to get back to work as quickly as possible. We are carrying on all right and wish you to take the necessary time to get completely healed.

Best wishes from us all,

Yours sincerely,

Dear Ms McEwan,

I was sorry to hear from your travelling companion, Ms Evelyn Mitchell, that you had had an acute attack of appendicitis on the last lap of your holiday and had to fly to England for an emergency operation.

This is no way to end a holiday! However, knowing your resilient nature – not to mention your sturdy Scottish constitution – I have no doubt you will come out of the operation splendidly and will be flying back home to us in next to no time. Too bad about your projected tour of the British Isles, though!

Do please drop me a line as soon as you can, letting me know how you are and when we may expect you back. Don't worry about things this end, the important matter is to have you back all in one piece.

All your colleagues at the office send their best regards and are sorry they can't pop over and bring you some grapes!

Yours sincerely,

Dear Rex,

I was most surprised and distressed to hear that you had to be rushed to hospital for an emergency operation. Your brother tells me the worst is over and that you should be as right as rain again within a few weeks.

Please don't worry about things at the office. Everything is running smoothly and, in fact, your colleagues have volunteered to share your work out between them. You therefore haven't a worry in the world except to mend your health.

We shall be out to see you as soon as you're able to have visitors and meanwhile our warmest wishes go to you.

Sincerely,

12

Requests

Letters making requests vary all the way from writing in for a piece of advertising literature, which a company will be only too happy to send you – to writing to a friend or business associate for a loan. The latter request is obviously a great favour to ask, regardless of the sum involved, and the letter should be written accordingly. In addition, it is imperative to mention when the loan will be paid back. It is amazing how many people omit this very important detail when asking for a loan, whether verbally or in writing. Where it might be perfectly convenient to lend a friend £5, £10 or even £100 for a week or a month, it might be highly inconvenient, or even impossible, to make the same loan for six months.

When writing for literature or information the only two requirements are brevity and clarity. If you require two or more pieces of literature, or want clarification of two or more points, it is helpful to list them separately, one item on each line, numbering them consecutively. This helps the recipient both to see quickly what is wanted and to check each item off as he or she puts it in a return envelope or writes a reply.

As to asking for a business appointment, it is important to give sufficient notice and, especially in the case of very busy and important people, to give them as much freedom as possible in the choice of day and time.

When asking for permission to reproduce written material or illustrations, always remember to mention that you will give credit to their author and when you <u>do</u> use the material, do not forget the acknowledgement.

For charge account

Dear Sirs,

I visit your store almost every day and would therefore like to open a charge account with you. Would you kindly send me the appropriate application form?

Yours faithfully,

Dear Sirs,

I would greatly appreciate your opening an account in my name to facilitate my purchases at your store.

Lloyd's Bank PLC, Piccadilly, are my bankers and both my business and private addresses are given hereunder. If you require any further reference, kindly let me know.

Yours faithfully,

Dear Sirs,

I am considering opening a charge account at your store and would appreciate your kindly letting me have details on how this works. More specifically I should like to know how much credit I could get, how long to pay, and so on.

I look forward to hearing from you soon, as I would like to get the matter settled in good time for Christmas shopping.

Yours faithfully,

For business appointment*

Dear Mr Dale,

I am somewhat dissatisfied with the performance of my portfolio of securities and would therefore rather like to overhaul it completely and make quite a few changes.

May I come in and see you about it some time next week? I shall be in town both Wednesday and Thursday morning and either would suit me well.

Yours sincerely,

Dear Mr Bartholomew,

I happened to mention to Mr Smith of the Ealing Job Centre that I was writing a book on selling and would like to track down a company with a good sales training programme.

Mr Smith told me that your company was outstanding in this respect and I am therefore wondering whether I might come in to see you one day and learn more about your sales training school and, indeed, about your sales organization in general.

I look forward with great interest to hearing from you.

Yours sincerely,

Dear Mr Jones,

My marriage next summer will mean quite a few changes and several new provisions will have to be made, including a new will. May I come in and see you about these various matters early next month?

If you let me know the time and day which will best suit you, I will fit in my other appointments accordingly.

Yours sincerely,

---

* Some of these letters are very similar to those contained in Chapter 2, under Introducing Yourself.

Dear Mr Bayley,

Thank you for your letter of yesterday with your comments on the various colour schemes and other details concerning the house.

There are so many points involved that I feel it would be better if we got together rather than try to decide by correspondence. I could take a quick trip to Maidenhead either late Wednesday afternoon, or late on Friday. Will you please let me know which of the two days suits you better?

Yours sincerely,

Dear Mr Williams,

I shall be taking a trip to the Midlands early next month in an attempt to tie up the various pending agency agreements. I should be in Birmingham by about May 6.

Do you think I might come in to see you then? If so perhaps you would kindly let me know what time would be most convenient for you.

I look forward to hearing from you soon.

Yours sincerely,

Dear Signor Bianchi,

We have now had an opportunity of examining the last prototype refrigerator you sent us and I am afraid there are still various important details which need attention before the model is suitable for marketing in the UK.

The Board has therefore decided that it would be best if I came over to Italy to iron out these details with you personally. I could fly in next Monday if this would suit you. Perhaps you would be good enough to telex your reply, so that I can make a few last-minute preparations before leaving.

Kindest regards,

Yours sincerely,

Dear Mr Young,

Our Company has devised a means whereby you can cut down your business correspondence costs by as much as 30 per cent.

May I explain our plan to you when I'm in Nottingham next week? I'm sure you will find it well worth considering.

I will call your secretary for an appointment as soon as I arrive and hope you will be able to spare me a little time.

Yours sincerely,

Dear Mr Carter,

Would you like to cut your spraying costs by as much as 20 per cent? I'm sure you would and I'd like to come in and explain to you just how you can accomplish this.

I shall be in Leicester next Monday and am hoping that 3 p.m. would be convenient for you. In order to save you time, if I don't hear from you to the contrary, I shall be with you at 3 p.m.

Yours sincerely,

Dear Mr Britten,

The plans for the new building are now ready and I am wondering whether I might come up and show them to you on Wednesday? Would 2.30 to 3 p.m. suit you?

I shall be in Reading for the rest of the afternoon, however, and if you prefer to see me later, that would suit me equally well.

Yours sincerely,

For information

Dear Mr Page,

I am writing a book on personnel management and am rather keen on mentioning in it Boots' training programme for girls, which began in 1961. I read about it in the Industrial Training Council booklet and I trust you will not mind my referring to the programme.

By now you will have had ample opportunity of assessing results and I should very much like to know whether the programme has been a success. Have efficiency and productivity improved? Has morale risen? Has staff turnover been reduced?

I look forward with interest to your good news, and thank you for any assistance you care to give me.

Yours sincerely,

Dear Mr Brown,

I am doing some research on my second book and it will have a chapter on sales aids. I have seen your Du Kane and Salesmate equipment in action and would like to mention in my book the service you give.

May I have full details of your service, including an idea about costs? Is your service country-wide?

Many thanks for your kind assistance.

Yours faithfully,

Dear Sirs,

I have just read your advertisement in the Sunday Times and am wondering whether you ever have any call for senior marketing executives.

While I am fairly content in my present position as marketing manager in a large electronics company, I feel that, for various reasons, any further progress will be blocked for many years to come.

I would therefore be quite interested in getting on your books, quite confidentially of course, with a view to seeking an opening enabling me to move upwards towards the directorial chair.

Enclosed is a copy of my curriculum vitae and I look forward to hearing from you just how your service works and whether you feel you could do something for me.

Yours faithfully,

Dear Sir,

I am endeavouring to get in touch with Dr W. C. Watson, who taught at your University some years back. I wrote to him care of the University of Southern California, but the letter was returned to me marked: 'Not on U.S.C. Faculty'.

Would you be good enough to let me have Dr Watson's private address? He was a very elderly man even a few years ago, so I am wondering whether he has retired or, indeed, whether he is still living.

Many thanks for your kind help.

Yours faithfully,

Dear Mr Wright,

I am preparing material for an article on management training and feel I cannot omit a mention of the world-famous G.E. Management Institute at Ossining.

Would you be good enough to let me have some details of the Institute, e.g. how many people are trained there every year, how long the course lasts, what the syllabus consists of, etc.?

If you have any printed matter on the subject, I'd greatly appreciate your sending me a copy.

I should be most grateful for any assistance you care to give me in my work and look forward to hearing from you.

Yours sincerely,

Dear Sirs,

I understand that you make up roller-blinds in customer's own material. I am thinking of having such a blind in the living-room, since the view is a beautiful one and I want as little curtaining as possible to be in the way.

Will you kindly let me know whether you have a selection of materials to choose from or whether I should send you the material myself? In the latter case, how much material do you need? The window measures 5 feet square.

I should also appreciate receiving details as to cost and delivery.

Yours faithfully,

Dear Sirs,

I am planning to have my living/dining-room re-carpeted and before I come in with my wife to look at the carpets you have in stock, I would appreciate your letting me have the following information:

1 Is the price of cutting and laying the carpet included in your quotation?
2 How soon can you do the job once you receive the order?
3 Do you have any clients in the Marlow area to whom I can refer?

I look forward with interest to your early news.

Yours faithfully,

Dear Sirs,

I have frequently seen your small advertisement in The Times and have often wondered just what kind of investments you handle.

Since I am now contemplating making a change in some of my investments, I would greatly appreciate your letting me have details of the kind of business you do. I have in mind investing something in the region of £8,000–£10,000.

Yours faithfully,

For printed matter

Dear Sirs,

I would very much appreciate your sending me the following material, as mentioned in the current issue of Campaign:

1 Brochure on your chalkboards and screen units
2 Leaflet on your lecture theatres
3 Booklet on your slide and filmstrip projectors

Many thanks.

Yours faithfully,

Dear Mr Cunningham,

Our company is contemplating putting out a staff newspaper or magazine. I have always admired Entre nous, which your company publishes for its staff and I am wondering whether you would be good enough to let me have a recent issue or two to help us decide on format, contents, and so on.

Many thanks for your kind assistance.

Yours sincerely,

Dear Sirs,

I would greatly appreciate your sending me a copy of Cutting Corners with Conveyors. I understand you make no charge for these excellent Technical Aids, but if I am mistaken, I'd be happy to make the appropriate remittance.

Yours faithfully,

Dear Mr Lynn,

I am doing some research on labour turnover and am wondering whether you have any material on the subject in your library. I understand that a survey on labour turnover was carried out not too long ago in the County of Gwent.

I hope you will be able to track down something for me and thank you for your help.

Yours sincerely,

Dear Sirs,

I wonder whether I might have a complimentary copy of your useful booklet Authors' Alterations Cost Money and Cause Delay . . .?

I have found it quite invaluable when correcting proofs of my books and would like to have a copy permanently by me.

Many thanks.

Yours faithfully,

For permission to reproduce material

Dear Sirs,

I am writing a book on personnel management and would like to reproduce in it the first page of Dr McMurry's 'Patterned Interview Form'. I already have his permission to do so, but notice on the form itself – which Dr McMurry sent me – that you hold the copyright.

May I therefore have your kind permission to reproduce the first page only of the form? I shall, of course, give proper credit to Dartnell Corporation.

Many thanks for your kind co-operation.

Yours truly,

Dear Mr Dolan,

Further to our exchange of correspondence last spring, I have now finished the first draft of my book and would like your permission to quote your 'Ten Commandments' of personnel policy, as well as your permission to reproduce the illustrations of how job grading works from your booklet Western Electric's Pay Policy in Action.

I would, of course give full credit to Western Electric for the material and illustrations reproduced in my book.

May I thank you once again for your splendid co-operation? It has been a great help to me in my work.

Yours sincerely,

Dear Mr Green,

I am preparing an article to be called 'Advertising the Truth' and would like to mention in it some of the very pertinent remarks you made last week at the IPA dinner.

I wonder if you happen to have a written copy of your talk and whether I might quote from it in my article? It was an excellent talk and I found myself nodding agreement all the way through it.

Yours sincerely,

Dear Mr Kirk,

Many thanks for the excellent material you sent me. May I quote from the following passage from the IPM Golden Jubilee Statement:

The personnel manager should be qualified by training and experience to advise directors and senior managers on personnel policies; to exercise certain controls on behalf of management, for example, over wages and salary structures, systems of communication and conditions of work generally; to administer certain employee services and arrangements for training and further education; and to give a specialized service to managers and employees at all levels.

I will, of course, make the usual acknowledgement to the Institute of Personnel Management in the preliminary pages of the book.

Many thanks for your kind co-operation.

Yours sincerely,

Dear Sirs,

Modern Personnel Management

The above book is to be published by Gower Publishing Co Ltd in late summer or early autumn and I am anxious to include in it an appendix containing the following material:

1 The Equal Pay Act (1970)
2 The Health and Safety at Work Act (1974)
3 The Employment Act (1980)

May I have your permission to reproduce these three items in my book?

I look forward to hearing from you soon.

Yours faithfully,

Dear Sir,

I am anxious to reproduce in my forthcoming book a cartoon which appeared on page 14 of your January 2 issue. It is the one showing a lady mounting a horse. The caption reads: 'Now, Mrs Mulligan, let's think this thing through'.

If you are able to give me permission to reproduce the cartoon, will you kindly let me know how you would like the acknowledgement to read?

I look forward to hearing favourably from you.

Yours faithfully,

For loan from business associate or friend

Dear George,

As you know, I'm moving into my new house this week. I'm afraid I've allowed my imagination to run riot and let myself in deeper financially than I ought to have done.

I wonder if you could possibly lend me £50 to help me keep my accounts straight? I could let you have it back at the end of the year when royalties from my book come in.

I'm sorry to bother you with this and please do not hesitate to turn me down if it is difficult for you.

Sincerely,

Dear Jim,

I have been thinking about your kind offer to lend me the money to make a down payment on that car we were looking at the other day and I've decided to take you up on it.

I've never done this kind of thing before and it makes me feel rather odd, but since you mentioned that it made no real difference to you I've decided to be a devil and go ahead.

I'm sure I'll be able to pay you back within six months – unless something ghastly happens, that is.

Will you please make the cheque payable to Modern Motors Ltd?

Thanks, Jim, you're a real pal.

Sincerely,

Dear Ray,

I was good to hear from you. Your cheery letter brought a little sunshine to my hospital bedside.

You ask if there is anything you can do. It is kind of you to offer and I hope you don't mind my saying 'Yes, there is'. The fact is that my mortgage becomes due the first Tuesday in the month and I'm lying here worrying about it. It's only £175 and if you could lend me the sum until I'm back on my feet I'd be very grateful indeed.

If it hadn't been for the whole series of disasters that has befallen me of late, I'd have been well able to carry on for several months, but as it is, things look a bit sticky.

Apart from these sordid financial matters, I'm beginning to feel a little stronger and hope to be out of here soon.

Sincerely,

Dear Geoffrey,

I hope everything is under control at the office and very much wish I could be back with you. The days and nights seem to drag on endlessly as I lie here unable to move yet so well able to worry about all my financial commitments still coming up regularly in spite of my inability to meet them.

Both the children need new school uniforms and I just don't know how I am going to provide them. Do you think you could see your way to helping me out with a £100 loan? No doubt this long illness will be over one day and then I can pay you back, by instalments if necessary.

It really would relieve my mind if you could help. Thanks, Geoffrey.

Sincerely,

Granting requests

Letters granting requests will be every bit as varied as those making requests, depending once again on the nature of the request and the degree of friendship between the correspondents.

Some such letters are not strictly speaking necessary at all. If, for instance, someone writes in for a folder of some sort, all you really need do is put one in an envelope with a compliment slip and send it on. If you did do this, however, you would be missing a splendid opportunity of creating goodwill.

Likewise with requests for information or permission to reproduce material. Since you are complying with the request, it is all to your advantage to do so graciously and willingly, putting your correspondent at ease and making him or her feel the request was a welcome one. Such an attitude on your part cannot help but build goodwill for you and your company.

For charge account

Dear Mrs Holmes,

Many thanks for your letter asking us to open an account in your name. We are delighted to do so. Your charge-card is enclosed and we hope it will make shopping in our store all the more pleasurable and convenient for you.

Yours sincerely,

Dear Mr Barton,

We are pleased to enclose your charge card, as requested, and welcome you as a charge account customer.

We very much appreciate your expression of confidence in Hartman's and assure you that we shall do our best at all times to merit your continued support.

Yours sincerely,

Dear Mrs Feltham,

Thank you for requesting a Freeman's charge account. Your charge card is enclosed and our staff is eager to welcome you.

Statements are sent out at the end of every month and become payable by the 10th day of the month following.

As a charge customer you will be notified in advance of our sales and other special events and we have already put your name on our special mailing list.

If at any time you prefer to shop by telephone, by all means do so. If you ask for 'Telephone Service' you will be sure of prompt and courteous attention.

We hope you will find shopping in our store a pleasant and satisfying experience.

Yours sincerely,

Dear Mrs Field,

We are enclosing the charge card you requested and look forward to seeing you in the store soon.

We hope you will make yourself at home at Hearn's whenever you drop in, whether it be to make an important purchase or merely to browse.

No extra charge is made for this added convenience. All we ask of you is kindly to send us your prompt remittance when you receive your statement on the 10th of every month, for goods purchased the previous month.

We are sure you will understand why our auditors require such an arrangement and that you will co-operate with us.

May we take this opportunity to wish you many years of carefree shopping at Hearn's?

Yours sincerely,

Dear Mrs Colman,

Your new Murrycard is enclosed and we wish you many happy shopping days at Murry's.

We should like to remind you that, while you will receive monthly itemized accounts, you do not need to pay the whole of the amount outstanding right away. In fact, you may pay as little as £5.00 or 5% of the amount outstanding, whichever is the lesser. In this way you have a charge account and budget account in one.

We look forward to serving you as a charge customer for many years to come.

Yours sincerely,

Dear Mr Hardy,

The charge account you requested in your letter of April 12 is now ready for you. Enclosed is your charge card for your use whenever you make a purchase.

We are happy indeed to welcome you to our large circle of special customers and will do everything possible to make shopping at our store a pleasure.

Yours sincerely,

For business appointment

Dear Bill,

I was very pleased to learn that you'll be in Birmingham early next month and will certainly make time to see you on the 3rd, as you mention. Any time after 3 p.m. will suit me fine. Just come along.

I very much look forward to seeing you.

Sincerely,

Dear Mr Haynes,

Thank you for your letter of April 15.

I'd be delighted for you to come in and talk to us about our sales training programme. In fact our Sales Manager would like to have a word with you too.

Perhaps you would ring my secretary, Ms Everett, to arrange a mutually convenient time.

Yours sincerely,

Dear Mr Reynolds,

I was very glad to learn that the plans for the new building are finally ready. Yes, by all means come in next Wednesday, 3 o'clock suits me fine.

My partners and I are very anxious to press on with the work.

Yours sincerely,

Dear Mr Finney,

As a matter of fact, spraying is quite a small part of our finishing operation. None the less, I'd be happy to see you while you're in Leicester. If you could make it 4 o'clock, rather than 3, it would suit me better.

Yours sincerely,

Dear Mr Wallace,

Thank you for your note announcing your arrival in Liverpool on May 26.

I'll be very pleased to see you and I think the afternoon would be a better time to discuss our project, as I would like our chief accountant to be present too. Shall we say 2.30–3?

I look forward to seeing you then.

Yours sincerely,

Dear Joan,

I have just had your letter telling me you'll be in Manchester next week. I very much look forward to seeing you and have reorganized my day in order to be free at the time and place you mention.

See you then.

Sincerely,

Dear Ms Savage,

Your book project sounds most interesting.

My partner and I would be delighted to see you when you're in town next Wednesday. The time you mention would suit us well.

We look forward to meeting you and hope we can be of some assistance to you in your work.

Yours sincerely,

Dear Cavaliere,

I was happy indeed to learn that you will be making a quick business trip to England, arriving in London on the 21st.

Of course I'll find time to see you! Do please telephone me ahead of time, so that I can rearrange my day if necessary.

I very much look forward to seeing you.

Yours sincerely,

Dear Allan,

I have just got back from a trip North and found your letter waiting for me. I'll be very pleased to see you next Friday. Why not come straight over to my office from the station, since your time is so short? I'll be at my desk all morning, so don't worry if the train is late.

I look forward to seeing you again after such a long time.

Yours sincerely,

For information

Dear Ms Wilkes,

Thank you for your letter asking for information on our school.

It was founded in 1921 by our then managing director, Mr Sydney Hughes. Since then approximately 175,000 students have taken our courses. We are now embarking on an expansion programme overseas and have just opened schools in Cape Town and New Delhi. We are also considering branches in Canada and Australia. Our ultimate aim is to have a network of schools reaching across the world.

I hope this letter has gone some little way towards helping you and shall be pleased to give you any further information you may require.

Yours sincerely,

Dear Mr King,

I have your letter requesting further details of our training programme for young people.

I am pleased to say that the programme has been a complete success. When it began in 1961 we trained a total of 24 youngsters.

Now, more than 20 years later, the number trained is over ten times as many.

While morale is a very difficult thing to measure, we do feel that it has improved over the years. Perhaps the youngsters feel they are getting attention – which indeed they are – and that they can see more clearly where they are going.

We appreciate your interest in our personnel training programme and hope our answers to your questions will be of some assistance to you.

Yours sincerely,

Dear Ms Mayer,

I have your letter asking for information on the Management Institute which our Company runs.

As a matter of fact the courses have been completely revised this year in the light of our experience over the past 10 years. The courses now last three whole months and the syllabus is somewhat different.

The enclosed booklet will give you all further details on the revamped course.

Please do not hesitate to get in touch with me again should you require any further particulars.

Yours sincerely,

Dear Mr Smith,

I am happy to supply the private address of Dr W. C. Watson:

Dr W. C. Watson
2124 Barton Avenue
Los Angeles 57, California

He is still very much alive, but retired from our University some five years ago. I'm sure he will be pleased to hear from you.

Yours sincerely,

Dear Mrs Gregg,

The finishing school I mentioned to you was the

Maison Maintenon
10 Rue Beau Rivage
Lausanne, Switzerland.

Our daughter Carole was very happy there and we found the fees quite reasonable, all in all.

I hope you manage to get your daughter fixed up all right.

Yours sincerely,

Dear Miss Mathews,

Thank you for your letter of July 12 and for your interest in my talk at the IPM last week.

The work curves I showed were actually taken from a 'Technical Aid' called Is Worker Fatigue Costing you Dollars? issued by the Small Business Administration, Washington 25, DC, USA. I am enclosing a small reproduction of all three. Please feel free to use them as you see fit. However, if you intend incorporating them in any printed matter, proper credit should be given to the SBA.

Yours sincerely,

For printed matter

Dear Ms Daniels,

Thank you for your kind words about Ballard and Wilkins. We hope the enclosed material will aid in the research for your book on personnel management.

The enclosures are:

1 A leaflet describing various personnel tests in use at Ballard and Wilkins.
2 A copy of our current employee handbook.
3 A copy of our annual report for last year.

If we can be of further help to you in your endeavour, please let us know. Good luck!

Yours sincerely,

Dear Miss Blair,

. It's a pleasure to enclose the March issue of Prisma, which you asked for during your visit to our office last week. We hope you will find it of interest.

We wish you the best of luck in your project.

Yours sincerely,

Dear Mr McCormack,

We are very pleased to learn that you have found our booklet on correcting proofs so useful.

Please accept the enclosed copy with our compliments.

Yours sincerely,

Dear Mr Jones,

We are happy to enclose a copy of Cutting Corners with Conveyors, with our compliments. All these 'Technical Aids' are supplied free of charge, as is our 'Management Aid' series.

We are also enclosing a complete list of both series so that you can order any one of them. You will also find listed a series of larger booklets. There is a small charge for these, as indicated beside each title.

We greatly appreciate your interest in our publications and are happy to be of service.

Yours sincerely,

Dear Mrs Lewis,

Thank you for your letter of February 28.

You will find enclosed the following materials:

1 Brochure illustrating and describing our chalkboards and screen units
2 Leaflet on our lecture theatres

In a separate envelope we are sending you a booklet on our slide and filmstrip projectors, as well as an illustrated brochure called The Industrial Training School, which we feel will be both interesting and useful to you.

We very much appreciate your interest in our teaching aids and look forward to being of further assistance to you.

Yours sincerely,

Dear Miss Gaynor,

I am delighted to send you, in a separate envelope, a specimen copy of <u>Selling</u>. I am sure you will find it interesting and may even decide to secure for yourself a copy every month.

With this in mind, I am enclosing our usual subscription form, together with a return envelope, to facilitate matters for you.

Thank you for your interest.

Yours sincerely,

Dear John,

I was glad to learn that your translation department is making steady progress and am only too delighted to make any small contribution to it.

In a separate parcel I am sending you half a dozen of the conversion booklets you mention. As a matter of fact our formidable Miss Schmidt – or Fraulein Schmidt, I should say – has compiled her own private glossary of engineering terms in English, German, French, and Italian. This mighty work is now being reproduced and when it is ready I will let you have a copy, with Miss Schmidt's compliments.

In great haste,

For permission to reproduce material

Dear Ms Wilkins,

Thank you for your letter of October 10.

There is no objection whatsoever to your quoting the passage indicated in your letter.

If there are any other points outstanding from previous correspondence, please let us know and we shall be happy to clear them up for you.

Yours sincerely,

Dear Mr Walker,

Thank you for your letter asking for permission to reproduce the cartoon showing a lady mounting a horse.

We have no objection to your using the cartoon, provided the words 'Copyright Hardwick Publishing Company Ltd' appear under it. In addition we make a reproduction charge of £15.

We hope you will have no objection to this fee and look forward to receiving your remittance.

Yours sincerely,

Dear Ms Murrey,

I am flattered to think that you should consider my remarks to the IPA worth quoting.

Enclosed is a typewritten copy of the talk. Please feel free to use any part of it as you see fit.

I look forward to reading your article when it is published.

Yours sincerely,

Dear Mr Freeman,

By all means feel free to reproduce the three letters you mention in your forthcoming book. I feel complimented to be represented in the book.

Do let me know if there is any other way in which I can co-operate with you in your project.

Yours sincerely,

Dear Miss King,

We are happy to grant you permission to reproduce the passages you mention in your book, Better Salesmanship.

We take this opportunity to wish you every success in your work and look forward to reading the book when it is published.

Yours sincerely,

Dear Dr Feldman,

My remarks at the Marketing Institute have already been published and you will find practically the whole talk in the September 11 issue of <u>Campaign</u>.

However, this does not mean that you may not use the passages you mention and I would be delighted that you should do so, in fact. Enclosed is a tear-sheet of the talk and I'm quite happy that you should quote whatever you like from it.

I always enjoy reading your marketing articles and look forward to seeing the next in the series when it is completed.

I am happy indeed to be able to co-operate with you in this way.

Yours sincerely,

For loan to business associate or friend

Dear Cyril,

Enclosed is my cheque for £175. Now please don't lie there worrying about paying it back. Being in hospital is bad enough in itself, without the addition of financial worries.

I quite expect you to be out of there in a couple of weeks and enjoying a recuperative rest at home. But do be assured in the meantime that we think of you often at the office, that I'll be in to see you again next week, and that another mortgage cheque awaits you if you need it. So don't worry, old friend, you just hurry up and get better!

Yours sincerely,

Dear Walter,

I was very distressed to get your letter and can imagine how worrying it must be for you to have financial commitments mounting up on you while you are on your back with a long, drawn-out illness.

My enclosed cheque should at least do something to take the worry off your mind. There's absolutely no hurry about my getting the money back. I'm happy to be able to help.

All of us in the marketing team send our regards and a small delegation will be in to see you later in the week.

Sincerely,

Dear Ed,

I am enclosing my cheque for just half the amount you asked for and therein lies a lecture. You see, being two years your senior I feel entitled to lecture you. But of course you already know chapter and verse of my stern little talk, so I'll say no more than 'Hold your horses, Ed, and remember Dickens's advice'.

Hope the new house is turning out just as expected and that you are happy in it.

Sincerely,

Dear Bill,

I'm glad you decided to get that car. It's the sensible thing to do in the cirumstances. My enclosed cheque is made out to the dealer, as you requested.

By all means send me a postal order every month if it makes it easier for you.

Best of luck and good driving in the new Metro.

Sincerely,

Refusing requests

Letters turning down requests must be very tactfully worded if they are to avoid offending the recipient and losing his or her goodwill. If you sincerely regret your inability to oblige, this must stand out clearly in the letter. The best way to prove your sincerity in the case of a business appointment, for instance, is to suggest a more suitable day or time for a meeting, where possible. In other instances, giving the reason for your inability to comply with the request will soften the blow. In the case of requests for literature, you might be able to offer a substitute or offer to help in another way.

Saying 'no' gracefully to an appeal for charity can be both difficult and embarrassing. Many companies solve the problem by having a written policy on charitable contributions as well as a budget earmarked for charities. This makes it very much easier simply to indicate that the charity in question is not included on your company's list or to mention that the budget has been fully allocated already. This method also has the advantage of removing the matter from the personal plane.

On the other hand, many companies simply ignore all appeals coming in by mail, unless they are addressed personally to one of the top executives.

For charge account

Dear Mrs Cartright,

We do appreciate your letter asking us to open a charge account in your name. This expression of your confidence and appreciation of our store is not lost on us.

Perhaps at some later date we shall be in a position to comply with your request and in the meantime we very much hope you will visit the store often and enjoy the high fashion, courteous service, and fair prices which it offers.

Yours sincerely,

Dear Miss Parker,*

Thank you for requesting a charge account with our store.

As you know, when such a request is received, a routine credit investigation is usually carried out and a decision made in each individual case. Unfortunately our information in support of your application is incomplete and we would therefore appreciate your calling in at the Credit Office to clear up one or two points.

We look forward to meeting you personally.

Yours sincerely,

Dear Mrs Jeffreys,

Thank you for your letter requesting a Whiting Brothers charge account. It is an expression of confidence and goodwill which we greatly appreciate.

While we are not at the moment in a position to comply with your request, we hope it will be possible later on.

We look forward to welcoming you in the store as always and assure you of our desire to serve you at all times to the best of our ability.

Yours sincerely,

For business appointment

Dear Bill,

I've just received your note telling me you'll be in Birmingham on Monday and asking if you could drop in to see me.

---

* This letter does not actually turn down the request for a charge account, but since statistics show that very few people actually do come in when asked in this fashion, the result is the same and, with a bit of luck, no hard feelings are caused.

There's nothing I'd like more, Bill, but unfortunately our national sales conference begins that very day and continues into Tuesday and Wednesday.

Had it been any other day I could easily have rearranged my appointments, but I'm afraid there's nothing I can do about the sales conference, as I'm sure you'll understand.

I'm very sorry to miss you. Don't forget to let me know next time you're in these parts, as I'd very much enjoy a chat with you.

Sincerely,

Dear Mr Green,

Thank you for your letter of September 11.

In the ordinary way, I'd be extremely interested in your proposition but, in fact, we have just set up a Word Processing Centre – at considerable cost, I may add.

In the circumstances, therefore, I see no point in taking up your time next Wednesday. Many thanks for thinking of Baxter's Ltd, none the less.

Yours sincerely,

Dear Mr Ross,

I'm very pleased to hear that the plans for the new building are finally ready and I'm most anxious to go over them with you. Unfortunately, however, I shall not be in the office at all on Wednesday. I'll be leaving for the North on Tuesday evening and will not be back until about midday on the Thursday.

Thursday afternoon, any time on Friday or the following Monday would suit me fine, however. I'm so sorry to have to ask you to make a special trip, and hope you will understand.

Yours sincerely,

Dear Ms Giles,

Your letter of the 12th has just reached me.

I'm afraid we shall miss each other when you come to Manchester early next month, because I shall be attending a conference in Scarborough on the date you mention.

However, I'll be back in Manchester on the 12th and have no further trips planned for a whole month. Do let me know, therefore, if you plan to be back again soon, as I'd very much like to see you.

Best wishes.

Yours sincerely,

Dear Tom,

I was delighted to get your letter announcing your fleeting visit to London and nothing would have pleased me more than a nice long chat with you. Unfortunately, however, I'll be leaving next Monday on a business trip to the Continent and won't be back until the end of the month.

It therefore looks as though we shall miss each other this time. I'm truly sorry about this. Do let me know when you'll be here again and perhaps we'll have better luck next time.

Best regards to you.

Sincerely,

Dear Mr Springer,

Your letter announcing your arrival in London next week reached me this morning.

Nothing would please me more than to get together with you on the date you mention but unfortunately I shall be leaving for a much needed holiday next Monday and will not be back until you have left.

I'm sorry indeed to miss you and hope you will be back soon. If there is anything anyone else in the office can do for you, please do not hesitate to call on them. I will leave word for them to expect you.

Yours sincerely,

For information or printed matter

Dear Ms Day,

Thank you for your letter of the 4th, requesting a copy of our catalogue of psychological tests.

We are, unfortunately, completely out of stock of the catalogue and the new edition will not be available for another couple of months.

If you will let us know which particular tests you are interested in, we shall be happy to quote you prices or furnish you with any other detail about them.

Yours sincerely,

Dear Mr Hardy,

Thank you for your letter of January 14 enquiring about our training courses for sales representatives.

As a matter of fact we are in the process of reviewing our training methods and devising new ones. We cannot therefore supply you with any useful information at this stage.

I do sincerely regret that we are unable to help you on this occasion.

Yours sincerely,

Dear John,

I'd be delighted to lend you my May 14 copy of <u>Business Week</u> if I had it. Unfortunately, however, I discontinued my subscription in January as I am usually able to read the office copy.

I do believe, however, that the Golden House library subscribes to the magazine. Why not try giving Ms Green a ring?

Sorry to be unable to help.

Sincerely,

Dear Mr Johnson,

I'm glad you found <u>100 Best Books on Business Management</u> so useful and I'd be very happy to let you have an additional copy for your home library if I had one.

The demand for the booklet has been so heavy that we are completely out of stock. I'm not at all sure whether we shall put out a new edition, but if we do, we will remember that you'd like to have a copy.

I'm very sorry to be unable to oblige you in this instance.

Yours sincerely,

Dear Ms Holland,

We have your letter of April 17 regarding our sales training programme.

We do appreciate your interest and would very much like to help you with your project, but the kind of training we give is of such a specialized nature that we do not feel it could possibly be of use to anyone in any other field.

We hope you will appreciate our position and sincerely regret our inability to help you on this occasion.

Yours sincerely,

For support of charities, co-operative arrangements, etc.

Dear Mr Fordham,

I appreciate your thinking of me in connection with your special 'Cancer Week' Appeal. I do not know of a more worthy cause, nor one to which I would more gladly contribute, the more so since you are personally connected with it.

Unfortunately, however, the funds I have set aside for charitable purposes have all been allocated already and I am therefore unable to respond this time.

I do, none the less, wish you the very greatest success in your wonderful work.

Yours sincerely,

Dear Mr Griffiths,

Your letter of January 27 on behalf of the Spastics Society has been given my very careful consideration.

I'm sure you will appreciate that a Company such as ours, with 80 branches covering the whole of the United Kingdom, receives a great number of requests for contributions to many very worthy causes.

Since it would be quite impossible for us to contribute to all of them, we have made it a policy to confine our support to a limited number of organizations.

For this reason, I am afraid that it will not be possible for us to lend our support to your Society.

I do hope you will appreciate our position and I take this opportunity of wishing you every success in your endeavours.

Yours sincerely,

Dear Mrs Smiles,

Thank you for your letter requesting some items of glass or china for your annual Church Bazaar.

Much as we would like to help, we regret to inform you that our budget appropriation for this purpose has been fully allocated for the current fiscal year. For this reason we are unable to contribute.

Please accept our very best wishes for the success of your annual event.

Yours sincerely,

Dear Ms Harrison,

I have carefully considered your request that our Company should place an advertisement in the United Churches Review and I personally appreciate that the Review is most worthy of support.

However, our Board of Directors wish us to restrict advertising expenditure to the absolute minimum at the present time. This is only a temporary measure and it may very well be relaxed in the not too distant future. None the less, it does mean that I am unable to comply with your request for the time being.

I hope you will understand.

Yours sincerely,

Dear Mr Gamage,

I very much appreciate your suggestion that we join forces in a co-operative advertising effort. It certainly has much to commend it. Unfortunately, however, our Board of Directors ruled against such joint efforts some years ago.

Because of the nature of our products, we are continually getting similar requests and in order to avoid any impression of favouring one company rather than another, the Board decided it was best for us to 'go it alone' at all times.

I hope you will understand the reason for my inability to take your suggestion further and thank you again for thinking of us in this connection.

Yours sincerely,

For loan to business associate or friend

Dear Frank,

I enjoyed your breezy, devil-may-care letter and am delighted to learn that things are settling down nicely in your new home. I'm sorry to learn, on the other hand, that you have so over-extended yourself financially and sincerely wish that I could help you.

Unfortunately, my commitments are very heavy too and I cannot possibly manage such a loan. I hope you will understand my inability to oblige you.

All best wishes.

Sincerely,

Dear Ron,

I was very sorry to get your letter of the 12th and only wish I could lighten your burden by helping you with your financial difficulties.

Regrettably, however, even the small sum you mention would be quite impossible for me to find at the moment. Meeting bills seems to be a difficult problem for all of us and there just never seems to be that bit over to enable us to breathe a little more freely.

I really am terribly sorry. If there is anything at all of a non-financial nature that I can do for you, please let me know. I hope you continue to make progress and that you will be out of hospital soon.

With all best wishes,

Yours sincerely,

Dear Ross,

I was delighted to learn that your business is doing so well and that you are busy drawing up expansion plans. There is nothing so satisfying as seeing one's business grow.

Knowing it and you as well as I do, there's nothing that would please me more than owning a slice of the pie, so to speak. Unfortunately, however, my various commitments are so heavy that I simply cannot entertain thoughts of new investments, even by way of a private loan to a very good friend.

Please don't take this amiss. I know you realize I'm not so well-heeled as not to miss a few hundred here or there! If I were, the money would be yours, do be assured of that.

The very best of luck to you and do let me know how you get along.

Sincerely,

Dear Jack,

I was very much interested to learn about the business venture you are thinking of undertaking. It certainly sounds like a fine proposition from what you told me.

As for my participating in it by a loan to you, much as I would like to help, I'm afraid I could not consider it. I simply do not have that kind of liquid cash to dispose of. What capital I have is invested in gilt-edged securities and the small cash balance in my bank account is for the proverbial rainy day.

I'm very sorry about this, Jack, and hope you will be successful in finding a financier for your venture.

Best of luck.

Sincerely,

13

Miscellaneous

Letters of apology

Occasionally pressure of events is such that we act in a discourteous or thoughtless manner. A prompt and sincere apology is the only way out at such times, yet how often do we take the trouble of making this? Far more frequently we act discourteously, then forget it, hoping that the slighted person will do likewise. How much more constructive to write a warm, friendly note, frankly admitting your failing.

If you do have a convincing explanation for your lapse, then by all means give it, otherwise honest admission of your error will often work wonders to restore you to the good graces of your correspondent.

For breaking appointment

Dear Mr Finley,

     I write to apologize for having had to put you off on Monday. As I hope my secretary explained to you, an emergency at our Midland Branch forced me to leave town unexpectedly and I have, in fact, only just got back.

     I sincerely hope that this last-minute cancellation of our meeting did not inconvenience you too much and that you will understand what prompted it. Can we meet next Monday instead, at the same place and time? Failing that, do please suggest a more convenient day, as I look forward to seeing you and discussing our 1986 programme with you.

            Yours sincerely,

Dear Ms Warren,

I am sorry indeed that I had to cancel our appointment yesterday. Unfortunately a visitor arrived unexpectedly from the Continent and it was incumbent upon me to entertain him.

I sincerely hope the postponement of our meeting did not inconvenience you too much. I shall be most happy to see you any time next week and will ask my secretary to ring you and set a convenient time.

Sincerely yours,

Dear Mr Preston,

Please accept my apologies for what happened yesterday. I fully expected to be back at the office by the time you arrived, but an appointment in the City kept me tied up until 3.30 and the exasperatingly slow-moving traffic delayed me still further.

I felt most contrite when I finally panted up the steps to my office only to learn that you had just left to catch your train back to Birmingham.

Do please give me an opportunity to make amends next time you come to London.

Sincerely yours,

Dear Ms Fletcher,

It was really most unfortunate that I should have chosen the day we were to meet to succumb to the 'flu. I sincerely hope our delayed meeting will not inconvenience you too much and that you will excuse my unavoidable absence from the office.

I am feeling quite myself again and would be happy to see you any afternoon next week. Perhaps you will let me know which day would be most convenient for you.

Yours sincerely,

For absence from meeting

Dear Robby,

I write to apologize for not turning up at yesterday's Research Committee meeting. I fully intended to come, but our Chairman called an emergency Board meeting owing to the sudden death of Lord Somerville, and, obviously, there was nothing for it but to attend.

I look forward to your bringing me up to date with the Institute's happenings and you can, of course, count on my usual regular attendance from now on.

Sincerely,

Dear Miss Stanley,

I write to apologize most sincerely for my dreadful lapse in missing the first meeting of your committee yesterday.

To be perfectly honest with you, the date completely slipped my memory and only this morning, as I was looking through my private diary, did I come upon the date which I had carefully jotted down last month.

I know this is a lame excuse, but it is the truth and I much prefer to make a clean breast of it. I do hope you will forgive me and I look forward to receiving a copy of the minutes of the meeting. I am still very enthusiastic about our Society's work and look forward to doing my bit towards making it a success.

Yours sincerely,

Dear Mr O'Sullivan,

I'm sorry I missed the Chamber of Commerce meeting on Wednesday and I hope you will convey my apologies also to Mr Gibbons.

I had hoped to return from my trip to the North in time to attend the meeting, but unfortunately my business up there took longer than expected and I only got back yesterday.

Please be assured that had it not been for this circumstance quite beyond my control, I would most certainly have been with you on Wednesday.

Yours sincerely,

Dear 'Dixie',

I can't tell you how disappointed I was to have missed the Ad Club meeting last night. I was looking forward to the evening as my train ambled towards London, but gradually, as the train lost time, I began to realize we would get to King's Cross too late for me to make a sprint for it.

Ultimately we arrived after two hours' delay and I decided it was pointless to get there at the tail end of the meeting.

I hope you will excuse me and look forward to making up for lost time at the next meeting.

Sincerely,

For belated acknowledgement of favour or courtesy

Dear Clive,

I want to thank you most sincerely – though belatedly – for the pamphlets, articles and book you sent me several weeks ago.

They really were most useful to me in my research for the book and I selfishly pressed on with the task, instead of first pausing to thank you for your kindness and generosity.

I hope that as a fellow-author who is every bit as busy, you will understand and forgive me. I should be finished with the material quite soon and will return it to you in good order.

Thank you again.

Sincerely,

Dear Dr Gordon,

Please forgive this tardy note of thanks for your
thoughtfulness in referring Michael Farringdon to me.

He turned out to be just the kind of young man we were
looking for and I really am most grateful to you for sending him
along.

Unfortunately the very day after he came I had to go to
Scotland unexpectedly and as soon as I got back the International
Symposium was about to begin. So it was that in the rush of
things I overlooked the pleasurable duty of writing to thank you.

Yours sincerely,

Dear Mr Norton,

I have just returned from my selling trip to Germany and
want to thank you warmly for the skilful and generous way in
which you paved my way there.

Everyone you recommended me to gave me a warm
welcome and was most receptive to ideas. Had I been visiting a
familiar country full of old friends I could not have expected a
finer reception.

My only regret is that I have waited so long to write and
thank you for such kindness. My only poor excuse is the rush and
tear of last-minute preparations for the journey. Of one thing you
may be certain, however, I blessed you and thanked you every inch
of the way, and I can assure you that it was a most successful trip.

Very sincerely yours,

Dear Mr Fletcher,

I hope you will accept my much-belated thanks for so kindly pointing out the article 'Pent-up Productivity' in your local Chamber of Commerce Journal.

I found myself agreeing wholeheartedly with its philosophy and it gave some valuable additional background material for my talk at the Institute of Directors.

Thank you again for your thoughtfulness.

Sincerely yours,

Dear John,

I have only just got back to the office after my seemingly interminable bout of 'flu and am therefore only now writing to say 'Thank you' for the splendid material on your last sales conference which you sent me.

I went through it at home while I was 'convalescing' and I know it will be invaluable to me in preparing my own sales conference for next February.

It was most generous of you to lend it to me and I really am most appreciative.

Sincerely,

For belated return of borrowed property

Dear David,

I have just addressed a parcel to you which contains all the books and other material which you so kindly lent me several months ago.

You <u>did</u> say I could keep the material as long as I liked, but I do feel none the less that I owe you an apology for keeping it so long. The fact is, it was so useful and I kept on referring to it as I wrote my book. But I have now written 'Finis' to the opus and your precious material is on its way back to you. Thanks, old friend!

As ever,

Dear Miss Mortimer,

The folder of 'Collection' letters which you generously lent me so long ago was most useful and has been put to good use in revising our methods of collecting overdue accounts.

In returning your folder so belatedly to you, I want both to thank you for your kindness in lending it to me and to apologize for keeping it so disgracefully long. I certainly hope that being without it for such a long time has not inconvenienced you in any way.

Thank you again for your thoughtfulness.

Sincerely yours,

Dear Ms King,

I am returning to you with this letter the minutes of the Institute's last meeting, which you so kindly sent me. They made very interesting reading and I am most grateful for your thoughtfulness in sending them along.

I realize I kept them a very long time and hope you will forgive this delay in returning them to you. I certainly hope that my laxity has not inconvenienced you.

I look forward to seeing you on March 4.

Yours sincerely,

Dear Mr Cooper,

I am returning to you by hand the original artwork which you lent me so long ago. I was able to use it and it saved me a great deal of additional expense.

I am most grateful to you for your generosity in lending the artwork to me and only hope you will not feel I have kept it too long. These printing jobs always take so long by the time all decisions are made and so on and your material only came back to my desk yesterday.

Do please, therefore, accept both my apologies and my most sincere thanks. As soon as the leaflet is off the press, I will send you a few copies.

Yours sincerely,

For delay in sending promised material

Dear Harold,

At long last I am sending you the promised material for your book. I had to search through various files to gather it together and this caused the delay.

I hope you will find the enclosed material useful and that its long delay in reaching you has not inconvenienced you. There is absolutely no hurry as far as returning it goes. Please keep it as long as you like.

Best wishes in your arduous task.

Sincerely,

Dear Mr Franklin,

You may recall that when I visited your Glasgow office in March I promised to send you a copy of our leaflet <u>Public Relations Makes Selling Easier</u>.

Upon my return to London, however, I found that we were completely out of stock of the leaflet and that a fresh supply had been ordered from the printers. The reprints have finally arrived and I am therefore keeping my promise to you, albeit belatedly.

I hope you will forgive the delay and that you will find the leaflet interesting.

Yours sincerely,

Dear Mr Kingsley,

I hope you did not think I had forgotten my promise to let you have a confidential copy of the market report carried out for us by Rubens and Jones.

What caused the delay was that upon my return to town I found my desk piled high with papers to be attended to. I have only now come up for air and am happy to enclose a copy of the promised report. As you will see, it throws a good deal of light on the present state of the women's footwear market in the United Kingdom.

Do please let me have the report back when you have read it, as it is my only copy.

Sincerely yours,

Dear Mr Amis,

Please forgive my brief delay in sending you the promised copy of my report on my selling trip to the Middle East. I have been quite overwhelmed with work since my return and I have simply had to take things in rotation.

I hope you will find the report interesting. Please keep it with my compliments.

Yours sincerely,

Dear Mrs Harbourn,

You must think I had completely forgotten my promise to send you a copy of the 'home-made' multilingual glossary of business expressions which we use in our export department.

The reason for my tardiness is that everyone in the export department has been going flat out for the past several weeks and I did not dare put them off their stroke with this small request.

All has now returned to normal and I am pleased to enclose a copy of the glossary, which I hope you will find as useful as we all do.

Yours sincerely,

Letters of regret

Sometimes the best-laid plans go wrong through no one's particular fault. Long-anticipated trips are cancelled, you are absent from the office just when one of your favourite out-of-town associates calls, or you are unable to attend a special meeting.

Such situations call for a friendly and sincere letter of regret. The very tone of your note should convey the feeling that the disappointment you may have caused your correspondent was very much shared by you. At times you may be able to express the hope that the occasion missed will re-present itself before too long.

Such a courteous note cannot help but strengthen a relationship which may have had cause to falter, yet it only takes a few minutes to write. It is a habit well worth cultivating.

To business friend absent from meeting or conference

Dear Mr Helpman,

I was disappointed not to see you at the Young Publishers' Club meeting yesterday and wondered what had kept you away.

It was an unusually interesting meeting and I'm sure you would have enjoyed it.

I certainly hope you will manage to attend next time, but no doubt we shall meet again before then, possibly at Leipzig.

Yours sincerely,

Dear Mark,

It was very disappointing not to see you at the International Symposium on Mental Health – I had quite looked forward to exchanging views with you.

I finally heard that the 'flu had kept you away. I certainly hope you are quite recovered by now and look forward to seeing you again soon.

Sincerely,

Dear Mr Kenmore,

I have just received your letter of September 4 telling me you will be unable to attend the Society of Chartered Accountants Annual Dinner this year owing to persistent ill health.

This is disappointing news indeed – and on both counts. The Dinner will certainly not seem the same without you and I know my keen disappointment will be shared by all our members. The other members will also share my concern about your health, I know. I believe myself that you have been working too hard and that in your anxiety to get back to your desk you have not allowed yourself to recover sufficiently.

Your zest for work is indeed commendable, but do remember that your health should be your first concern. Please take care of yourself. We shall all drink to your good health at the Dinner.

Yours sincerely,

Dear Jack,

I was very sorry not to see you in Glasgow for the Modern Homes Exhibition and feared at first that we had simply missed each other. I had greatly looked forward to a chat and a meal with you, but you were nowhere to be seen.

Finally I ran across Charlie Gifford and he told me you had been urgently called away to your French subsidiary and were therefore unable to attend.

I must confess the jaunt did not seem quite the same without you and I missed your high spirits and crazy stories. The exhibition was much the same as usual, of course.

See you soon.

As ever,

To business friend unable to call as planned

Dear Mr Melville,

I was sorry indeed to learn from your letter of March 6, that you will not be coming to London next week after all. I was looking forward to a long chat with you over a leisurely meal.

Please let me know in good time when your postponed trip finally materializes, so that I can reserve time for your visit.

Yours sincerely,

Dear Signor Franco,

It was most disappointing to learn that your proposed trip to the United Kingdom has had to be postponed. We were all looking forward to welcoming you to our plant and also to showing you some of the sights of London.

We do realize, however, that urgent business matters keep you in Milan and hope you will be able to get away quite soon, or at least before our dreary English winter sets in.

Yours sincerely,

Dear Joe,

Your letter brought me a double dose of bad news. I had very much anticipated the pleasure of seeing you later this week and it now appears you have had to cancel your trip altogether.

But when you tell me the reason for this cancellation is that Carole has fallen ill, you add sorrow to disappointment.

I'm happy to hear, at any rate, that she is much better already and hope this letter will find her well on the way to complete recovery. Do give her my best regards and let us hope that an opportunity to get together will present itself again quite soon.

As ever,

To business friend not called upon during visit to city

Dear Mr Frieden,

I was most disappointed not to see you during my recent visit to Glasgow.

I had fully intended to call at your office, but endless drawn-out complications in negotiating the new contract kept me on the go all day long and allowed me not a minute to spare for other matters.

I fully expect to be back in your city towards the end of October, however, and will certainly have a visit to your office very firmly planted on my agenda.

Yours sincerely,

Dear Mr Dinsmore,

It was very disappointing not to see you during my brief passage through London. I had hoped to have a few hours to spare before catching my train to Scotland, but unfortunately my flight from the Continent was delayed by fog and I only got into London in time to catch the train by the skin of my teeth.

We shall therefore have to postpone that meeting until I return from Scotland. I shall be spending a few days in London then and very much look forward to meeting you again.

Yours sincerely,

Dear Mr Smythe,

I was sorry indeed not to see you on my brief trip to Bath.

What happened was that my visit was unexpectedly cut short by an urgent call back to Head Office and I had to leave much unfinished business and hurry back.

Unquestionably I shall be in Bath again soon and will let you know in good time the date of my arrival.

Yours sincerely,

For absence during visitor's call

Dear Mr Brennan,

I was most disappointed to learn upon my return to the office last week that you had called to see me during my absence. I would have very much enjoyed seeing you.

I certainly hope that business will bring you to Birmingham again soon. Perhaps you will let me know in advance next time you come and we can have lunch together at the Club.

Yours sincerely,

Dear John,

When I got back to the office yesterday after three days in bed with the 'flu, my secretary told me you had dropped in to see me during my absence.

I was most disappointed to hear this, as there is nothing I would have enjoyed more than a long chat with you. Is there any chance of your coming back to these parts soon? Do let me know and I'll endeavour to be fit and well for the occasion!

I'm very sorry I missed you. Hope you had a nice trip here, none the less.

Sincerely,

Dear Mr Cooper,

On my return from my flying visit to the Continent I learned that you had been in to see me. I'm very sorry to have missed you, as I would have enjoyed a talk with you very much.

It has been many months since we got together and, unfortunately, I have no plans at the moment to go North. Certainly, if either business or pleasure brings you back to London soon, you must let me know so that I can be sure of not missing you.

Yours sincerely,

Dear Mr Simkiss,

It was very kind of you to call in to see me last week. If only I had known you were coming, I could very easily have rearranged my day accordingly. As it was I was at the printer's most of the afternoon, as no doubt my secretary explained to you.

I very much hope you will be coming this way again soon, and if you will let me know in advance, I will make a point of being in to receive you.

With best personal regards,

Sincerely yours,

Dear Peter,

I was most disappointed this morning when my secretary told me you had been in to see me yesterday. I'm very sorry we missed each other.

I hope all is going well with you in your new Company and that there will soon be another chance for us to get together to discuss matters of mutual interest.

Sincerely,

Letters explaining delays

At times you receive requests for information or material which you cannot attend to right away. Finding the material may require time or, indeed, you may be away from the office when the request is received.

In such cases it is a business courtesy to write and explain the delay. If you yourself are writing, you should mention the reason for the delay. If your secretary is writing in your absence, it is sufficient for her to mention the date of receipt of the request and that of your expected return to the office, assuring the writer that his letter will be put before you then.

If the delay involves the repayment of a loan, a letter is, of course, imperative. Try to say *why* you can't find the money and *when* you expect to do so. If you find this impossible, go at least some way towards answering these two questions for your generous friend.

Asking for extra time to supply final answer

Dear Ms Gordon,

I was very interested to read about your proposed book and will gladly lend you the material you mention.

I shall have to search for it in several files, some of them tucked away in the loft at my country home. As this will take some days, including one weekend, I thought I'd write to assure you that the material will be on its way to you as soon as I can lay hands on it.

Very best wishes for your book.

Yours sincerely,

Dear Mr Kennedy,

Your letter of March 12 reaches me just as I am about to leave on a business trip to Germany.

I shall be very happy to let you have the information you require, but hope you don't mind waiting for it until my return to England early in April.

Yours sincerely,

Dear Mr Lodge,

Thank you for your letter of March 2.

I shall be most happy to let you have the figures you require. Unfortunately your letter catches me in a frantic rush to prepare material for the next Board Meeting.

I therefore hope a few days' delay will not inconvenience you in any way. You can confidently expect the figures to be on their way to you by early next week.

Yours sincerely,

Dear Ruth,

I have just received your letter of April 2 and, much as I would like to help you, I am not at all sure I have the material you need.

If you give me a few days, I will search through my old papers at home and let you know then whether I can help you or not.

Sincerely,

Dear Frieda,

It was good to hear from you and I shall be very pleased to let you have the information you need.

It will take me a few days to gather it together, however, so I hope you don't mind waiting a while.

I'm very pleased to hear that everything is going so well with you and if I can help in any other way, do let me know.

Sincerely,

Dear Mr Maxwell,

I shall be very happy to lend you the material you mention to help you with your speech. It will take a little time to gather it together, but I feel fairly confident of getting it off to you by Friday. This should give you ample time to prepare your speech for the following weekend.

I wish you a very successful meeting and it is a pleasure to help you in this way.

Yours sincerely,

Asking for extra time to pay

Dear Ray,

I know you did not set a time limit on the loan you so kindly made me, but I had fully intended sending you a cheque early this month. I now find I cannot possibly do so, even though I have been out of hospital for over two weeks.

I hope you will forgive me if I admit that the squeaking wheels were attended to first. They have all now been taken care of and you may certainly expect a cheque from me next month.

Thank you again for your generosity and for your patience. I am beginning to feel much stronger now and I'm quite convinced that this nasty incident will be quite put behind me and forgotten very soon now.

Sincerely,

Dear Mr Smith,

As you will recall, I agreed to begin repaying the loan you so kindly made me at the rate of £50 per month, beginning this month.

In spite of my firm determination, I simply do not seem to be able to fit this sum into my budget. Skipping summer holidays was easy enough, but leaving the children unequipped to return to school was, of course, quite impossible and I cannot believe you would expect me to do this.

I have re-worked my figures yet again and feel confident that I shall be able to begin my repayments from January 1 of next year. Would you very kindly agree to this?

I look foward to hearing from you and thank you for your patience and forbearance.

Yours sincerely,

Dear Joe,

This is the day I promised to send you a cheque in repayment of the loan you so kindly made me.

I'm sorry to say that things have got worse rather than better since I came out of hospital. While I have worked hard to generate new business, it has been very slow in coming to fruition. To make matters worse, clients owing me money for services rendered before I fell ill have been inordinately slow in paying. Some of them simply will not budge in spite of several reminders.

I am therefore writing to ask you whether you will kindly bear with me a little longer. I know I should give you a firm date on which I shall repay you, but I do not feel confident enough to do so. Could we say February first if I can possibly manage it, otherwise March first?

I hate to do this to you, Joe, but I'm sure you will understand.

Sincerely,

Dear George,

I'm sure when you saw an envelope with my handwriting on it you immediately thought. 'Ah, this must be Peter sending me a cheque'.

I'm terribly sorry to disappoint you, George, but I'm afraid it's Peter telling you he's very sorry, but please will you wait patiently for another month?

I'm swimming through my sea of difficulties as hard as I can and I'm sure I can see the shore in sight, so be a pal and bear with me just a little longer. I won't let you down, I promise.

As ever,

Letters by secretary on behalf of absent superior

Dear Mr Irving,

Your letter of December 15 has just reached this office. Unfortunately Mr Stone has been away for the past two days with the 'flu and is not expected back until Monday, at the earliest.

Immediately he returns, your letter will be put before him.

Yours sincerely,

Dear Ms Britwell,

I wish to acknowledge your letter of January 10, addressed to Mr White.

Mr White is still on the Continent, but as soon as he gets back, probably early next week, your letter will be brought to his attention.

Sincerely yours,

Dear Mr Conran,

Ms Bridlow is at present in Harrogate attending our annual Sales Conference, but as soon as she returns, towards the end of next week, I will bring your letter of January 12 to her attention.

Yours sincerely,

Appendix

Forms of Address

Peers, Baronets, and Knights

To a Duke

Address on envelope: To His Grace, the Duke of . . .
Letter opening: My Lord Duke, (*Less formally:* Dear Duke, *or* Dear Duke of . . .,)
Reference in body of letter: Your Grace
Salutation: I am (or remain), My Lord Duke, Your Grace's obedient servant, (*Less formally:* Yours sincerely,)

To a Duchess

Address on envelope: To Her Grace, the Duchess of . . .
Letter opening: Madam, (*Less formally:* Dear Duchess, *or* Dear Duchess of . . .,)
Reference in body of letter: Your Grace
Salutation: I am (or remain), Madam, Your Grace's obedient servant, (*Less formally:* Yours sincerely,)

To a Marquess

Address on envelope: To the Most Hon. The Marquess of . . .
Letter opening: My Lord Marquess, (*Less formally:* Dear Lord . . .,)
Reference in body of letter: Your Lordship
Salutation: I am (or remain), My Lord Marquess, your Lordship's obedient servant, (*Less formally:* Yours sincerely,)

To a Marchioness

Address on envelope: To the Most Hon. the Marchioness of . . . *otherwise as for a Baroness*

To an Earl

Address on envelope: To the Right Hon the Earl (of) . . . *otherwise as for a Baron*

To a Countess

Address on envelope: To the Right Hon. the Countess of . . . *otherwise as for a Baroness*

To a Viscount

Address on envelope: To the Right Hon. the Viscount . . . *otherwise as for a Baron*

To a Viscountess

Address on envelope: To the Right Hon. the Viscountess . . . *otherwise as for a Baroness*

To a Baron

Address on envelope: To the Right Hon. the Lord . . .
Letter opening: My Lord, *or* Sir (*Less formally:* Dear Lord . . .,)
Reference in body of letter: Your Lordship
Salutation: I am (or remain), my Lord, Your Lordship's obedient servant, (*Less formally:* Yours sincerely,)

To a Baroness

Address on envelope: To the Right Hon. the Lady . . .
Letter opening: Madam, (*Less formally:* Dear Lady . . .,)
Reference in body of letter: Your Ladyship
Salutation: I am (or remain), Madam, Your Ladyship's obedient servant, (*Less formally:* Yours sincerely,)

To a Baronet

Address on envelope: To Sir John. . ., Bt.
Letter opening: Sir, (*Less formally:* Dear Sir John,)
Salutation: I am (or remain), Sir, your obedient servant, (*Less formally:* Yours sincerely,)

To a Baronet's wife

Address on envelope: Lady. . .
Letter opening: Madam, (*Less formally:* Dear Lady . . .)
Salutation: I am (or remain), Madam, Your Ladyship's obedient servant, (*Less formally:* Yours sincerely,)

To a Knight

Address on envelope: To Sir John ..., *if a Knight Bachelor or with the appropriate letters after the surname if a Knight of a British Order of Chivalry. Otherwise the same as for a Baronet. Bear in mind, however, that in addressing a Knight who holds more than one degree in one or more Orders of Chivalry, you must be careful to show only the senior appointment in each Order, i.e.* GCVO (*and not* GCVO, KCVO, CVO)

All the above may be addressed less grandiloquently as 'Sir' or 'Madam', closing simply 'Yours faithfully'.

The law

To the Lord Chancellor

Address on envelope: To the Right Hon. the Lord High Chancellor
Letter opening: My Lord, (*Less formally:* Dear Lord ...,)
Reference in body of letter: Your Lordship
Salutation: I am (or remain) your Lordship's obedient servant, (*Less formally:* Yours sincerely,)

To the Lord Chief Justice

Address on envelope: To the Right Hon. the Lord Chief Justice of England *or* (*according to rank*) To the Right Hon. the Lord ..., Lord Chief Justice of England
Letter opening: My Lord, (*Less formally:* Dear Lord ...,)
Reference in body of letter: Your Lordship
Salutation: I am (or remain), my Lord, your obedient servant, (*Less formally:* Yours sincerely,)

To the Solicitor General

Address on envelope: To the Right Hon. Sir John ..., Solicitor-General, QC
Letter opening: Sir, (*Less formally:* Dear Sir John,)
Salutation: I remain, Sir, yours truly, (*Less formally:* Yours sincerely,)

To a Judge of the High Court in England
Chancery, Queen's Bench or Family Division

Address on envelope: To the Hon. Mr Justice Brown, *or* To the Hon. Sir John Brown (*as the case may be*)
Letter opening: My Lord *or* Sir, (*Less formally:* Dear ..., *or* Dear Sir John)
Reference in body of letter: Your Lordship
Salutation: I am (or remain), my Lord (*or* Sir), your obedient servant, (*Less formally:* Yours sincerely,)

To a Woman Judge of the High Court

Address on envelope: To the Hon. Mrs Justice . . ., DBE (*this form is used even for unmarried judges*)
Letter opening: My Lady
Reference in body of letter: Your Ladyship
Salutation: I am (or remain), my Lady, your obedient servant, (*Less formally:* Yours sincerely,)

Civic dignitaries

To a Lord Mayor

The Lord Mayors of London, York, Belfast, Dublin, Cardiff, Sydney, Melbourne, Adelaide, Perth (WA), Brisbane, and Hobart only have the privilege of being styled 'Right Hon.'

Address on envelope: To the Right Hon. the Lord Mayor of . . ., *or* To the Lord Mayor of . . ., *otherwise as for a Baron*

To a Lady Mayoress

The wife of a Lord Mayor (Lady Mayoress) is styled the same as a Baroness, but only during her husband's term of mayoralty.

To a Mayor (man or woman)

Address on envelope: (*if of a City*) To the Right Worshipful the Mayor of . . .
(*if a Borough*) To the Worshipful the Mayor of . . .
Letter opening: Sir, (*or* Madam,) (*Less formally:* Dear Mr Mayor, *or* Dear Mr . . ., Dear Madam Mayor,)
Salutation: I am, your Worship's obedient servant, (*Less formally:* Yours sincerely,)

The diplomatic service

To a British Ambassador, abroad

Address on envelope: To his Excellency Mr Charles Brown, CMG (*or according to rank*), H.M. Embassy
Letter opening: Sir, (*or according to rank*) (*Less formally:* Dear Sir John, *or as the case may be*)
Reference in body of letter: Your Excellency
Salutation: I am (or remain), Sir, your Excellency's obedient servant, (*Less formally:* Yours sincerely,)

To a Foreign Ambassador to the Court of St James

Address on envelope: To his Excellency (or Her Excellency) the French Ambassador
Letter opening: Sir, (or Madam) (*or according to rank*)
Salutation: I am (*or* remain), Sir, (*or* Madam,) your Excellency's obedient servant, (*Less formally:* Yours sincerely,)

To a Consul

Address on envelope: G.J. Brown, Esq., (*or* Mrs/Miss/Ms) H.M. Consul-General/Consul or Vice-Consul (*as the case may be*)
Letter opening: Sir, (*or* Madam *or according to rank*) (*Less formally:* Dear Mr Brown, (*or according to rank and sex*)
Salutation: Yours faithfully, (*Less formally:* Yours sincerely,)

The church

To an Archbishop

Address on envelope: To the Most Revd the Lord Archbishop of . . .
Letter opening: Dear Lord Archbishop, (*Less formally:* Dear Archbishop, *or* Dear Archbishop of . . .,)
Salutation: I remain your obedient servant, (*Less formally:* Yours sincerely,)

To a Cardinal

Address on envelope: To His Eminence Cardinal . . ., Archbishop of . . ., (*if he is also an Archbishop*)
Letter opening: My Lord Cardinal, *or* Your Eminence, (*Less formally:* Dear Cardinal, *or* Dear Cardinal . . .,)
Reference in body of letter: Your Eminence
Salutation: I remain, my Lord Cardinal, your Eminence's most devoted and obedient servant, (*Less formally:* Yours sincerely,)

To a Bishop

Address on envelope: The Right Rev. the Lord Bishop of . . .
Letter opening: My Lord Bishop, (*Less formally:* Dear Bishop, *or* Dear Bishop of . . .,)
Reference in body of letter: Your Lordship
Salutation: I am, my Lord, your obedient servant, (*Less formally:* Yours sincerely,)

To a Dean

Address on envelope: To the Very Rev. the Dean of . . .
Letter opening: Very Reverend Sir, (*Less formally:* Dear Dean,)
Salutation: I have the honour to be, Very Reverend Sir, your obedient servant, (*Less formally:* Yours sincerely,)

To an Archdeacon

Address on envelope: To the Venerable the Archdeacon of . . .
Letter opening: Venerable (*or* Reverend) Sir, (*Less formally:* Dear Archdeacon,)
Salutation: I remain, Venerable (*or* Reverend) Sir, yours obediently, (*Less formally:* Yours sincerely,)

To a Rector, Vicar, Curate or Minister

Address on envelope: To the Rev. John . . .
In the case of a clergyman possessing a title, the clerical rank comes first,
e.g. The Reverend the Honourable C. G. Smith
Letter opening: Reverend Sir, (*Less formally:* Dear Mr Smith,)
To a Roman Catholic priest: Dear Father,
Salutation: I am, Reverend Sir, your obedient servant,

The armed services

To a member of HM Forces — commissioned ranks

Address on envelope: According to rank. Include either the full Christian name or initials of the addressee.
e.g. Lieutenant-General A. B. Mostyn; Air Commodore C. D. Lewis, RAF; Sergeant E. F. Richards, WRAF*

If an officer is titled, the Service rank is given first,
e.g. Admiral Sir George Cunningham, Squadron Leader the Hon. F. V. James.

Officers in the Army below the rank of Captain are referred to as Mr *and therefore their letters should be addressed* Esq. *with the name of their regiment afterwards,*
e.g. J. Jackson, Esq., Coldstream Guards.

Naval officers below flag rank have the letter RN *after their name, preceded by decorations, if any,*
e.g. Captain W. X. Mitchell, DSO, RN

The holder of a subsidiary rank is usually addressed in personal letters by the next rank higher up, e.g. Vice-Admirals and Rear-Admirals would both be addressed as Admiral; *Lieutenant-Generals and Major-Generals would both be addressed as* General. *The envelope is, of course, addressed with their proper rank.*

Letter opening: Sir or Madam, (*Less formally:* Dear Major Smith,)

---

* Women officers have the same Army titles as men officers. The appropriate initials always follow their name.

Other ranks

Address on envelope: Letters to all other ranks are usually addressed with the number and rank preceding the surname, which is followed by the initials of the addressee,
e.g. 196524 AB Freeman, D. W.; 896547 AC Copland, K.R.
The following is also correct usage: 165795 Private J. W. Atkins, RE; W/12345 Private H. P. Swift, WRAC.

The medical profession

To a Surgeon

Address on envelope: M. W. Stoddard, Esq., (*or* Mrs/Miss/Ms) FRCS
Letter opening: Sir, (*or* Madam,) (*Less formally:* Dear Mr Stoddard,)
Salutation: Yours faithfully, (*Less formally:* Yours sincerely,)

To a General Practitioner

Address on envelope: Dr F. J. Winter *or* F. J. Winter, Esq., (*or* Mrs/Miss/Ms) MD (*or other degree letters*)
Letter opening: Sir, (*or* Madam,) (*Less formally:* Dear Dr Winter,)
Salutation: Yours faithfully, (*Less formally:* Yours sincerely,)